Second Edition

The Sweater
WORKSHOP

By Jacqueline Fee

Knit Creative, Seam-Free Sweaters on Your Own with Any Yarn

Copyright © 1983, 2002 by Jacqueline Fee. All rights reserved.
ISBN 0-89272-533-8 sewn paperback binding
ISBN 0-89272-572-9 Wire-O binding
Library of Congress Control Number: 2001097401

The excerpt on pages 61–63 is from *Knitting from the Top,* by Barbara G.
Walker. Reprinted 1996 by Schoolhouse Press. Used by permission.

All photographs by Lynn Karlin, except as noted below:
    Photos on pages 73, 104, and 105 by Nancy Cook.
    Photos on pages 139 and 143 by Thatcher Cook.
    Page 84 photo from the Hamburger Kunsthalle in Hamburg,
       Germany. © Elke Walford. Used by permission.
    Page 85 photo reproduced by permission of the Museum
       of London Picture Library, image courtesy of Plimoth
       Plantation.
    Photos on pages 87 and 88 reproduced courtesy of Smithsonian
       Institution Press.

Printed in China
RPS

2   4   6   8   9   7   5   3

Down East Books
P.O. Box 679, Camden, ME 04843

Book orders: 1-800-766-1670
www.downeastbooks.com

Contents

Acknowledgments

First, and still foremost, I must express a special thank-you to my daughter, Nancy, my very best friend and helpmate, whose "ESP" brings her to my side when I need one of her many talents. Nancy's love of early textiles and her pursuit of their reproduction filled our home with old looms and wheels and our lives with weavers and spinners. This association with true creators made me want to hide my knitting. It became suddenly unsatisfying and took on an air of inferiority. It seemed a copycat craft, akin to painting by numbers. The question began to nag: "Why don't knitters knit as spinners spin, as weavers weave, or even as quilters quilt, as potters pot, as sculptors sculpt—with a choice of materials and a few guidelines to follow? The answer? There were precious few guidelines—no book of blank stitches. You now have it: the bare bones, skeletons of sweaters to knit of any yarn and to embellish to your heart's content.

In memoriam, I also thank another Nancy, Nancy Latady, who was there to guide me through my first wheel turnings. I also am grateful to my handspun yarn itself, for not conforming to a prescribed gauge.

To Barbara Fairchild and Gloria Cohen for typing the rudimentary beginnings of *The Sweater Workshop* for my first classes. Subsequently, to the talented members of our South Shore Spinners Guild—collectively for energy and enthusiasm, individually for encouragement. And most grateful thanks to one particular talent in that group, Patricia LaLiberte, for her very special kindness in rendering the charming stitch illustrations.

Thanks also to Connie Pearlstein—my devil's advocate on the West Coast since we met at Elizabeth Zimmermann's 1978 Knitting Without Tears Workshop at Shell Lake, Wisconsin—and to Anne Gould, Jeanne Haviland, Marlies Price, and Toni Trudell, her counterparts in the East, for reading, testing, and commenting.

To Miriam Chesley and Linda Lincoln—thank you for always

listening, and to Linda also for her many years as my faithful booth assistant at the New Hampshire Sheep and Wool Festival.

I am indebted to every one of my students, those first adventurous six—Debby Blanchard, Pat Curtin, Jean Dionne, Carolyn McKenna, Kathleen Ouellette, and Elizabeth Reardon—and all those who have followed. You are all here in the pages of this book. You were its inspiration.

To Linda Ligon, my former editor at Interweave Press, publisher of the first edition of *The Sweater Workshop*, for recognizing the need for an "on your own" knitting instruction book and for following through with its many printings.

And to the tens of thousands of knitters who have spread the words of *The Sweater Workshop* by recommending or giving the book to their friends, family members, and even strangers whom they may have seen with needles in their hands (in this category, I must thank former Rhode Island School of Design students Louise Vance and Ellen Longo, in particular). To those on the Internet's knit and spin lists who have praised the book's value via comments and e-mail.

To Carole Wulster, mathematical genius, who understands the depths of *The Sweater Workshop* book better than I and who put the text in Windows 3.1 for Linda Skolnik at Patternworks in Poughkeepsie, New York.

To Andrew Batt, at the Museum of London, and Jill Hall and Die Modlin Hoxie, at Plimoth Plantation, for the image of the 300-year-old knitted infant's vest that appears in the chapter titled "Unravel Your Thinking."

To Neale Sweet, publisher, and the staff at Down East Books, and in particular to my editor, Karin Womer, for her warm, perceptive advice. I am deeply grateful for their faith and kindness in bestowing upon *The Sweater Workshop* a second life for those who have patiently awaited its return to shop shelves.

And again, to the rest of my family: always to my husband, Peter, for his thoughtfulness, help, and constant understanding; to our son, John, his lovely wife, Lynn, and our two precious granddaughters, Emily and Kayla, for their cheery good wishes; to Nancy's husband, Peter Cook, for his exuberant optimism, and, in memoriam, to dog Gus, for waiting all those minutes so many years ago.

Preface to the Second Edition

My 30-Year Search for a Seamless Sweater

You will notice as you work your way through *The Sweater Workshop* that I avoided using the pronoun *I*. This reluctance, I believe, is a throwback to my very strict eighth-grade English teacher, a Miss Hough, who detested reading our elementary writings, as we were prone to start every sentence with "I" this and "I" that. This goal of "no *I*s" was accomplished with two exceptions—once in the Acknowledgments, for I was the one who had to thank my daughter for her significant role in my ending up writing a knitting book, and again in the Introduction, where I had to thank Elizabeth Zimmermann for her inspiration and permissions—no one else could speak for me in either case.

Invariably, in my workshops and lectures, someone asks how and when I started to knit, and I give a brief summary. So, here and now, I break my "no *I*" vow for you knitters who have not already heard the tale in person. Further, I was reminded of the value of my first project after a visit to Barbara King's shop, The Yarnwinder, on Newbury Street in Boston, for she had her beginners—both male and female, I might add—knitting socks in the round on four needles, exactly the way I had learned to knit too many years ago. And her students were having a lively, fun time of it.

I know my story starts the same way as many of yours. My introduction to the knitting process came in a Junior Girl Scout Troop in my hometown of Braintree, Massachusetts. We were working on our Textiles badges. Our leader, the late Mary Page, either deliberately or by chance, handed out four needles, a skein of blue yarn, and directions for spiral socks. To this day, I wonder whether I was blessed or cursed by this beginning: blessed because working with four needles became second nature—they became an extension of the fingers—and, even more important, the spiral pattern of K4, P4 gave *equal* billing to the purl stitch. It wasn't a second-class stitch taking a back seat to the knit stitch. So many beginners start with thick yarn, big, fat needles, and a knit-every-row garter stitch scarf. Then, some weeks later, they hear, "Oh, by the way, there is another stitch involved in this craft called knitting; it's the purl stitch"—and forevermore the purl stitch is treated as a pest, something to be tolerated and not enjoyed. As a right-hand knitter, i.e., one who holds the working yarn in her right hand, I love the purl stitch and on occasion will work a sweater on the purl side then turn it knit-side out.

Take heed, all who teach beginning knitters, and start your students off on the right foot, or the left foot, or both feet; you may have to help with the initial casting on to four needles, but soon these knitters will be going merrily around and around and have a completed sock—no sewing or finishing involved. As a public service, I am including the directions here.

SPIRAL SOCKS

These tube-shaped socks are adaptable to fit any foot, from infant's size to Paul Bunyan's extra, extra large. This particular pattern calls for a multiple of 4 stitches, as a knit 4, purl 4 rib has a good amount of elasticity. For beginning knitters, a generic 4-ply worsted-weight yarn is fine for practice; after that, a finer sock yarn may be desirable. The sock may be made short or long, and the decrease rounds should start when the sock reaches the base of the little toe.

Note: These directions are for the 4-ply yarn. If using a finer sock yarn, you might want to work a size larger and drop down one or two needle sizes.

Yarn: 4-ply worsted weight

Needles: set of 4 double-pointed needles, #4 or #5

> *Infant:* Cast on 32 stitches. Divide among 3 needles (12, 12, 8).
>
> *Small:* Cast on 40 stitches. Divide among 3 needles (12, 12, 16).
>
> *Medium:* Cast on 48 stitches. Divide among 3 needles (16, 16, 16).
>
> *Large:* Cast on 56 stitches. Divide among 3 needles (20, 20, 16).
>
> *Extra Large:* Cast on 64 stitches and divide among 3 needles (20, 20, 24).
>
> *Paul Bunyan:* Cast on 72 stitches and divide among 3 needles (24, 24, 24).

Cuff: Join your work, being careful not to twist stitches. Work ribbing of K2, P2 for about 2½ inches. Change to spiral pattern and work until the sock will reach to the base of the little toe when tried on the foot (or estimated).

Spiral Pattern

Rounds 1–4: *K4, P4* around.

Rounds 5–8: P1, *K4, P4* around, ending K4, P3.

Rounds 9–12: P2, *K4, P4* around, ending K4, P2.

Rounds 13–17: P3, *K4, P4* around, ending K4, P1.

Rounds 17–20: *P4, K4* around.

Rounds 21–24: K1, *P4, K4* around, ending P4, K3.

Rounds 25–28: K2, *P4, K4* around, ending P4, K2.

Rounds 29–32: K3, *P4, K4* around, ending P4, K1.

Repeat from round 1 for pattern.

Spiral socks are an ideal first knitting project, as beginning knitters immediately become accustomed to working with four needles, the purl stitch is given equal billing with the knit stitch, and the finished seamless socks are instantly wearable.

When sock is desired length to little toe (or you are tired of going round and round), begin decrease:

Round 1: *K6, K2 tog* around.

Rounds 2 & 3: Work even.

Round 4: *K5, K2 tog* around.

Rounds 5 & 6: Work even.

Continue working decrease rounds (each time with one less knit stitch before the K2 tog) followed by 2 even rounds until 12 stitches remain. Divide the stitches, 6 each on 2 needles, and graft toe stitches together. (See Sampler, p. 71.)

Now, to get to the curse part of this spiral sock experience: I was spoiled by the simplicity of the socks' construction and the fact that they were instantly wearable. Though I did upgrade to socks with turned heels, from that time on it was socks, socks, and more socks; I did not tackle my first sweater until freshman year in college. It was a *Woman's Day* pattern for a short-sleeve cardigan with collar, worked in a yarn-over design using yellow nylon yarn. I should say *is*, not *was*, as several years ago I found it tucked away with some old prom gowns—too much blood, sweat, and tears involved to simply toss it, I guess. Well, this little number was worked in six pieces: two fronts, one back, two sleeves, even the tiny collar was knit separately.

From the very beginning, I fought flat knitting; it didn't make sense to knit what seemed like six puzzle pieces and then try to fit them together. The shoulders, bound off "in steps," weren't conducive to a neat looking "seam"; the set-in sleeves didn't seem to want to set in; the tiny collar didn't want to fit around the neckline; the side seams interrupted the yarn-over pattern; and grosgrain ribbon had to be sewn under the front openings.

In retrospect, the only useful technique I learned from that sweater was the way the buttonholes were made—they were simply yarn-over holes at the edge of the right front. I remember wearing the faulty (I thought) sweater a few times under a suit jacket to hide the seams, but then I obviously packed it away, to be discovered again all these years later. (Now it travels with me when I teach workshops, serving as a perfect introduction to my seamless-knitting philosophy.) As sewing was another pastime of mine, it did occur to me at some point that it would have been much easier to knit a length of fabric, plunk down some pattern pieces, cut them out, and machine-sew them together, but by then the search was on for a seamless sweater, and I never again worked one with set-in sleeves.

After that unpleasant first sweater experience, I entered what I call my "Brunswick Period" as I turned to a Brunswick pattern with raglan sleeve shaping. This sweater was still worked in pieces, but it was easier to sew in sleeves along straight lines.

This period was also responsible for my adhering to three golden rules:

1. *Always* slip the first stitch of every row as if to purl, for a chain selvedge. (Sampler, p. 31.)
2. *Never* tie in a new ball of yarn at the end of the row, as most knitting directions suggest (unless you are changing color or yarn type). (Sampler, p. 23.)
3. *Never* decrease or increase the edge stitches—always move the decrease or increase one or two stitches into the fabric.

The reasoning behind these golden rules is to keep the selvedge neat and tidy, with no strange bumps or knots to interfere with the sewing of a flat seam. Yes, catching a stitch from one side of a piece of work to the other made a visible seamline, but it formed a pattern of its own as long as there were no irregularities with which to contend. This method was more acceptable to me than working a backstitch through both thicknesses of fabric—I can't stand lumpy seamlines. Of course, this method of sewn-in raglan sleeves is tolerable for sweaters worked in stockinette, but the seams do interrupt any all-over pattern work.

So my search continued. I searched in all the yarn shops I happened across, but they all carried the same line of pattern books, to be coordinated with a specified yarn, and all the directions called for piecework. How I hated to see the words *front, back,* and *sleeves*! Then, in the early 1960s, The Country Needle opened right in the very next town—Cohasset, Massachusetts— and so I entered my "Candide Period." The new shop carried Candide Yarns and Candide's matching designs, but that was all right, as one of the pattern booklets was for seamless top-down raglans. Over the next few years, that four-page leaflet was worn beyond belief, as it was my salvation from seams, and the sweaters could be worked to any size.

Everyone in my family soon had top-down raglans galore, and some sweaters even kept on going down to become dresses. But the plainness of stockinette stitch began to bother me, and (except for being able to fit in a small all-over pattern or a cable here and there) the top-down concept was limiting. I found it difficult to think and plan in reverse. The more I thought about this method, the less sense it made, for nothing on earth starts at the top and is worked downward (except socks!). I felt like I was defying gravity. The yokes of the sweaters worked up rather quickly while the increases kept the brain busy, but after that exercise, boredom set in. It seemed to take forever to get through the body of the sweater and down to the bottom ribbing.

For the next decade, I kept searching. Then I made the most exciting discovery in 1974. At that time, daughter Nancy was a junior in high school and had taken a weaving course in Hingham's excellent art department, with instructor Christopher Brown. One evening she sent me to the library for a particular weaving book, and so I ended up in the textile section. I'd veered off to Dewey Decimal 746.43, when what to my wond'ring eyes should appear, but a real, hardcover book on knitting—*Knitting Without Tears,* by Elizabeth Zimmermann. You young knitters perhaps don't realize that back in those days knitting books were practically non-existent, except for *Mary Thomas's Knitting Book* and *Mary Thomas's Book of Knitting Patterns,* and Barbara Walker's two stitch-pattern books, *Treasury of Knitting Patterns* and *Second Treasury of Knitting Patterns.* Not much like today, with a new knitting book hitting the stands weekly, but these four classics have stood the test of time.

There, in Elizabeth's book was exactly the construction that I had been seeking for so long—a seamless crew neck sweater worked from the bottom up. Even more incredible, it could be knit of any yarn in any size, with the dimensions calculated by percentages. Here, in this book, was the long-sought object of my quest. The timing couldn't have been better, for Nancy and I had just started spinning our own yarns and were wondering what to do with them because they looked like they would not work to a pre-scribed gauge.

So intrigued was I with this woman and her brilliance that I immediately wrote to the publisher for her address and penned my first letter of thanksgiving to her. By return mail, I learned of her Knitting Without Tears Workshop in Wisconsin, and so, in August of 1978, I ventured west to meet this ingenious lady and study with her for a much too short week.

The moment we met, Elizabeth handed me her original manuscript for *Knitting Without Tears* and allowed that I might keep it overnight to marvel at it—talk about a very special moment in one's life!! Handwritten and crammed into a blank book were her years of ideas. She explained that the original title was going to be *Knit One, Purl None,* but Scribner's thought it too confining. As a left-hand knitter, she really did dislike working the purl stitch. Hooray that she did, for her goal when she designed her Seamless Raglan Sweater was a minimum of purl stitches. She achieved this by arranging the neckline so only five short rows of purl were required once the neck shaping started. I, on the other hand, loved the sweater for its seamlessness and for the fact that it allowed me to work without a given gauge, using my own set of measurements.

I returned home excited and inspired by being able to knit "on my own," and soon the concept of the sampler began to develop in my mind—an opportunity to practice techniques needed when not following the directions of others. Then I made a few changes to Elizabeth's original Seamless Raglan Sweater. Since I love to purl, I kept lowering the neckline to plackets and Vs, and then lowered it all the way down to include cardigan styles. With Elizabeth's very kind permission, I put the ideas to paper and started teaching classes, beginning with a six-page handout that kept growing and growing into *The Sweater Workshop*.

As it grew, I kept stopping to ask myself, "Do I really have to say that?" "Do I really have to add that detail?" "Do I really have to bother with that description?" Every time, I would answer myself, *Yes, I really do.* So I took the time and the space to be as specific as possible, and my reward has been the hundreds of appreciative notes, cards, and letters that now fill eight very fat notebooks. I have loved reading every one of them, and share a few containing pertinent (and sometimes humorous) comments in the Introduction and on the back cover. However, one note from an appreciative Texas knitter sums up the rest. On a sheet of paper, five inches by eight, were these few words:

> *Your book,* The Sweater Workshop, *is absolutely the best. Thank you for writing it and helping the rest of us.*
> — *June P., Mesquite, Texas*

Thank you, June, and everyone. Knitters are the best people!

Introduction

From yarn shop to supermarket, you, the knitter, are confronted with various species of patterns for sweaters: sweaters designed by others for you to work to their specifications, the trend of the knitting industry today. This book veers from the current trend. It is a retreat from dependence upon others, an alternative for you who wish to knit sweaters on your own. This retreat begins in the literal sense of the word. It means taking a giant step back to the first cast-on stitch and thoughtfully working step by step through construction possibilities. By so doing, you will become an independent, *thinking* knitter. Your reward will be perfect-fitting, perfectly constructed, seamless sweaters knit of any yarn you choose.

The Sweater Workshop contains no specifics, a detail your sharp eye may have already noticed. Brands of yarn are not stipulated; the customary comparison chart is missing; needle sizes are not recommended; gauge is not prescribed; and there are no columns of sizes and numbers (some in parentheses).

The elimination of these restrictions allows you to design a sweater in an atmosphere of creativity, and with a spirit of adventure. The most enjoyable aspect of this release from rigid attention to written instructions is the freedom to select the yarn of your choice. The energy conscious and the fashion conscious may select yarns for snug, warm shelters, or designer adaptations. The handspinner may create a spectacular original with skeins of handspun yarn that defy categorization; and the weaver is, at last, granted the intelligence to knit a sweater that will be a smashing match for her handwoven skirt. Whether the yarn is handspun or millspun, cotton or wool, thick or thin, its selection is your prerogative.

To knit in this mode, using any desired yarn, a gauge sample is a necessity. Though now you may regard this exercise as a dull chore, in the future, as you grow accustomed to knitting on your own, it

---

— Notes from Knitters —

I now understand knitting in the same way I do weaving, and feel much freer to create something the way I need it to be, not robotically following a line-by-line-pattern!
(Nancy A., Lenoir, N.C.)

will become second nature and an exciting excuse for experimentation. In fact, and properly defined, a gauge sample is a sample piece of fabric, a preview of the delightful sweater to come.

The Gauge Page (p. 98) replaces the usual number systems and provides you with an individual formula for each sweater. The arithmetic is simple and is based on your sample's stitches to the inch and your preferred sweater measurements. Each sweater deserves its own Gauge Page, and you may want to add more specific information, such as yarn type, date, recipient, pattern stitch, and so forth. Kept in a notebook, with samples attached, these pages are a permanent record of projects undertaken, or to be undertaken—a memory book, if you will. If organized papers are not your cup of tea, and if you write small, the Gauge Page can be reduced to a hang tag, or further reduced to one number on file in your head.

The format of *The Sweater Workshop* is the result of years of practical application in classes and workshops attended by novice and veteran knitters of every age, race, color, creed, and sex. Its division into three segments, "The Sweater Sampler," "The Basic Sweater," and "The Sweater Variations,' has naught to do with your ability and experience as a knitter, but to the success of your sweaters. Therefore, this book, as any book, starts on page 1—for all. It is, first, a guide to lead you through the actual mechanics of the processes, and second, a manual to be used over and over as you vary your sweaters' component parts. The directions do presuppose that you can knit and purl (see pp. 47 and 51).

The Sweater Sampler most certainly fits the general definition of a sampler: a piece of ornamental needlework made as an exhibition of skill. Ornamental it is, not with bobbles and cables but with good, sound, tried-and-true construction techniques—the pick of the crop, especially selected for sweater knitting. It incorporates all the skills needed for any sweater you will ever want to design and knit. This unusual piece is a much-loved accomplishment of knitters at all levels of ability. No one is excused from working it.

The Sampler is a "sweater" worked from the bottom up and in the round, as is the Basic Sweater to follow—thus, its correlation to that sweater is obvious. The Sampler paces, in sequence, the options available to you for fit, styling, and originality. Instructions are given for the mechanics of each technique. However, while it's important to learn the mechanics, it's even more crucial to become aware of the peculiar characteristics of stitch combinations. This awareness comes from knitting one after the other, in the same

— Notes from Knitters —

A friend sent me The Sweater Workshop. *I read it like a novel, cover to cover, made the Sampler, and have been knitting sweaters ever since.*
(Shirley Z., New Port Richey, Fla.)

piece of work, not in isolated squares unrelated to each other. A comparison can be made, and the best combination selected for use in a particular situation. The Sampler is an original concept, its contents gathered and culled from myriad sources throughout many knitting years. Most are common-knowledge techniques assembled with a sense of order and meaning; some are of my own invention, and some are borrowed with kind permission.

For the principles of the Basic Sweater I owe a debt of gratitude to Elizabeth Zimmermann and her nemesis, the purl stitch. Tucked in her book *Knitting Without Tears,* pp. 73–75, is a seamless raglan sweater of pure, logical construction—a masterpiece of fabrication. Worked to one's own gauge using percentages, the sweater develops proportionally to any size, with any yarn. With Elizabeth's very kind permission, the Basic Sweater presented here is an adaptation of her Seamless Raglan Sweater.

This *Sweater Workshop* version varies somewhat from the Elizabeth Zimmermann original; most noticeably, the neckline has been lowered and shaped to a true crew neck—a change that requires ten, rather than five, short rows of purl stitches. These extra rows allow for a rounding of the crew neckline by decreasing four stitches on each side of the neck edge every other row.

Built into the directions and not as immediately noticeable to the eye is the fact that in these adaptations the yoke has been deepened by decreasing at the raglan seamlines every fourth round three times, before starting the decreasing every other round. This staggered rate of decrease lengthens the yoke, for more ease and comfort. Also, the start of the raglan seamline decreases—or, as it is called in this version, "GO"—has been moved from the left back raglan seamline to the right front raglan seamline, so that all seamlines may be decreased in proper order when the back-and-forth rows begin for the neck shaping.

Also presented here are six choices of raglan seamlines. Depending on the style and the yarn of the sweater, one choice may be better than the others. On one sweater you may want the raglan seamline to "hide," but on another you might want it to be a prominent feature to complement a design. In addition, you are given a choice of six different sleeve styles, from "fitted" to the "even fuller, fullest"—a decision to base on your intended use of the garment: will the sleeves be slid into a blazer jacket or allowed to gracefully flutter and be admired?

A clear understanding of the Basic Crew Neck Sweater construction and the concept of the Gauge Page will provide you with the framework for many a variation, stir your imagination for other sweater designs, and make it possible for you to knit them on your own.

The sweater variations beginning on p. 130 developed as the result of Elizabeth's inspirational sweater. The motivation was compelling to knit another and another from its mold. Offered in this section are directions for varying the neckline and for varying the style from pullover to cardigan. Then, if worked in an appropriate pattern, either style may be worn inside out, a tribute to the sweater's pure and simple seamless construction.

In summary, *The Sweater Workshop* is a viewpoint. Its aim is to cause you to take an analytical look at sweater knitting with your yarn as the starting point. As you work through the progressive steps, my hope is that you will realize the satisfaction of knitting on your own. The purpose of this book is to hint at potentialities, to stimulate your ideas, and to foster a keen appreciation for the knitted fabric.

No effort has been made to present novelties. Rather, great care has been taken to present selections that you may interpret and develop. The sweaters are purposely photographed *sans* models, in the flat, so their construction details are clearly visible. Through choice, you, the knitter, as any fine craftsman, may strive for originality, quality, and perfection. Your gain will be a true sense of achievement.

Think knitting,

— J.M.F.

— The Famous Sweater Sampler —

Jackie suggests you make a thing called a Sampler—for your head. It looks like a hat one of Dr. Seuss's characters would wear. But "for your head" doesn't mean a hat; it means, for your brain. (Linda W., Benicia, Calif.)

The technique Sampler is a hoot! (Deb K., Philadelphia, Penn.)

I made the Sampler and endured my family's teasing—they insisted it was a sweater for a three-legged dog! (You have to see one to understand.) (Judy S., Shoreline, Wash.)

I learned gads and gads of information from doing the Sampler. I actually modified it a tad. I knitted up a square bottom for it and added an I-cord strap to the top and made it my "on-the-go" knitting bag—talk about an attention-getter! (Crystal B., Milford, Conn.)

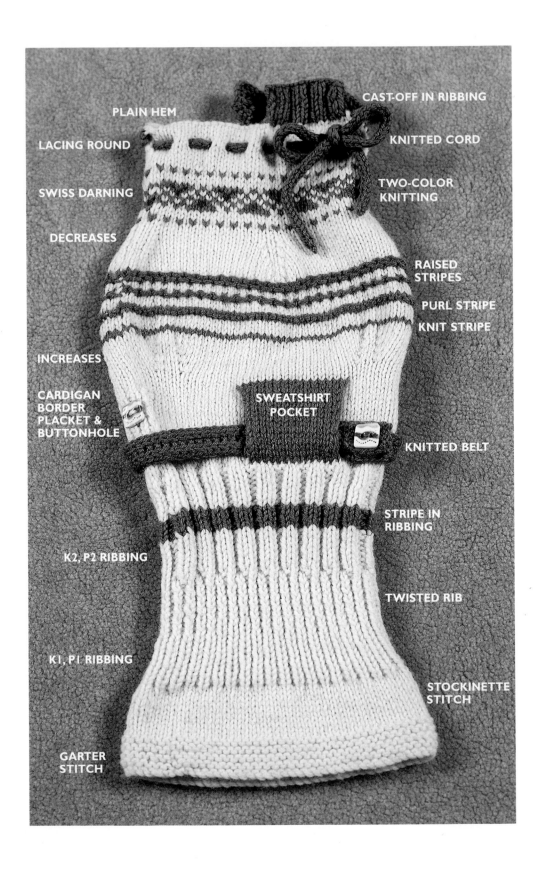

PLAIN HEM

LACING ROUND

SWISS DARNING

DECREASES

INCREASES

CARDIGAN
BORDER
PLACKET &
BUTTONHOLE

K2, P2 RIBBING

K1, P1 RIBBING

GARTER
STITCH

CAST-OFF IN RIBBING

KNITTED CORD

TWO-COLOR
KNITTING

RAISED
STRIPES

PURL STRIPE

KNIT STRIPE

SWEATSHIRT
POCKET

KNITTED BELT

STRIPE IN
RIBBING

TWISTED RIB

STOCKINETTE
STITCH

The Sweater Sampler—
front view

The Sweater Sampler

The Sampler is your opportunity to experience the whys, the wheres, and the whens of knitting a sweater. As you work from stitch to stitch exploring the more obvious how-to's, this underlying focus becomes apparent; reason emerges as the key to a perfectly constructed sweater. Combine this perspective with your own wits, wisdom, and natural flair, and you'll have the makings of many a variation. And varied they will be, for timidity and hesitation will be gone. Proudly, and without a second thought, you'll be adding a pocket here, a bit of lace there. This new "nothing-to-it" attitude will spark your enthusiasm for knitting.

To stir your imagination even more, why not make a fresh new start? Before getting underway with the Sampler, organize a knitting niche. Search the house. Poke through the bags and baskets. Gather all your knitting gear together: the yarns, the needles, and the books. (With luck, you may find the Sampler makings, or even enough yarn for a sweater or two.) Then, confiscate a chest of drawers, a wicker hamper, or a trunk—think big. Station this windfall beside your favorite chair and add a good light. Your space is defined; settle in with contentment.

Just one last thing before you sit down—you'll need paper and a pencil. Not only for your hen-scratchings, but primarily for a list— a list of who wants what sweater, of what yarn, with what pockets where. Your hands will never be idle again.

Now, for the Sampler you will need:

Yarn. Use a *light color* 4-ply knitting worsted-weight yarn—the common, ordinary garden variety. Dark shades obscure technique, which is a blessing sometimes, but not advantageous in the Sampler. One 4-ounce skein is ample, or, as so many have shrunk to 3½ ounces, that amount will just do it. Ply is more important than price, so whether it is 100% virgin Orlon, or 100% virgin wool, be sure the four strands are twisted together tightly, else you will spend too much time dealing with split stitches. You will also need about an ounce of yarn in a contrasting color; those new-found scraps are fine as long as they are approximately the diameter of the base yarn.

Needles. The Sampler is worked on a 16" circular needle, metal, if you can possibly find one, in size #6, or #7, or #8—whichever is most comfortable for you with your yarn. This one-piece tool may seem awkward if you and it are strangers. As you get better acquainted, your hands will adjust to its mold and you will wonder how you ever managed without its convenience for sleeves, hats, scarves, baby garments, and other small knittings.

Also find a set of double-pointed needles in about the same size, one fine double-pointed needle, two stray buttons, the few items listed in Miscellany (p. 81), and that's it. You're ready to start.

Format. The directions for the Sampler are specifically written for right-hand knitters. You left-hand knitters have your own wonderful ways of working the yarn and the needles, and you should have no problem translating the yarn positions from right to left. If a specific right-hand technique is impracticable, such as the cast-on, substitute your own best left-hand method.

The Sampler is worked basically in the round. However, directions for flat knitting are also included, where applicable, for the day you knit a cardigan, or start the neck shaping in a pullover—a move that requires back-and-forth knitting from that moment on. In the few instances where both round and flat directions are given, keep an eagle eye out for, and on, the ROUND—that is the method to follow in the Sampler.

Carefully read through the comment and the ROUND method for each technique before following the actual instructions that will take you through the Sampler. In no time at all, you will have completed your Sampler and assembled the skills for many a sweater on your own.

Good luck, and enjoy! Hold it high when you're through for all to admire—and tell anyone who will listen what it all means. Then tuck it beside you for reference, or better still, hide it. Embroidery samplers seem to endure a haughty fate, lovingly framed and carefully hung, but this one has a tendency to walk by you on a leg, to hang by the chimney (with care), or to prance about as a puppet with eyes above its Afterthought Pocket mouth. On great insistence, it may lead to a mate for sleeves, or with the addition of feet, the fanciest pair of stockings in town. And, who knows, it might even wind up warming a cold fish. But, after all, isn't turnabout fair play? If it weren't for fish, would the sweater exist? What will "they" think in 200 years—a windsock, an urn cozy, a sleeping bag for a Care Bear? A knitter out west wrote that she had to knit *two* Samplers, as one granddaughter discovered it made a perfect doll's dress, and the other granddaughter just had to have one too!

The Sweater Sampler— back view

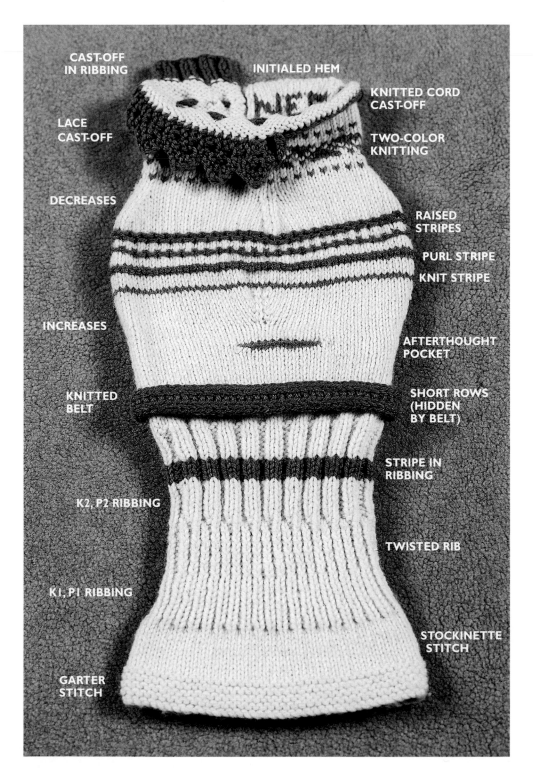

CAST-OFF IN RIBBING

INITIALED HEM

KNITTED CORD CAST-OFF

LACE CAST-OFF

TWO-COLOR KNITTING

DECREASES

RAISED STRIPES

PURL STRIPE

KNIT STRIPE

INCREASES

AFTERTHOUGHT POCKET

KNITTED BELT

SHORT ROWS (HIDDEN BY BELT)

STRIPE IN RIBBING

K2, P2 RIBBING

TWISTED RIB

K1, P1 RIBBING

STOCKINETTE STITCH

GARTER STITCH

THE CABLE CAST-ON

The Cable Cast-On, as its name implies, resembles a smooth cable or rope of yarn, and (significant to an inside-out sweater) it is reversible. More important, it is strong and elastic. In a sweater constructed from the bottom up, the cast-on automatically becomes the base of the body and sleeve ribbing. As part of the ribbing, this row, or round, must have give. Otherwise, the elasticity of the ribbing will be restricted, the edge will wear from stress and strain, and the whole sweater will feel uncomfortable.

The Cable Cast-On guarantees the correct tension; the spacing of the stitches forces looseness.

METHOD

1st Stitch: Make a slip knot, leaving a good 6" tail of yarn. Insert one end of the 16" circular needle through the loop of the slip knot and adjust the loop to fit the needle by pulling down on the ends of the yarn. This first stitch is on the left needle. The slip knot gives easily to insert the right needle.

2nd Stitch: Insert right needle into slip-knot stitch as if to knit.

   ◆ Take the yarn around the right needle as if to knit.
   ◆ Pull the loop through, but do not drop the slip-knot stitch off the left needle.
   ◆ Insert the left needle straight down into the center of the loop.

This straight-down move may be a change if you have previously used the knitting-on method and inserted the left needle from under the loop, thus twisting the stitch before putting it on the left needle. That move tightened the stitch to avoid a row of holes. For the Cable Cast-On, the stitch must **not** be twisted. To repeat: insert the left needle straight down into the center of the loop.

   ◆ **Pull gently** on the yarn as you transfer the loop to the left needle. Do not let the second stitch snuggle up to the slip-knot stitch; keep good distance between them.

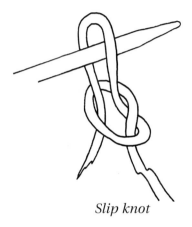

Slip knot

Insert right needle into slip knot.

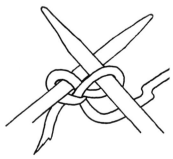

Pull loop through, but don't drop slip-knot stitch off left needle.

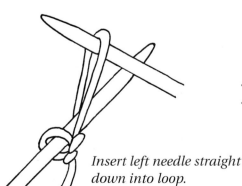

Insert left needle straight down into loop.

Gently transfer loop to left needle.

3rd Stitch: Insert the right needle *between* the first and second stitches. Yes, right smack out *between* the two.

- ◆ Take the yarn around as if to knit.
- ◆ Pull the loop through, but do not drop the second stitch off the left needle.
- ◆ Now, position your left forefinger on the left needle *ahead* of the second stitch.
- ◆ Pull gently on the yarn as you transfer the loop to the left needle. Again, do not let the third stitch snuggle up to the second.

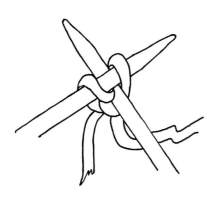

Insert right needle between first and second stitches.

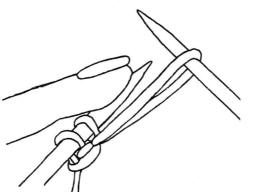

Position left forefinger on left needle ahead of second stitch.

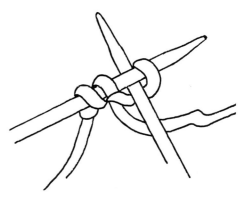

Insert right needle between two previous stitches.

And, it won't, if your left forefinger is on the left needle as it should be. This finger acts as a buffer and holds the new stitch away from the previous stitch—a necessary move for tension as well as speed. To pick up a rhythm casting on in this manner, you must be able to insert the right needle quickly *between* the stitches; having to hunt and peck for the opening will not only slow you down, but will result in an uneven tension and a ragged looking selvedge.

From 4th Stitch on—Continue the third-stitch technique—i.e., insert the right needle *between* the two previous stitches on the left needle—and proceed from there.

> ### *Cast 64 stitches onto the 16" circular needle.*

In the recommended 4-ply knitting worsted-weight yarn, this number of stitches should fit comfortably around the needle. However, if 64 stitches will not reach from end to end for the first round—or if, once underway, you find you must push the stitches around the needle—feel free to add a few more, in multiples of 8. Increase to 72 or 80; that should do it. The more stitches, the easier they flow around the needle, but the longer it will take to work through the Sampler and get on with the sweater.

Imagine for a moment that the stitches you have cast on are for a sweater. In that case, you have arrived at the first Decision Point: is the sweater to be a pullover or a cardigan?

>>> **Decision Point**

The Pullover. Follow directions below for The First Round— Round Knitting.

The Cardigan. Follow directions below for The First Row—Flat Knitting. Also see the Crew Neck Cardigan, p. 194.

The Sampler falls into the pullover category. Follow the directions for round knitting.

THE FIRST ROUND

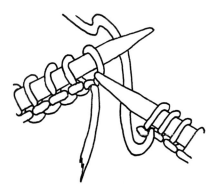

The first stitch—round knitting

Round Knitting. Round (or circular) knitting is worked in "rounds." A round is once around the needle, starting from the slip-knot stitch around to it again. As your work progresses, the knitting will grow toward you and eventually will land in your lap—just as in flat knitting. Do **not** push it out through the center of the circular needle in an effort to "get it out of the way," or you will be effectively turning your work inside out.

METHOD: Transfer the end of the needle with the slip-knot stitch to your left hand.

♦ Untwist and straighten all the stitches on the needle; the bottom of each stitch should head down and be under the needle.

♦ Hold the end of the needle with the last cast-on stitch and the working yarn in your right hand. (The yarn is on the front of the needle. Pay no attention to that; it's where it should be.)

♦ Insert the right needle into the slip-knot stitch on the left needle, and knit the stitch. This joins your knitting.

(For Future Reference: The First Row)

Flat Knitting. Flat knitting is worked in "rows." A row is once across the needle. Turn your work at the end of every row the same as when working on two needles.

METHOD: The end of the needle with the last cast-on stitch and the working yarn remains in your left hand.

♦ Hold the end of the needle with the slip-knot stitch in your right hand.

♦ Insert the right needle into the last cast-on stitch on the left needle, and knit the stitch. This does *not* join your knitting. The stitches will untwist and straighten themselves as you work across the row.

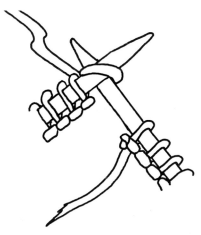

The first stitch—flat knitting

> ***Knit one round.*** (The last 2 stitches at the end of the first round are intertwined. Dig them apart; there are two.)

Stop at the end of the first round—before the slip-knot stitch. The slip knot loosened when you inserted the right needle to join your work. Tighten it by pushing up on the knot as you pull down on the tail. Don't, by the way, grab the tail and work it in with the next few stitches; this is a habit you must break, if you have it. For the tail of the slip knot is crucial to a sweater worked in the round. It identifies the right side seamline of the sweater when the sweater is on. Thus you will know the front from the back as you work. It is the very last end to be tucked in and neatened, for without it a rapid assessment of where you are is not possible.

The term *seamline* is used figuratively as a point of reference to designate either the right or the left side lines of the sweater. The same holds true for the Sampler. And, to further identify its right-side seamline:

> ***Put a marker on the right needle.*** Always start and end the rounds at this marker. Slip it from the left needle to the right needle as you work.

Take one last check to be sure the stitches are all straight on the needle. If you do find a twist, correct it now by reversing the last stitch of the round and taking the yarn through the needle to the back. Beyond this point, it's the start-all-over-again department.

And, yes—in round knitting, one round is always ahead of the other. This shift at the seamline is noticeable only if you change color or are working a pattern. You are the only one who'll be aware of it; when the garment is complete, the tiny jog will disappear.

With the first round worked, it's on to garter stitch.

GARTER STITCH

Garter stitch produces a weft fabric (one having horizontal tendencies). The surface of a garter stitch fabric is bumpy, and the fabric is reversible.

On a given number of stitches, garter stitch makes a *wider* fabric than stockinette stitch. Therefore, to be used as a border or a trim on a stockinette stitch garment, it must be narrowed—either by working it on a smaller needle than that used for the body of the garment or by reducing the number of stitches by 10%.

To count garter stitch rows, each bump equals 2 rows of knitting.

An interesting idiosyncrasy of garter stitch is that, worked in the flat, it will produce a perfect square if you work twice as many rows as you have stitches on the needle.

Always start a gauge sample with 6 or 8 rows of garter stitch to prevent the edge from curling. The sample will then lie flat for the "stitches to the inch" count. Otherwise the job will take three hands: one to hold the edge flat, one to hold the gauge measure, and one to count the stitches.

METHOD

Round: Knit one round, purl one round. Repeat these 2 rounds.
Flat: Knit every row.

> ***Work 7 rounds of garter stitch.*** You have already knit one round, so start with a purl round.

STOCKINETTE STITCH

Stockinette stitch produces a *warp* fabric (one with vertical tendencies). On a given number of stitches it makes a *narrower* fabric than garter stitch. It is the most common and basic knit fabric. The surface of stockinette stitch is smooth on one side, usually the outside, and bumpy on the other, usually the inside. For design purposes, or simply to get two different looks for the price of one sweater, the fabric can be used inside-out.

METHOD

Round: Knit every round.
Flat: Knit one row, purl one row. Repeat these two rows.

> ***Work 5 rounds of stockinette stitch.*** As you work, you should feel your Sampler pulling in a bit.
>
> ***Knit a few stitches into the 6th round, and break your yarn, leaving a 6" tail.*** (You may have to cut it if it's a synthetic.)

MAKING CONNECTIONS

A break can occur in the yarn in any place, at any time, and for a variety of reasons (usually all wrong, inconvenient, and a jolt to one's sense of continuity). Coming to the end of a ball of yarn is final; there is nothing to do but accept it. Not as readily accepted are knots. It's a great temptation to let them slide right by, pretending—or preferring—not to see them. No more. From now on, treat that knot for what it is, a natural break in the yarn, and break it again. You must get rid of the knot. If you are using a commercial yarn, look a few yards ahead of the knot; where there is one, there may be two, and you can rid the yarn of them both at once. Granted, you will be wasting the few yards of yarn in between, but this is certainly preferable to another interruption as soon as you are underway again.

Handspinners, early on, become accustomed to knots in their yarn and tend to be more understanding. After all, the tools of the trade are limiting; a bobbin will hold only so much yarn, and there is no alternative. Knots tied with one's own hand are more readily recognized as a temporary connection to be rectified at some future time.

In the case of overly thick or extra-thin spots in the yarn, the unintentional ones that are not supposed to be there, you'll have to make your own decision about whether to break or not. The circumstance may occur more often with handspun, but commercial yarns are not above having a stray tuft or twit. Be disciplined, and deal with the imperfection as it comes along. That the flaw is there doesn't mean it should be. Why have a thick spot mar the regularity of your knitting—or worse, a thin spot break in the finished garment? If there is any doubt in your mind, break the yarn.

Changing color or yarn type at a seamline also necessitates breaking the yarn. To add a one-round stripe, you might get away with carrying the base yarn up inside your work, but for anything deeper, a clean break is best. Then each end can be eased to tension at the intersection and knotted; this will better control the aforementioned jog at the seamline.

If there is a break in the progression of your knitting, i.e., if you must start anew at a different location in the same piece of work, either in the same color or a contrasting color, treat the new beginning as a change of color.

Now, it's time to get you and your yarn back together. To connect yarns at a break, follow directions for the particular circumstance, either joining the ***same color*** or making a ***change of color***.

Same Color

METHOD

Round or Flat: Make the connection *near* a side seamline.

Flat knitters: Are you listening? *Never* (*never* except to change color) connect the yarn at the end of a row; make the connection a few stitches in from the edge. Keep that selvedge intact whenever possible. (End of aside to flat knitters.)

- ◆ Work to within 6" of the end of the old yarn, or leave more if you must in order to be near a side seam.
- ◆ Hold the old yarn parallel to the stitches you have just worked, its end heading right.
- ◆ Hold the new yarn parallel to the stitches you are about to work, its end heading left.
- ◆ Snatch up both strands of yarn at the stitch you have just worked, and knit, or purl, whatever the case may be, the next two stitches with both strands.
- ◆ Drop the old strand and continue working with the new.

On the next round, or row, don't forget you have made a connection. The tails will serve to remind you to work these two "double" stitches as one; else you will wonder from where the extra stitches came. If you are working with a slippery yarn, work three or more stitches with both strands. In the final analysis, these double stitches are undetectable.

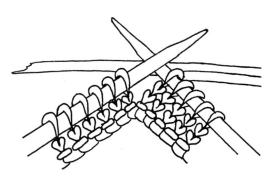

Making connections—same color

Change of Color

METHOD

Round or Flat: Leaving a 6" tail, break the old yarn at the right side seamline, or at the end of a row, or wherever you want to change color.

- ◆ Insert the right needle into the next stitch to be worked.
- ◆ Make a loop with the new yarn 6" from the end.
- ◆ Bring the loop down over the tip of the inserted needle, and pull the yarn through as a stitch. Knot the ends and adjust to tension later.

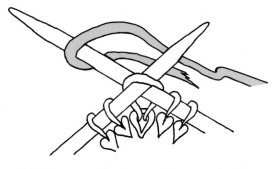

Making connections—change of color

> *Reconnect the Sampler yarn, following directions above for "Same Color."*
>
> *Finish knitting the 6th round.*
>
> *Work 4 more rounds of stockinette stitch.*

THE RIBBINGS

Until now, you may have blithely followed written directions for a ribbing style or, on your own, substituted one for another because you thought it might look better. Looks aside, you must discover how each ribbing acts and feels. The ribbing is the most significant factor in the shaping of a sweater. Your choice of style determines whether the sweater hangs loose, fits snug, or is somewhere in between. As you work the three most common ribbings, one after the other, notice their pull-in tendencies. Then stop and think: Is that the type of ribbing I want? Will it do the job in this weight yarn? Do I want more or less elasticity? The choice is yours.

Knit 1, Purl 1

K1, P1 is the least elastic of the ribbings. It is best used with fine yarn for baby wear, as shape is not of consequence. It does not have the elasticity to hold in a medium- or heavy-weight yarn, and will not snap back into shape once stretched. The knit stitches tend to have a crooked appearance no matter how skillfully the tension is controlled.

METHOD
Round: On an even number of stitches, K1, P1 around. Repeat for as many rounds as desired.
Flat: On an uneven number of stitches, repeat these 2 rows:
   Row 1—K1, P1 across the row, end K1.
   Row 2—P1, K1 across the row, end P1.

> **Work 10 rounds of K1, P1.**

Knit 1b, Purl 1— The Twisted Rib

Worked correctly, K1b, P1 is a decorative ribbing, as the twisted knit stitch gives it a pleasing appearance. Its elasticity factor is practically nil, which explains why Aran Isle sweaters, where it's most often used, simply hang with no shape at all. For a cardigan style that is more jacket than sweater this ribbing is fine, but if you'd rather your pullover had a bit more pull-in, see K2, P2, which follows.

K1b, P1 is a tricky rib, and the method must change in order to work it correctly in the round. You may have discovered this peculiarity of K1b, P1 rib already. Have you ever worked a sweater with this ribbing in the flat, and then worked its neck ribbing in the round? If you have, note the difference in the knit stitches. In the neck ribbing, they are tense; in the body and sleeve ribbings, they are at ease. The reason for this dissimilarity is that in flat knitting the K1b stitch of the outside row is purled on the inside row, and thus has a chance to straighten up. In round knitting, the K1b stitch is twisted every round. Who can blame it for becoming stiff, tight, and slanted? It is being strangled.

Therefore, in round knitting, to obtain the same soft, relaxed decorative twist as in flat knitting, you must alternate a round of K1b, P1 with a round of plain K1, P1. To keep track of these alternating rounds, it might be wise to put a second marker on the needle at the seamline as you start the K1b, P1 round, and remove it as you start the plain K1, P1 round. Then if the phone rings or the paper boy knocks, you will know where you are when you return—rather a "one if by land, two if by sea" sort of reminder.

K1b: With the tip of the right needle heading left, insert it out through the *back* of the knit stitch, and complete the stitch as usual. This gives a twist to the knit stitch.

METHOD

Round: On an even number of stitches, alternate these two rounds:

> *Round 1*—K1b, P1 around.
> *Round 2*—K1, P1 around.

Flat: On an uneven number of stitches, repeat these 2 rows:

> *Row 1*—K1b, P1 across the row, end K1b.
> *Row 2*—P1, K1b across the row, end P1.

The K1b stitch for twisted rib

> ***Work 10 rounds of Twisted Rib.***

Knit 2, Purl 2

K2, P2 is a good, snug, all-purpose rib for use with any weight yarn. Be generous: the more of it you do, the more elasticity it will have. Work at least 2", if not 3", on the body of a sweater; 3" to 4" on a sleeve cuff, especially for the small set. If the ribbing does stretch out of shape, a good washing—or, if time is short, a good lengthwise tug—will snap it right back to its former state; you can't destroy it.

And, to give more shape to that Aran Isle pullover, work a round of K2b, P2 alternately with a round of plain K2, P2—a ribbing that retains the decorative twist but with more pull-in.

METHOD

Round: On a number of stitches divisible by 4, K2, P2 around. Repeat for as many rounds as desired.

Flat: On a number of stitches divisible by 4, plus 2, repeat these 2 rows:

> *Row 1*—K2, P2 across the row, end K2.
> *Row 2*—P2, K2 across the row, end P2.

Work 8 rounds of K2, P2.

Did you feel that knitted fabric pulling in? What a difference a stitch makes; K2, P2 hardly seems related to K1, P1. And that statement is the key to the elasticity of ribbings. The higher the number of *equal* alternating knits and purls, the greater the amount of pull-in to the fabric.

If you thought K2, P2 was an improvement over K1, P1, try some K3, P3. The Scottish fishermen's ganseys were all ribbed with K3, P3. For looks? No, for the purposeful, hug-the-body qualities of this ribbing. The last thing these hard-working salts needed was a loose sweater flopping about as they struggled with their catch. (And, to avoid chafed wrists, the gansey sleeves were three-quarter length. Oh, were they smart. Why push up a wet, soggy sleeve when a shorter one is the cure?)

So, if you want a very snug ribbing, use K3, P3. Just remember that it must be worked over a number of stitches divisible by 6 in the round, and a number of stitches divisible by 6, plus 3, in the flat. And, on it goes—from K4, P4 to K5, P5 to K6, P6—each with a greater amount of snap and bounce than the one before.

Sometime—and you may put the Sampler aside to try it now, if you wish—heed the advice of Mary Thomas (in *Mary Thomas's Book of Knitting Patterns*) and work the two fabric samples described in the sidebar that follows, on p. 28. Not only will you see how alive K4, P4 is, but you will clearly see how the choice of a pattern stitch will change the width and the height of a knitted fabric.

Then, it's on to add a bit of color.

VERTICAL RIBBED FABRIC vs. HORIZONTAL RIBBED FABRIC

Sample A—Vertical Ribbed Fabric

METHOD: Use 2 double-pointed needles. Cast on 32 stitches. Work K4, P4 for 40 rows. Cast off.

Sample B—Horizontal Ribbed Fabric

METHOD: Use 2 double-pointed needles. Cast on 32 stitches.

Row 1: Purl.	**Row 5:** Knit.
Row 2: Knit.	**Row 6:** Purl.
Row 3: Purl.	**Row 7:** Knit.
Row 4: Knit.	**Row 8:** Purl.

Repeat these 8 rows 5 times for a total of 40 rows. Cast off.

Incredible? Do you see why a sweater in a vertical ribbing pattern fits like a second skin? Can you also see why a sweater in a horizontal ribbed pattern would not?

These gauge samples—worked on the same number of stitches for the same number of rows on the same size needles—demonstrate the importance of always working test swatches in your chosen pattern. The vertical (warp) fabric of K4, P4 ribbing is about ⅓ the width of the horizontal (weft) fabric of 4 knit rows, 4 purl rows.

Alternating one row or round of K4, P4 with one of plain knit or purl results in Garter Stitch Rib (on right)—a fabric with the look of a rib but without the extreme elasticity. A sweater knit entirely in Garter Stitch Rib is shown on p. 155.

STRIPES IN RIBBING

For a neat, clean-cut stripe in a ribbing, an all-knit round, or row, must be worked on the outside of the fabric to introduce the new color. This all-knit round, or row, prevents the new color from dropping below the old color in the purl stitches. The interplay of colors then borders the stripe on the inside. Keep this phenomenon in mind if you intend to roll up a sleeve cuff or the brim of a cap. On the other hand, if you intend to keep it rolled up forever, and if you are working in the flat, reverse the procedure and work an all-purl row on the outside. Remember to make use of this technique whenever there is a purl stitch involved in a color change; don't restrict its use to ribbings per se. All-over sweater patterns, such as K6, P2, or P7, K1, are variations of ribbing patterns, and their stripes should be treated in the same manner.

METHOD

Round or Flat: With the new color, and on the outside of the fabric, *knit every stitch* around the round or across the row. In other words, forget momentarily that you are working a ribbing pattern. On the next round or row, resume the ribbing pattern. Continue ribbing in the new color for the desired depth of the stripe.

To return to the original color, or to change to still another, repeat the all-knit round, or row, on the outside.

> *Work a 4-round stripe in the K2, P2 ribbing.*
>
> *Work 8 rounds of K2, P2.* (Take a peek inside; design possibilities?)
>
> *Work 3 rounds of stockinette stitch, adding a marker after the 32nd stitch.*

The Sampler now has two side "seams." The marker at the tail is the right seamline. The marker you just added is the left seamline.

SHORT ROWS

Short rows can be used to add extra length, a detail that allows a custom fit for those who are always tugging down the back of their sweater. Working the technique once adds two rounds or rows to the back, and for this reason, once is generally enough. Consider the diameter of your yarn, and consequently, your number of rows to the inch (a measure you can usually ignore). In a medium- to heavy-weight yarn, two rounds or rows could add one-half inch or more, an ample amount. In a fine yarn, four extra rounds or rows may be needed.

In any case, work the short rows about 3" above the ribbing, and again 3" above that, if a second set is applicable. If short rows are added, put a large safety pin somewhere in the back of the sweater as a reminder. You don't want the short rows ending up in the front.

Short rows do have their limitations. Confine them to a plain sweater, or one in which the extra rows will not interfere with a pattern. The directions for working short rows are the same for both round and flat knitting, except for the last step. For the Sampler, be sure to follow the *round* directions at that point.

METHOD

Round or Flat: Work around (or across) to within 3 stitches of the left seamline.

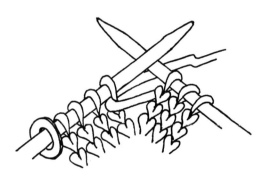

Short rows—the wrapping.

 ◆ Put the yarn forward (as if to purl), slip 1 stitch as if to purl, put the yarn back, put the slipped stitch back on the left needle.

 ◆ *Turn your work.* (You are now looking down into the Sampler, or if this were a sweater in the round, the sweater.)

 ◆ Purl across to within 3 stitches of the right seamline, put the yarn back (as if to knit), slip 1 stitch as if to purl, put the yarn forward, put the slipped stitch back on the left needle.

 ◆ *Turn your work.* You have wrapped the yarn around 1 stitch at each turn to avoid a hole in the fabric. The wrapping is in a horizontal position. Now, to stand it up:

 ◆ Work across to within 3 stitches of the left seamline. *With the tip of the right needle, lift the front of the wrapping and put it on the left needle with the stitch it was wrapped around. Knit the two together as one stitch.*

 ◆ **Round only:** Continue working around to the 3rd stitch after the right seamline. Repeat * to *. All done. Finish the round.

 ◆ **Flat only:** Continue working to the end of the row. On the next row, work to within 3 stitches of the right seamline. Repeat * to *, except *purl* the two together as one stitch. All done. Finish the row.

> *Work the short rows once.*
>
> *Work 2 rounds of stockinette stitch.*
>
> *Stop at the right seamline.*
>
> *Remove the marker.* For a short while you will be working back and forth on the circular needle—flat knitting.

Read about Chain Selvedge, then move on to Cardigan Border, below.

CHAIN SELVEDGE

A neat selvedge is essential to the front edges of a cardigan sweater and the sides of a sweatshirt pocket. For that matter, it is essential to anything knit in the flat. Pity the knitters of sweaters in pieces who attempt to sew an even seam without the consistency of even selvedges. (This pity extends back a few pages to include those who connect their yarns at the end of the row.) It might be possible to hide an irregular selvedge in a seam, but it's not an enviable job.

By slipping the first stitch of every row as if to purl, you will be rewarded with a uniform edge—the chain selvedge. Practice this "slip one" move until it becomes second nature whenever you are working in the flat. Pay particular attention to the position of the yarn, for though you are slipping as if to purl, the yarn is not always in the front. If a chosen pattern doesn't have an extra stitch to slip, add one. A simple solution, a world of difference, and vital if the edge is to be exposed to the naked eye.

METHOD

Flat: In flat knitting, always slip the first stitch as if to purl. This refers only to the position of the needles; the position of the yarn varies from front to back:

- ◆ If the first stitch was knitted at the end of the previous row, slip as if to purl with the yarn in *front*.
- ◆ If the first stitch was purled at the end of the previous row, slip as if to purl with the yarn in *back*.

The slip-one selvedge resembles a chain of stitches, each chain stitch being equal to two rows of knitting. Because of its appearance and ratio, the chain of stitches clears up a sometimes perplexing chore for all knitters; that is, knitting up the stitches for the neck ribbing of a sweater. Even a sweater worked in the round must be worked back and forth on the needle once the neck shaping starts, but by slipping the first stitch of every row, you will be rewarded with a visible chain of stitches. No longer will you have to wonder what, where, or how many to knit up; they will be right there looking at you. The added bonus is that the proportion will be correct and the neck ribbing will lie flat.

Jumping ahead a bit, but while we're on the subject—

Knitting into the chain selvedge

Knitting into the Chain Selvedge
METHOD

♦ Hold the edge of the fabric horizontally in your left hand so that the edge is up straight and the chain doesn't roll to the back.

♦ Put the tip of the right needle under both strands of the chain stitch, take the yarn around as if to knit, and pull the loop through onto the needle.

♦ Repeat for the length of the chain.

THE CARDIGAN BORDER

The Cardigan Border is a 6-stitch border of K1, P1. It is worked at each end of the needle right along with the body of the sweater. The obvious advantage to a knit-along border is that once the sweater is done, it's done; there are no strange additions to be made. The K1, P1 rib makes an edge sturdy enough to support a button; its heftiness is more visible inside than out. Garter and seed stitch borders, though perhaps more decorative, lack stability. Confine them to your afghans and scarves.

In a medium- or heavy-weight yarn, a 6-stitch border should be wide enough. However, in a fine yarn you may want to increase to 8 or 10 stitches in K1, P1. If that sounds like too many, remember that the purl stitches hide, so the actual border is only half that width. For some reason, the K1, P1 acts more like it should in a border than in an all-around ribbing.

The Cardigan Border in the Sampler is worked on a mini version of a placket neck opening. To prepare for this, turn the Sampler so that you are looking down into it. The stitch with the working yarn should be in your left hand. Insert the right needle between the first two stitches on the left needle, and proceed to:

> *Cast on 6 stitches.*
>
> *Purl the 6 cast-on stitches and all the others around to the opening you have created.* (Do not slip the first one, as it is not yet an established stitch.)
>
> *Turn your work.*

You are now in a position to work the Cardigan Border over the first and last 6 stitches on the needle. You will be working back and forth on the needle—flat knitting. Keep the stitches in between the borders in stockinette stitch. This means that you will knit these stitches on the outside rows and purl them on the inside rows. If this were a sweater with a pattern stitch between the borders, you might very well have to reverse the knits and purls for the inside rows. Hence the word *work* in the phrase "work across to the last 6 stitches." It means to do whatever you must do to keep your pattern in order.

One final caution—carefully watch the position of the yarn for the slip stitch (selvedge) at the beginning of each row. Notice also that in the instructions below the slip stitch takes the place of what should be a K1 at the beginning of row 1 (outside row) and what should be a P1 at the beginning of row 2 (inside row).

METHOD

Row 1—The outside row: Slip 1 (slip as if to purl with the yarn in *back,* bring the yarn to the front), P1, K1, P1, K1, P1, work across to the last 6 stitches, P1, K1, P1, K1, P1, K1. *Turn your work.*

Row 2—The inside row: Slip 1 (slip as if to purl with the yarn in *front*, bring the yarn to the back), K1, P1, K1, P1, K1, work across to the last 6 stitches, K1, P1, K1, P1, K1, P1. *Turn your work.*

Repeat rows 1 and 2 for the length of the border.

> ***Work 4 rows with Cardigan Border.***

BUTTONHOLES

Of all the methods that exist for making buttonholes, there is only one that will do the job swiftly and neatly: the Yarn Over, or YO for short. This quick maneuver, followed by an equally quick "knit two together" (or K2 tog, for short), guarantees a proper buttonhole because the size of the hole changes with the weight of the yarn. The opening is therefore proportionate for an appropriate button.

LARGE BUTTONS are distracting. So are LARGE BUTTONHOLES. How sad to see those sweaters, particularly Aran Isles, with a row of great wooden buttons marching up one side front, paired with a row of misshaped holes marching down the other. Weeks, perhaps months, of knitting vanish before your very eyes. Do away with these offenders. Use proper-sized buttons color-matched to the yarn, and replace those complex slots with a simple YO. Then all your beautiful knitting will be the focal point.

Now, how do you space the buttonholes? To begin with, put two in the ribbing, the area that takes the most stress and strain. Make one about half an inch after you start the ribbing, and the other about half an inch before you stop the ribbing. When buttoned, the two will equalize the pressure and hold the bottom closing straight—no gap. Space the rest about three inches apart, or use another sweater for a guide. These little fellows hide in the purl groove; if one does end up in the wrong spot, stitch him together— no one will know.

An alternative solution to the button problem is to eliminate the embellishment entirely. Work buttonholes at each end of the needle, and with a coordinating or contrasting knitted cord, lace the sweater as you would a shoe (see photo on p. 176). This option admittedly changes the nature of the garment from cardigan to pullover—unless you have the time and patience to lace and un-lace for each wearing. Nevertheless, the idea has merit; kept laced, the sweater has a chance of being worn. How many cardigans are? They are thrown over the shoulders, draped around the neck, or tied at the waist and sat on; a shawl or a blanket would be more practical and present a better picture. No wonder that, nine times out of ten, the sweater that stands out in a crowd is a pullover. Displayed on the body proper, as intended, it makes a positive statement and thus attracts attention. At the same time, it reflects its wearer's positive qualities. Not the type to hem and haw, this one—do I need a sweater, or don't I? A decision was made, the sweater pulled on, and worn out the door to catch eyes.

METHOD

To make a buttonhole, substitute the following beginning or end-ing for the beginning or ending of Row 1 of Cardigan Border:

Woman's: Begin Row 1 with Slip 1, P1, K1, YO*, K2 tog, P1.

Man's: End Row 1 with P1, K1, YO*, K2 tog, P1, K1.

*To a right-hand knitter, YO simply means to put the yarn forward as if to purl. The yarn then goes over the needle by itself from this position as you knit the next two stitches together, thus adding one stitch to compensate for the one you are losing by knitting two together. On the next row, work the YO stitch as K1.

The buttonhole—YO, K2 tog

Work a buttonhole row. (Woman's: Begin Row 1.)

Work 2 more rows of Cardigan Border. (All this seem-ingly blank knitting in between the borders will be the home for pockets.)

At the beginning of the next row, cast off* the 6 added stitches, then purl across to the last 6 stitches and work the border.

> **To cast off:* Slip 1, K1, pass the slipped stitch over the knit; P1, pass the knit over the purl; K1, pass the purl over the knit; etc.

At the beginning of the next row, work the border, and then knit to the end.

Now it's back to circular knitting to re-join the Sampler. *Insert the right needle (the one with the working yarn) into the first stitch on the left needle.*

Knit one round.

Put a marker back on the needle at the right seamline. Check to be sure the left seamline marker is still there.

A placket neck in a sweater would, of course, not be joined back together, but worked straight and open to the top. By joining your work, you have created a side placket (or, if it were in the front, a fly?). Sew a button on the flap under the buttonhole to keep it closed and out of your way while you finish the Sampler.

THE SWEATSHIRT POCKET

This pocket certainly needs no introduction. It's always right there with you, ready to warm your hands in an instant—a built-in muff, if you will. And, this one is truly built-in, or rather knit-in, without a single stitch to sew. Though the concept is not new to you, the construction might be: the pocket grows out of the ribbing and then joins forces with the sweater in progress. The principle of its construction remains the same for any size sweater.

The sweatshirt pocket in the Sampler is a mini version of the one in the sweater on pp. 183–87.

Work the following directions line by line for the Sampler's mini version of the sweatshirt pocket.

METHOD: The front of the Sampler has 32 stitches. The pocket will cover the center 12.

◆ Starting at the right seamline, work 10 stitches beyond the *left* seamline marker.

Stop.

◆ With your finger trace the 11th stitch down to its source in the row above the ribbing.

◆ Slide a fine double-pointed needle under one half of this 11th stitch. Each stitch has two sides; it doesn't matter which one.

◆ Aiming to the left, slide the needle under one-half of each of the next 11 stitches. You should have 12 "stitches" on the fine needle.

◆ Connect a *new* yarn at the first stitch on the right end of the fine needle. ***Do not*** break the working yarn of the Sampler itself; you will need it right where it is in a minute. Use the other end of the Sampler yarn—or, better yet, a scrap of a contrasting color.

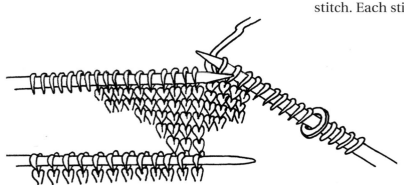

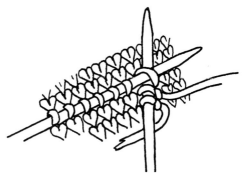

Slide the fine needle under one-half of each of the next 11 stitches.

◆ Using a Sampler-size (or close to it), double-pointed needle, knit the 12 stitches from the fine needle. Put the fine needle aside; it has done its job, which was to pick up this bottom row of stitches without stretching them any more than necessary. The flap that is to be the pocket is worked in flat knitting on two Sampler-size double-pointed needles.

◆ ***Turn your work,*** and purl the 12 stitches. You will now be working back and forth on the 12 stitches, knitting a row, purling a row. To practice chain selvedge:

Knit rows—Slip the first stitch as if to purl, yarn in back.

Purl rows—Slip the first stitch as if to purl, yarn in front.

◆ Work until the pocket knitting reaches the top edge of the Sampler knitting.

Stop after a purl row.

◆ Break the pocket yarn and secure it.

◆ Hold the pocket needle so that the 12 stitches of the pocket are lined up in front of the next 12 stitches to be knit on the Sampler needle.

◆ With the Sampler yarn and needle, join the pocket to the Sampler by knitting together a stitch from the pocket needle with a stitch from the Sampler needle.

◆ ***Finish the knit round.***

Knit the 12 stitches from the fine needle.

Knit together a stitch from the flap with a stitch from the sweater.

Did you survive? Do you have a pocket? Wasn't it easy? This Rube Goldberg creation is the result of my being too lazy to get up and search the books for sweaters with pockets and then wade through directions to see how others have tackled the job. This piece of ingenuity seemed logical, and the end product is a success.

Important: In a sweater, work the first and last 6 stitches of the pocket in Cardigan Border (p. 32) so the pocket will have firm edges. In the Sampler, you only had 12 stitches to begin with so . . . oh well, you can figure that one out. Notice the curl to the stockinette stitch edge. Worked to be sewn, it would be fine; but for an edge to be on view, it doesn't pass muster. Nor would it wear; it's too flimsy. The Cardigan Border provides the sturdiness needed on the edges.

For future reference: If for some other flat project a 6-stitch border is too wide, work just the second and next-to-last stitches as purls on the knit row. These purl stitches will keep the edges flat.

THE BAR INCREASE

Though there are many styles of increases, the Bar Increase is the one used to shape the body and the sleeves of the Basic Sweater. It is worked in two ways, either evenly spaced or in pairs. Worked evenly spaced, it is used to increase the number of stitches from the body and sleeve ribbing to the body and sleeve proper. Worked in pairs, it is used to gradually shape the sleeves.

The Bar Increase produces a visible horizontal bump, or bar, to the left of the original stitch. Worked evenly spaced in the last round of ribbing, these bumps mingle nicely with the purl stitches. Worked in pairs in a sleeve, the bumps form a pattern, or track, at the seamline and can easily be counted.

In the Sampler, the Bar Increase is worked in pairs to somewhat simulate the sleeve seamline possibilities.

METHOD: Knit the stitch but do not drop the stitch off the left needle, knit out through the back of the same stitch, and then drop the stitch off the left needle.

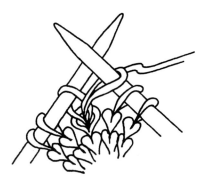

Knit the next stitch. Do not drop the stitch off the needle.

Knit out through the back of the same stitch.

Then, drop the stitch off the needle.

> *Read through the following directions for Increases*
> *Evenly Spaced and proceed to Increases in Pairs.*

Increases Evenly Spaced

In a sweater, evenly spaced increases are worked in the last round, or row, of the body and/or the sleeve ribbing while you are still on the ribbing-size needle. Keep the round, or row, in your ribbing pattern except for the stitch you increase. Work the Bar Increase into that stitch as described above, regardless of whether the stitch is a knit or a purl. (Working a purl increase into a purl stitch will leave a hole.)

METHOD: To increase evenly spaced throughout a round or across a row, divide the number of stitches on the needle by the number of stitches you must increase. The quotient is the stitch in which to work the Bar Increase.

Example: If you have 56 stitches on the needle and you must increase 8 stitches, divide 56 by 8. The quotient is 7. Therefore, work the Bar Increase into every 7th stitch throughout the round or across the row. *In round knitting,* start counting at the seamline marker. *In flat knitting,* start counting at the beginning of the row, unless you are working a border. In that case, position the increases in the body of the sweater only, without counting the border stitches.

The division won't always come out even, of course. If it doesn't, don't worry about it. Increase into the quotient stitch, but not into any part of the remainder. The remainder takes care of itself.

Increases in Pairs

To shape fitted and semi-fitted sleeves (p. 106), pairs of Bar Increases are worked at the seamline with 0, 1, or 2 stitches between. As the "bar" of the Bar Increase is always to the left of the original stitch, it will look as if there is an additional stitch for separation.

Seamline increases A, or B, or C (below) differ only in their width. In the Sampler, you will work all three simultaneously. In a sleeve, select *one* of the three and work it at the seamline.

METHOD

Seamline Increase A: Knit to within 1 stitch of seamline marker, *increase,* slip marker, *increase.*

Seamline Increase B: Knit to within 1 stitch of seamline marker, *increase,* slip marker, K1, *increase.*

Seamline Increase C: Knit to within 2 stitches of seamline marker, *increase,* K1, slip marker, K1, *increase.*

To prepare the Sampler for working increases:

> *Knit one round, removing the marker at the left seam-line. Knit one round, putting markers after the 20th, 40th, and 60th stitches. Note:* it will be easier to work these make-believe seamlines if the markers are of different colors and differ too from the one at the right seamline. Mark in the spaces provided in the box below which increase will be worked at what marker color. Then you can talk and knit at the same time without losing track of where you are.

In a sleeve, the pairs of increases are worked about an inch apart where desired for a particular style. To save time here in the Sampler, the increases are worked every other round. Therefore, the track will not look exactly as it does in an actual sweater.

If you happen to prefer another style of increase, work it instead of the Bar Increase, or work them side by side in your Sampler for comparison.

> *Knit one round, working:*
>
> Increase A at 1st marker, _____ (marker color).
>
> Increase B at 2nd marker, _____ (marker color).
>
> Increase C at 3rd marker, _____ (marker color).
>
> *Knit one straight round.*
>
> *Repeat these 2 rounds 3 times.* On the last round, remove all markers except the one at the right seamline.
>
> You now have 88 stitches on the needle.

STRIPES

What's your pleasure? How do you see them? Are they bold and bright, or mellow and subdued? Single-round statements, or an all-over thesis? Flat and smooth, or full of texture?

From the earliest times, individuals have personalized their fabrics in this most elementary manner. And, as the proverbial duck takes to water, sweaters take to stripes. Scraps would remain scraps without stripes.

The Knit Stripe

There are so many variables, but for the average size 40 sweater, a single-round stripe will take about 3 to 5 yards of yarn. If you are using scraps and want a more accurate measure, try this: Stop at the seamline a few rounds before the stripe. Pull out about 5 yards of your working yarn—you don't need a yardstick, just nose to fingertip—and tie a knot at the end of this measure. Start at the seamline and work one round. How far are you from the knot?

METHOD *(round or flat):* At the beginning of a round or an outside row, using another color or another yarn, knit every stitch around the round or across the row. Continue in stockinette stitch for the desired depth of the stripe. To return to the original yarn, or make another change, repeat the above.

The Purl Stripe

The humble purl, in another color or another yarn, produces a proud stripe. Hark back to stripes in ribbing and remember what happens with a change of color or yarn when there is a purl stitch involved. The same holds true in a stockinette stitch fabric, for what looks like a simple purl stripe, isn't. A round or row of knit must be worked in the stripe yarn first. This round or row of knit stitches disappears under the next round or row of purl stitches, thus making a clear purl stripe. You must figure on using double the amount of yarn for a "single" purl stripe.

METHOD
Round
- ◆ Knit 1 round with another color or another yarn. Purl 1 round with the same.
- ◆ Continue working purl rounds for the desired stripe depth.
- ◆ To return to the original yarn, knit the next round.

Flat
- ◆ Starting on the outside, knit 2 rows with another color, or another yarn.
- ◆ To continue, purl the outside rows and knit the inside rows for the desired stripe depth.
- ◆ To return to the original yarn, knit it in (on the outside) or purl it in (on the inside).

> *Work a one-round knit stripe.*
> *Knit three rounds with the Sampler yarn.*
> *Work a "single" purl stripe* (actually worked over two rounds, as explained above).

> *Knit three rounds with the Sampler yarn.*

The Raised Stripe

Weavers, move over; you no longer have a corner on the market for texture. The Raised Stripe is the knitter's answer to your soumak and twining. The yarn loops along above the fabric, the more contrast to the background the better.

The Raised Stripe makes a perfect haven for odd lengths of lumpy handspun or other novelty yarns, yet don't discount the idea of working this stripe in the self-same yarn, for it offers a subtle swag in relief, tone on tone, to decorate an otherwise plain fabric.

To achieve that subtle swag, you work only rounds, or rows, *1 and 2* in the directions below. To produce a linked chain of texture, work all 4 rounds or rows. The steps are the same, regardless of whether you are working these rounds or rows in the same yarn, in another color, or in another yarn.

METHOD

Round: Work on an even number of stitches.

> **Round 1:** *Slip 1 (as if to purl, yarn in back), K1* around.
> **Round 2:** *Slip 1 (as if to purl, yarn in front), P1* around.
> **Round 3:** *K1, slip 1 (as if to purl, yarn in back)* around.
> **Round 4:** *P1, slip 1 (as if to purl, yarn in front)* around.

Flat: Work on an uneven number of stitches.

> **Row 1:** *Slip 1 (as if to purl, yarn in back), K1*. Repeat * to * across row, ending with slip 1.
> **Row 2:** Repeat Row 1.
> **Row 3:** *Slip 1 (as if to purl, yarn in back)*. Repeat * to * across row, ending with K1.
> **Row 4:** Repeat row 3.

Try the Raised Stripe in your Sampler this way:

> *Work rounds 1 and 2 in another color.*
> *Knit 2 rounds with the Sampler yarn.*
> *Work rounds 1, 2, 3, and 4 in another color.*
> *Knit 2 rounds with the Sampler yarn.*

That gives you the idea of, first, the swag and then, the chain. By all means, experiment further in the Sampler with different yarns and colors, if you want.

THE RAGLAN SEAMLINE DECREASES

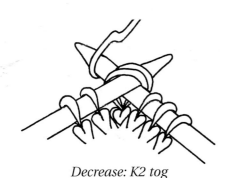

Decrease: K2 tog

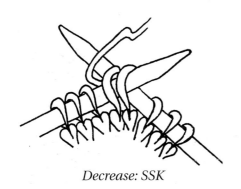

Decrease: SSK

To shape the yoke of the Basic Sweater and all its variations, you must decrease at the four raglan seamlines. Offered here are six different methods of working the seamlines. Your choice depends on the style of the sweater, whether fancy or casual; the yarn of the sweater, smooth or textured; and the design of the sweater, plain or patterned.

You will practice four basic raglan seamlines in your Sampler. Directions for two other, more decorative, raglan seamlines follow the basic four.

Each method has its own characteristics and appearance, and the seamline widths vary—being two, three, or four stitches wide. Think of each seamline as a whole, the sum of its parts.

All these raglan seamlines are constructed with a combination of decreases, one worked before the marker and one worked after the marker, with 0, 1, or 2 knit stitches in between. The first four seamlines are worked using K2 tog in combination with SSK:

> **K2 tog:** Insert the right needle into the front of 2 stitches and knit them together as if they were one. K2 tog leans **right**.

> **SSK:** Slip as if to knit, slip as if to knit, insert the left needle into the front of the two slipped stitches (from left to right), and knit them together as if they were one. SSK leans **left**.

Raglan Seamlines A, B, B-Reverse, and C

METHOD *(round or flat)*: The seamlines are worked on the outside of the sweater.

Raglan Seamline A: Knit to within 2 stitches of the seamline marker, K2 tog, slip marker, SSK.

Raglan Seamline B: Knit to within 2 stitches of the seamline marker, K2 tog, slip marker, K1, SSK.

Raglan Seamline B-Reverse: Knit to within 2 stitches of the seamline marker, SSK, slip marker, K1, K2 tog.

Raglan Seamline C: Knit to within 3 stitches of the seamline marker, K2 tog, K1, slip marker, K1, SSK.

Their Characteristics

Raglan Seamline A "comes together" as a perforation. Use it whenever you do not want a seamline interfering with a pattern. This two-stitch seamline hides, and in a textured yarn it disappears altogether. However, in a plain stockinette stitch yoke, the fact that SSK does not exactly match K2 tog is evident. This

6 Styles of Raglan Seamlines

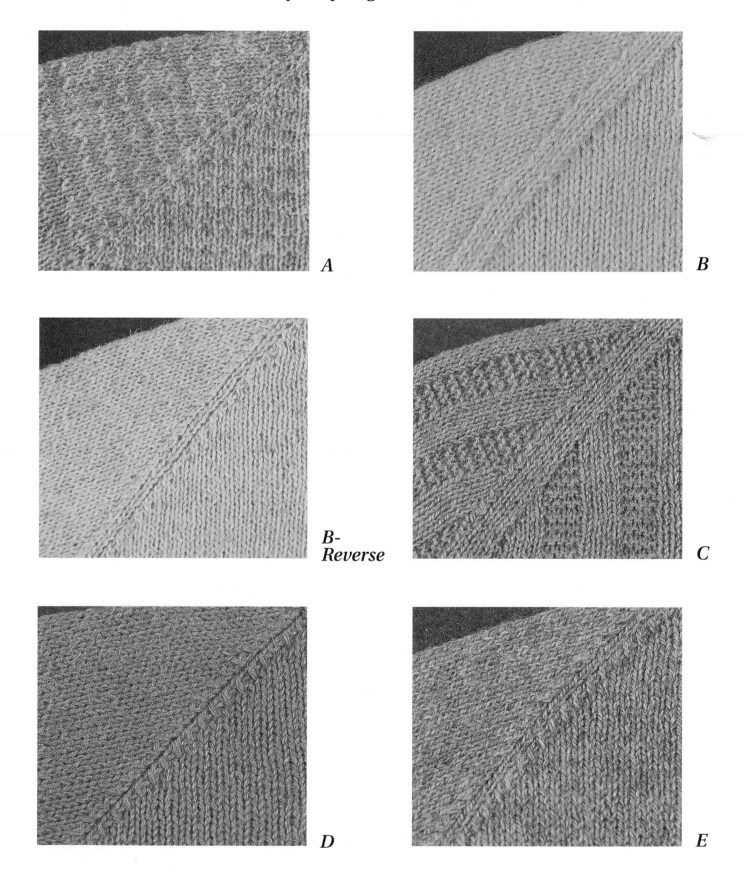

A

B

B-
Reverse

C

D

E

discrepancy points up the problem with decreasing in pairs—nothing exactly matches K2 tog. But, in the completed garment, the focus is on the seamline as a whole, so this fact is not of primary importance. The seamline is presentable.

Raglan Seamline B is a three-stitch-wide raised seamline. Give it a tug after a few rounds to shape it up. This is the best all-purpose seamline, and it is suitable for any weight yarn.

Raglan Seamline B-Reverse is flat, with one center knit stitch visible. B-Reverse makes a daintier seamline than B and is suitable for a lightweight yarn. It is named B-Reverse because the SSK decrease is worked before the marker, and the K2 tog after the marker—just the opposite of B.

Raglan Seamline C is a wider version of B. As a four-stitch raised seamline, its use is best confined to a sweater worked in a fine yarn.

For a sweater, select one of the four styles and use it at each raglan seamline. In the Sampler, you will try all four in one round, so—as you already did with the seamline increases—devise a color code with your markers.

To prepare the Sampler:

Knit one round, putting markers after the 22nd, 44th, and 66th stitches. Use the right seamline marker for the fourth raglan seamline.

As you work the seamlines, pay particular attention to the positions of K2 tog and SSK relative to the markers.

Knit 1 round, working seamlines in this order:
   A at first marker, _____ (marker color).
   B at second marker, _____ (marker color).
   B-Reverse at third marker, _____ (marker color).
   C at fourth marker, _____ (marker color).

Knit 1 round straight.

Repeat the 2 rounds 3 times. On the last round remove all the markers except the one at the right seamline.

Give each of the four seamlines a lengthwise tug to shape them up, and compare their appearance to the preceding descriptions. If you want, hang a small tag on each for quick reference.

The raglan seamline in a sweater has a halting beginning, as you will be working a decrease round every 4th round or row, three times. Once underway, however, you will be working the decreases every other round or row, as you did in the Sampler. From that point on, the seamlines in the sweater will look the same as they do in the Sampler.

In a plain stockinette stitch sweater, a little more detail at the raglan seamline might be in order, as this could be the sweater's only discernible feature. Though not included in the Sampler itself, try seamlines D and E at your leisure, and keep their characteristics in mind for just such an opportunity. These more decorative seamlines are constructed with a combination of the decreases PSSO and PSSO-R.

> ***PSSO:*** Slip 1 stitch as if to purl (yarn in back), knit 1 stitch, insert the left needle into the front of the slipped stitch, and pass the slip stitch over the knit stitch, dropping it off the left needle. PSSO leans ***left***.

> ***PSSO-R:*** Knit one stitch. Put it back on the left needle. Insert the tip of the right needle as if to purl into the stitch to the left of the returned stitch and pass it over the returned stitch and drop it off the right needle. Slip the resulting stitch back on the right needle. PSSO-R leans ***right***.

METHOD *(round or flat)*: The seamlines are worked on the outside of the sweater.

> ***Raglan Seamline D:*** Knit to within 2 stitches of the marker, PSSO, slip marker, PSSO-R.

> ***Raglan Seamline E:*** Knit to within 2 stitches of the marker, PSSO, slip marker, K1, PSSO-R.

Their Characteristics

Raglan Seamline D results in a feather-stitch seamline. Use it as an alternative to A for a two-stitch seamline. The decreases match, heading in the opposite directions, and the feathery appearance dresses up the yoke.

Raglan Seamline E is a wider version of D with the feather stitches more pronounced, as they are separated by a knit stitch. This seamline is quite prominent: in a plain sweater it is fine; in a patterned or striped sweater it could be distracting.

(For future reference: Decreases Evenly Spaced)

Though decreases are not used evenly spaced in the construction of the sweater itself, they are here for the record if you decide on a hem at the neck.

Raglan Seamlines D and E

Decrease: PSSO

Decrease: PSSO-R

METHOD: To decrease stitches evenly spaced across a row, or in a round, divide the number of stitches on the needle by the number of stitches you must decrease. Knit the stitch that matches the quotient figure together with the stitch before it.

Example: If you have 64 stitches on the needle, and you must decrease 8 stitches, divide 64 by 8. The quotient figure is 8. Therefore, knit the 7th and 8th stitches together across the row or in the round.

Again, don't worry about the remainder if your division doesn't come out even.

Now, to be ready for Two-Color Knitting, you must have a number of stitches divisible by 8 to work the pattern. Currently, in your Sampler, you have 56, which is a multiple of 8. However, on a 16" needle, more is better. So, turn back to Increases Evenly Spaced, on page 38, and:

> **Knit 1 round, increasing 8 stitches.**

TWO-COLOR KNITTING

Two-color knitting is as ancient to the knitted fabric as striping; it was another means of incorporating a refreshing note of a second color, or more, into a garment while, no doubt, enlivening a knitter's daily chore. Until very recent times, knitting, as well as all the steps leading to the creation of the yarn itself, was always on some family member's "to do" list—a necessary task, unheard of as a "hobby." What better way to make the job more stimulating and the garment more cheerful than to work with multiple colors?

Perhaps issue could be taken with the term *two-color knitting*, for a fabric striped with a color is, in effect, two-color knitting. What the phrase implies but does not say is that both colors are worked **in the same round or row**. Those who describe the process as double-knitting are more on the mark, for the resulting fabric is layered—one strand of yarn behind the other. This fact offers the third and most plausible explanation for the existence of two-color knitting—added warmth.

A word to the handspinners among you: Don't be hesitant to use unevenly spun and/or dyed yarns for two-color knitting. Though your handspun may not produce the distinct color sequence typical of today's smooth commercial yarn, the resulting design will have a soft, mysterious beauty of its own, the look of its past. The only dissuading factor is that after all that spinning and dyeing, half of the handspun will be hidden from view.

Two-color knitting is neater and less complicated if worked in the round and executed with two hands, one color in each. This allows you to concentrate on the outside of the fabric while the yarn behaves itself on the inside. You may not become an accomplished knitter with the "other" hand, but you can certainly manage the technique for a few rounds to add a color design to a sweater.

There are two basic types of knitters—so called right-hand (English) and left-hand (Continental)—and a myriad of variations of each. In both types, the right hand controls the mechanics of making the stitch. What designates whether one is a right- or left-hand knitter is which hand holds the yarn and controls the tension. A right-hand knitter holds the yarn in the right hand, a left-hand knitter holds the yarn in the left.

The choice of style is not based on being right- or left-handed. Many right-handed individuals knit the left-hand style. However, most left-handed individuals find left-hand knitting more to their liking.

Left-hand knitting is much quicker, as a whole step is eliminated in the process of making a stitch. To a right-hand knitter this may seem like cheating, yet there on the needle is a perfect stitch with one-third less effort.

METHOD

Refer to the illustrations at right.

To knit a right-hand stitch:
- ◆ With the yarn in back, put the right needle in.
- ◆ Put the yarn around the tip of the right needle.
- ◆ Pull the yarn through.

To knit a left-hand stitch:
- ◆ Put the right needle in and go over the left yarn with the tip of the needle.
- ◆ Pull the yarn through.

Working Knit Stitches

Right-Hand:

Put right needle in,

wrap yarn around tip,

pull yarn through.

Left-Hand:

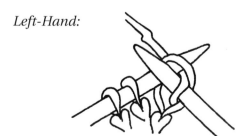

*Completed stitch; working yarn is in **left** hand.*

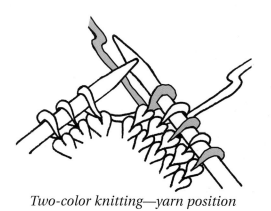

Two-color knitting—yarn position

Now, try a practice round.

Place the ball of yarn you are using on your right side, with the yarn over the right forefinger. Place a ball of contrasting yarn on your left side, with the yarn over the left forefinger.

> *Alternate a right-hand stitch with a left-hand stitch, starting at the right seamline marker and working around to it again. Work 2 rounds of stockinette stitch with your original color.*

A simple practice round, yet effective in its own right. These little heart-shaped stitches would brighten any sweater quickly and easily. Imagine that round worked in the flat, both colors in one hand, and the tedious crossing of yarns for each stitch; there is no comparison.

Designs with as many as 4 or 5 stitches of one color in a series can be worked in the same manner and with as little effort. Make it a practice, however, to spread the stitches on the right needle to their full width before working the alternate color. This move allows the waiting yarn to strand completely behind the just-worked stitches, and your two-color knitting won't pucker.

Weaving—Knit Stitches

If you select a design with a series of 5 or more stitches in one color, you may weave the waiting yarn rather than stranding it on the inside. The longer the strand, the harder it is to control tension.

To weave the color not in use is to carry it along, catching it up as you work; it is never more than one stitch back. Thus, there are no strands.

Weaving, as you know, is an under/over/under/over movement. The good news is that you are already doing the unders, unconsciously, as you work a normal right- or left-hand stitch. That means you have to be conscious only of the overs. In a series of 5 stitches of one color, for example, work stitches 1, 3, and 5 normally and use the weaving technique on stitches 2 and 4.

METHOD: Work only on *every other* stitch in a series. The dark yarn is in your right hand.

To weave the left yarn while knitting with the right:

◆ Put the right needle in.

◆ Put the left yarn gently over the tip of the right needle.

◆ Put the right yarn around to make a stitch.

◆ Bring the right stitch through.

Weaving the left yarn: (1) Put the right needle in and put the left yarn gently over the tip of the right needle.

(2) Put the right yarn around to make a stitch, and bring the right stitch through.

To weave the right yarn while knitting with the left:

◆ Put the right needle in.

◆ Put the right yarn around as if to make a stitch.

◆ Put the left yarn over the tip of the right needle—from under.

◆ Take the right yarn back to the back—the way it came.

◆ Bring the left stitch through.

Weaving the right yarn: (1) Put the right needle in, put the right yarn around as if to make a stitch, put the left yarn over the tip of the right needle—from under.

(2) Take the right yarn back to the back, bring the left stitch through.

Two steps are essential before two-color knitting is started:

◆ Put a marker on the needle to identify the absolute beginning of the rounds. This marker should be at the right seamline.

◆ Count **and recount** to be certain you have the correct multiple of stitches on the needle. (The practice design in the Sampler is worked over a multiple of 8 stitches; be sure you have 64.)

The two-color Scandinavian border design coming up has a series of 5 stitches in one color in rounds 1 and 5. In order to practice both of the procedures, switch yarns from hand to hand for round 5; the day may come when you must work 5 dark stitches followed by 5 light stitches.

To work the design, the colors have been translated to dark and light. Rename your yarns. One must be darker than the other. To start, put the dark yarn in the right hand. For round 5, switch the dark yarn to the left hand.

> **Work the 5 rounds of the two-color Scandinavian border design, following the graphed or written directions at left.**
>
> **Work 2 rounds of stockinette stitch in original color.**
>
> **Repeat the round of alternating stitches to balance the border design.**
>
> **Work 6 rounds of stockinette stitch in original color.**

If using "the other hand" does not come naturally, be selective in your choice of color design. Scrutinize the patterns and settle for one in which one color predominates. Put the predominant color in the hand with which you usually knit, and put the color that works the fewer stitches in the other hand.

Directions for two-color knitting are often written with the colors denoted as "main color" and "contrasting color." Rather than mentally struggling with that confusion, rewrite the pattern using dark and light; or, as you know the colors you are using, spell them right out—2 red, 1 white, etc. This aforethought step clears the air.

Designs may also be set up on graph paper, one square being equal to one stitch. This arrangement eliminates the need for words altogether, and the pattern may be used over and over in different color combinations. Many ready-made designs exist in this form; even a cross-stitch design can be called into service. For further mileage and a totally different effect, reverse the colors—work the dark as light, and the light as dark.

Scandinavian Border Design

A multiple of 8 stitches.
D = dark, L = light.

Round 1: 3D, *1L, 1D, 1L, 5D*, repeat * to *, ending 2D (instead of 5D).

Round 2: 2D, *1L, 1D, 1L, 1D, 1L, 3D*, repeat * to *, ending 1D (instead of 3D).

Round 3: *1D, 1L*, repeat * to *.

Round 4: *1L, 1D, 1L, 3D, 1L, 1D*, repeat * to *.

Round 5: *1D, 1L, 5D, 1L*, repeat * to *.

8-STITCH REPEAT

("Bordar 18," from Hans M. Debes, *Foroysk Bingingarmynstur*.)

In round knitting, work a graph from the bottom up, reading the squares from right to left—unless otherwise directed. For flat knitting, work the graph from the bottom up, alternating the rows from right to left, and left to right.

Two-color designs written specifically for flat knitting may include an extra stitch for the end of the row that is excess baggage in round knitting. For the most part, a design that states it is a multiple of 8, plus 1, for example, can be trimmed to the exact multiple of 8. Please note the words *may* and *for the most part*; this is not an absolutely consistent occurrence.

Before ending two-color knitting, check the "hand" of this area of your Sampler. If the fabric feels stiffer than in other sections—not thicker (which it is), but stiffer—work looser next time. Tension is of prime concern when working with two colors; too tight is more common than too loose. There's truth in that old adage about practice.

This tendency for two-color knitting to have a tighter tension means that it is not wise to fill a sweater yoke with two-color designs in a sweater, because the tighter tension interferes with the raglan shaping. (This problem is discussed in more detail in the Basic Sweater chapter.)

(For future reference: Working Two Colors in Purl)

Refer to the illustrations at right.

To purl a right-hand stitch:
- With the yarn in front, put the right needle in.
- Put the yarn around the tip of the right needle.
- Push the yarn out through the back.

To purl a left-hand stitch:
- Follow the same 3 right-hand stitch steps, with the working yarn in your left hand.

If your heart's desire is to knit a two-color cardigan, you will need to work some two-color rows in purl, and further, if your pattern has a series of five or more stitches in one color, you may need to weave the waiting color on a purl row, as described on the following page.

Working Purl Stitches

Right-Hand:

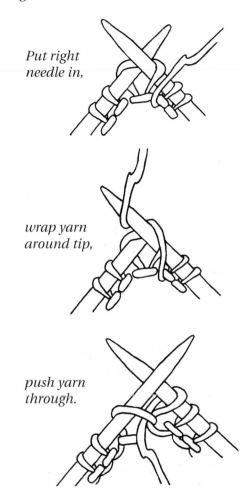

Put right needle in,

wrap yarn around tip,

push yarn through.

Left-Hand:

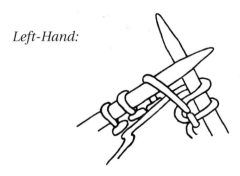

*Completed stitch; working yarn is in **left** hand.*

METHOD: Work only on *every other* stitch in a series. The dark yarn is in your right hand.

To weave the left yarn while purling with the right:

◆ Put the right needle in.
◆ Put the left yarn gently over the tip of the needle.
◆ Put the right yarn around to make a stitch.
◆ Bring the right stitch through.

To weave the right yarn while purling with the left:

◆ Put the right needle in.
◆ Put the right yarn around the needle from below.
◆ Put the left yarn over as if to make a stitch.
◆ Take the right yarn back to the front—the way it came.
◆ Bring the left stitch through.

Final step in weaving the left yarn while purling the right: bring the right stitch through.

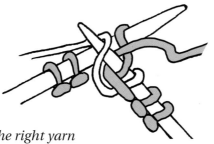

Weaving the right yarn while purling with the left: (1) Having put the right yarn around the needle from below, put the left yarn over as if to make a stitch.

(2) After taking the right yarn back to the front, bring the left stitch through.

SWISS DARNING

Swiss Darning, also known as duplicate stitch, is an easy way to add more color to a completed sweater, embroider a monogram, create a plaid, or simply put a third color into a design worked with two. For the latter, select a logical stitch to cover, one that can be quickly spotted as you work.

To avoid long strands spoiling the neatness of the inside, wiggle the yarn from one stitch to the next under the purl bumps.

The disguising powers of Swiss Darning will correct a color error or a stubborn nonconforming stitch at a seamline. And when you're using an unevenly spun yarn, it will camouflage a too-thin stitch.

METHOD: Thread a Braidkin or a blunt needle with a yarn of the same diameter in the desired color.

- ◆ From the inside, pull the yarn to the outside up through the center of the stitch below the one to be covered.
- ◆ Slide the Braidkin under both sides of the stitch above the one to be covered.
- ◆ Take the yarn back to the inside through the center of the stitch below the one to be covered—where it came up.
- ◆ Adjust the tension of this cover stitch.

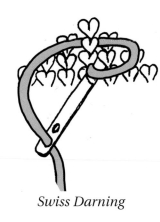

Swiss Darning

> **Work a third color into the Scandinavian design.** Cover the center stitch of the triangle formed by the dark yarn with a third color.

Now, take a brief break from the Sampler.

THE KNITTED CORD

The uses of the three-stitch Knitted Cord are endless, depending on how much of it you can stand to do: tie bows, thread cables, lace cardigans, connect mittens, form monograms, tie hats, or work drawstrings, to name a few. (The technique comes from Elizabeth Zimmermann's *Knitter's Almanac*, p.105.)

METHOD: Use 2 double-pointed needles—garment size.

- ◆ Cast on 3 stitches. (For this special technique, do not slip the first stitch.)
- ◆ *K3. **Freeze. Do not turn your work. Slide** the 3 stitches to the other end of the needle. Give the yarn a gentle tug.*
- ◆ Repeat * to * for the desired length.
- ◆ To bind off: K1, K2 tog, pass the first stitch over the second, secure the yarn, and tuck in the tail.

The Knitted Cord

> **Work about 2 feet of cord in the dark yarn.** Then it's back to the Sampler. You need a place to put your cord.

(For future reference: The Twisted Cord)

A quicker cord, but not as substantial, is the Twisted Cord.

METHOD

- ◆ Measure a strand of yarn 4 times the desired length of the finished cord.
- ◆ Double the strand.

◆ Tie one end around a doorknob, shut it in a drawer, or find someone to hold it.

◆ Walk as far away as the doubled strand allows.

◆ Twist, twist, and twist some more, until the twist runs tightly to the end in your hand.

◆ If the doubled strand is short enough (or, your arms long enough), hold it taut, grab it in the middle, and walk to the secured end. Hold the secured end with the loose end and release your grip on the middle, allowing the doubled strands to twist together.

◆ If the doubled strand is too long (or your arms too short), find someone else to grab the middle.

◆ Tie an overhand knot one inch from each end. Cut the folded end and trim the ends an equal distance from the knot.

THE LACING ROUND OR ROW

At wrists, necks, waists, or wherever you want or need a lacing, work the YO, K2 tog. The YO leaves an opening large enough for a Knitted Cord of the same yarn—complementary proportioning, the same as for a buttonhole. (Or, if you and the sweater prefer, the lacing may be a Twisted Cord, velvet ribbon, or length of rawhide; whether it is truly functional or merely decorative is up to you.)

Due to their very stretchy nature, cotton sweaters benefit from a lacing above the body ribbing—a better accent and a quicker solution than threading their innards with elastic.

METHOD: The lacing round or row is worked on an outside round or row.

Round: On an even number of stitches, work YO, K2 tog around. On the next round, knit all the stitches.

Flat: Work on an uneven number of stitches.

> **Row 1:** Slip 1, *YO, K2 tog *. Repeat * to * across the row.
>
> **Row 2:** Slip 1, purl all the stitches across the row.

> *Work a lacing round in the Sampler.*
>
> *Work 5 rounds of stockinette stitch.* You have reached the top!

The technique for a picot edge on a hem is the same as for a lacing round or row. Take a minute to fold the last few plain rounds to the inside. Check the appearance of the edge and file it in your visual memory, then unfold the edge and stand the top right back up again.

> **Insert the Knitted Cord into the lacing round.** Don't pull it tight yet.

Coming up next is the Knitted Belt, a close relation of the Knitted Cord. Put the Sampler aside again for a minute.

THE KNITTED BELT

The Knitted Belt is so much more than just a belt; think of it also for straps, suspenders, belt loops, and trims. Like so many other useful items, it is from Elizabeth Zimmermann (*Wool Gathering*, #21, Sept. 1979). As in the Knitted Cord, the yarn comes from the third stitch back at the beginning of every row to give nicely rounded edges to this sturdy, reversible belt. You must work 2 or 3 inches of it before it begins to shape up—keep tugging down.

METHOD: Use 2 double-pointed needles—garment size.

- ◆ Cast on 7 stitches. (For this special technique, do not slip the first stitch.)
- ◆ *K4, bring the yarn to the front, slip the next 3 stitches as if to purl. Turn your work, and give the yarn a gentle tug.*
- ◆ Repeat * to * for the desired length.
- ◆ On the last row, knit all the stitches.
- ◆ To bind off: Slip 1, P2 tog, pass the slip stitch over the purl; P1, pass the purl stitch over the purl; P2 tog, pass the purl stitch over the purl, P1, pass the purl stitch over the purl. Secure the yarn, and tuck in the tail.

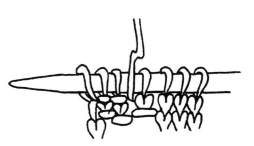

The Knitted Belt

> **Using the dark yarn, work the Knitted Belt long enough to button through that gigantic belt loop, alias Sweatshirt Pocket.**
>
> **Add a buttonhole in the last inch:** K3, YO, K2 tog, bring the yarn to the front, slip 2 as if to purl.

In the Sampler, the mini version of the Sweatshirt Pocket serves double duty as a wide belt loop through which to thread the Knitted Belt. In real life, a skinny Sweatshirt Pocket would make an inadequate belt loop, but a proper belt loop may be worked using the pocket technique—if you are able to judge the correct position of the loop, or loops, as you work the sweater.

(For future reference: The Belt Loop; Mock Placket)

METHOD: The belt loop is worked across 7 stitches. Work to within 7 stitches of where the top of the loop is to be, and stop.

- ◆ Trace the next stitch down to where you want the loop's bottom.
- ◆ Slide a double-pointed needle through one-half of the next 7 stitches, heading left.
- ◆ With new yarn, and garment size double-pointed needles, work the 7 stitches using the Knitted Belt method.
- ◆ When the loop is long enough, hold one needle in front of the other and knit the belt loop stitches together with the sweater stitches; presto, a sturdy belt loop to match that sturdy belt.

A fool-the-eye placket neck, or a mock cardigan for that matter, can be engineered in the same manner on a crew neck sweater. Briefly, as you must have the idea by now:

- ◆ Work the pick-up round for the neck ribbing to within the center 7 stitches of the front.
- ◆ Travel down as many inches as you want for placket length, or go all the way back to the row above the ribbing for a cardigan.
- ◆ Knit up the next 7 stitches, and work the Knitted Belt to the top. Join it to the waiting stitches and complete the neck ribbing.
- ◆ Don't bother to work buttonholes—simply sew buttons at appropriate intervals through the belt and the sweater itself; a move that also attaches the two.

Now, back to the Sampler and on to its various endings.

To work the last round of any circular-needle project, use an independent double-pointed needle in place of the right end of the circular needle. Your ending, whether it be a simple cast-off or something more elaborate, will proceed much more quickly and steadily because you will have more control over the tension; a circular needle tends to drag as it empties. For the Sampler (or for a sweater), with the outside facing you, take the right end of the circular needle and tuck it down into your work. Find a double-pointed needle the same size, and use it in your right hand.

The Sampler has 4 "endings," each worked over 16 stitches. As the first three are worked in the dark yarn, take your working yarn and send it down into the Sampler with the needle; don't break it off, for you will need it again when you work the hem ending to the Sampler.

THE KNITTED CORD CAST-OFF

In a sweater worked from the bottom up, the use of the Knitted Cord Cast-Off is limited to trimming necklines. An alternative to ribbing, it magically surrounds the openings with a welt-like edge of yarn as you cast off the stitches—a soft and gentle ending for a sweater. Once implanted in the knitting mind, the application of the Knitted Cord will certainly expand to other projects that would benefit from its finishing touch. (The technique comes from Elizabeth Zimmermann, *Knitter's Almanac*, p. 110.)

Now that you have worked the Knitted Cord on its own, you will better understand how it works as a cast-off. Set-up is important, so check it before you start.

With the outside of the Sampler facing you, and with the right end of the circular needle and the working yarn tucked down inside, take the dark yarn, and this time, for security, knot it through the first stitch on the left needle.

(1) Cast 3 stitches onto the left needle with the dark yarn.

METHOD: Insert the double-pointed needle in your right hand between the first two stitches on the left needle and cast 3 stitches onto the left needle (with the dark yarn).

- ◆ *K2 (dark), K2 tog (1 dark, 1 light). Slip the 3 (dark) stitches back onto the left needle, being careful not to twist them.*
- ◆ Repeat * to *.

It may seem strange to be casting on in order to start casting off, but it helps to think of the cord as an extension of the fabric. The 3 dark stitches should be sitting ahead of the other stitches on the left needle. Each time you knit the last dark stitch together with a light stitch, you are getting rid of, or casting off, 1 stitch of the Sampler and at the same time adding a round knitted edge.

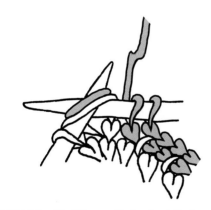

(2) K2 (dark), K2 tog (1 dark, 1 light).

The Knitted Cord can, of course, be worked in self-same color; the dark yarn is used here for clarity.

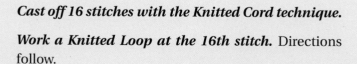

> ***Cast off 16 stitches with the Knitted Cord technique.***
>
> ***Work a Knitted Loop at the 16th stitch.*** Directions follow.

THE KNITTED LOOP

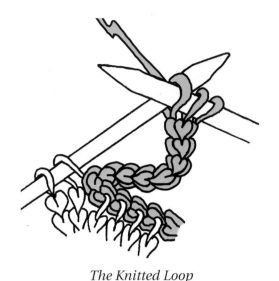

The Knitted Loop

After casting off the 16th stitch, do not return the 3 stitches to the left needle.

- ◆ Take another double-pointed needle and work the Knitted Cord alone; that is, *K3, slide *, and repeat for 2".
- ◆ Put the empty double-pointed needle aside.
- ◆ Insert the left end of the circular needle into the 16th stitch again. You will be reworking this stitch to draw the base of the loop together.
- ◆ Slip the 3 stitches from the double-pointed needle onto the left end of the circular needle and K2, K2 tog.
- ◆ Immediately cast off the cord: slip 1, K2 tog, pass the slipped stitch over the knit stitch.
- ◆ Break the yarn and snug the base of the loop together even more while tucking in the end.

The loop deserves a home in your knitting bag of tricks, perhaps not as part of a neckline cast-off—but then again, why not? The lucky sweater might spend less time lying on the floor. And how about the cap that's lying there beside it, a useless pompom affixed to its peak? Think of all the time (and yarn) a loop would save. You can complete one in the time it takes to rummage up a piece of cardboard for making a pompom. On your next cap worked in the round, decrease to a final 3 stitches, work a 2" cord, cast it off, bend it over, and secure it to the inside with the tail. Then, side by side, cap and sweater will find their place hanging on a peg.

Hang everything: the mittens, the scarves, the wash cloths, the pot holders, and, by all means, the Christmas stockings. If you don't have 3 convenient stitches at the ready, find them. Dig around in the edge of whatever, and with a double-pointed needle manufacture 3 stitches. The Shakers had the right idea—if it's not in use, hang it, assign it to a wall—their credo for a neat and tidy house.

(For future reference: Knitted Cord Edge—After the Fact)

It is never too late to add a Knitted Cord edge to a garment. This versatile trim may be worked on an existing cast-on edge or a previously bound-off edge—or, for that matter, up and down or right around the middle of a finished sweater. Proceed stitch-by-stitch in whichever direction you decide to go. If perchance you do use the cast-off version for a neckline trim, the other sweater edges can be made to match. Plan ahead, and start the body and the sleeves without a ribbing pattern—though (who knows?) a Knitted Cord might settle onto a ribbed edge too.

There are no specific directions for working this after-the-fact edging onto the Sampler; however do try it someplace when you're through, either around the cast-on or anywhere around the middle. METHOD: Use 2 double-pointed needles—garment size.

- ◆ Cast on 3 stitches.
- ◆ Slide the left end of the left needle (the one with the stitches) under one-half of the stitch that marks the starting point for the trim. Slide the 4 stitches together, in a row, to the right end of the left needle.
- ◆ *K2, K2 tog. Do not turn your work. Transfer the empty needle to your right hand. Again, slide the left end of the left needle under one-half of the next stitch to be worked.*
- ◆ Repeat * to *.

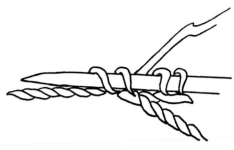

Knitted Cord edge—after the fact

LACE CAST-OFF

Nothing changes the picture of a sweater more quickly than a dash of lace. Whether the yarn is a shimmering synthetic, a rough wool, a fluffy angora, or a smooth cotton, the impact is instant; the sweater goes from plain to fancy. Yet the real beauty of this lace edge is in its working, for as it imparts its very special touch, inching its way around a neckline, it also is casting off the stitches. What more could you ask?

Lace edgings are usually worked, and consequently pictured, in very fine cotton thread. Keep this fact in mind when selecting a pattern to trim a sweater, for, in a heavier yarn, they will naturally be much deeper and could be overwhelming. The pattern you are about to work is the very first, and the narrowest, in Barbara Abbey's book, *Knitting Lace*. Though worked with a base of only five stitches, this "#1 Very Narrow Edging" provides ample width for a lace edge on a sweater.

Lace Cast-Off is worked in the same manner as Knitted Cord Cast-Off, except you are working back and forth over the lace stitches, turning your work.

The odd-numbered rows must be worked heading away from the fabric. The even-numbered rows must be worked heading in toward the fabric. It is only on the even-numbered rows that the last stitch of the lace pattern is worked together with a stitch from the fabric itself. Therefore, it takes 2 rows of lace pattern to cast off one stitch.

On the Sampler, the lace edge is worked with the contrast color so it's easy to see how the casting-off proceeds.

Every row starts with a "slip 1." Work this slip 1 as if to purl, yarn in front, then take the yarn to the back for the next stitch. The YO2, to a right-hand knitter, is: put the yarn forward as if to purl, and then take it around the needle back to this position again.

Make note of one trouble spot: The only purl stitches are in rows 2, 4, and 6. These purl stitches are worked into the second half of the YO2 from the row before. Don't drop these long diagonal stitches off the needle by mistake; no matter what they look like, purl into them. Notice, too, that the YO in row 3 is followed by K2 stitches, not K2 tog as in rows 1 and 5.

Again, set-up is important, so check before you start: With the outside of the Sampler facing you, and with the right end of the circular needle and the working yarn still tucked down inside, take the dark yarn, and again, for security, knot it through the first stitch on the left needle.

METHOD: Take the double-pointed needle in your right hand and insert it between the first two stitches on the left needle.

- ◆ Cast 5 stitches onto the left needle (with the dark yarn).
- ◆ Knit the 5 stitches. Turn your work.
  - **Row 1:** Slip 1, K1, YO2, K2 tog, K1. Turn your work.
  - **Row 2:** Slip 1, K2, P1, K1, K2 tog (1 dark, 1 light). Turn your work.
  - **Row 3:** Slip 1, K3, YO2, K2. Turn your work.
  - **Row 4:** Slip 1, K2, P1, K3, K2 tog (1 dark, 1 light). Turn your work.
  - **Row 5:** Slip 1, K1, YO2, K2 tog, K4. Turn your work.
  - **Row 6:** Slip 1, K5, P1, K1, K2 tog (1 dark, 1 light). Turn your work.
  - **Row 7:** Slip 1, K8. Turn your work.
  - **Row 8:** Cast off 4, K3, K2 tog (1 dark, 1 light). Turn your work. (5 stitches)
- ◆ Repeat rows 1 through 8.

As you will be only casting off 1 stitch every other row, you must work the 8 rows 4 times. At the end of row 8, you will be back down to the original 5 dark stitches. Turn your work, and start right in with row 1 again. (The knit row you worked immediately after casting on was a one-time measure to get you started in the right direction—row 1 must head out, away from the garment.) On the very last row, cast off all 9 stitches of lace. At the last cast-off stitch, pull out a large loop, pass the whole ball of yarn through, and secure—this will save having to reattach the yarn.

> ***Work Lace Cast-Off over the next 16 stitches.***

(For future reference: Lace Edging—After the Fact)

The sleeve and body edges of a sweater (as well as shawls, scarves, baby clothes, blankets, and other fancy goods) are all candidates for a lovely, lacy edging. As you now know, worked directly as a cast-off, the lace practically applies itself, and the "give" of the fabric extends from one area to the other without any constriction in between. To duplicate this effect so that sleeve and body lace look and act the same as neck lace requires the elimination of the cast-on row or round. This move can be accomplished in two ways: (A) think of it ahead of time, or (B) don't think of it ahead of time.

A. Think of it ahead of time and begin with an invisible cast-on.

For those of you who are organized and know exactly where you plan to eventually add lace, you may start the sleeves and/or body with the Invisible Cast-On. This cast-on allows you to work in reverse, and ceases to exist once you do, leaving nothing in its wake but an available round, or row, of stitches heading in the opposite direction.

However, even some of the most organized knitters would rather run and hide than work this cast-on; the very mention of its name sends them scurrying. If you are one of these, take heart; Barbara Walker (in *Knitting from the Top*) has come to your rescue. A picture is supposedly worth a thousand words, but, in this case, a picture would not even come close to her written description of the process. She clarifies it in words that number just over eight hundred. Put yourself in her hands and relax. The cast-on is not invisible until you take it out; you can see it as you work it.

---

1. Take a length of string, more than enough to hold comfortably all necessary stitches.

2. With one needle and the end of your yarn, cast on one stitch, and place it near the needle point. Hold this needle in your right hand.

3. With the same hand, hold the end of the string under, and against, the needle, so that the string passes in front of the ball end of the yarn. Keep hold of the string and needle together, throughout.

4. Put the left hand around the long strands of both yarn and string, and keep hold of both, henceforth. Put the left thumb between yarn and string, below the point where the string

BARBARA WALKER'S INVISIBLE CAST-ON

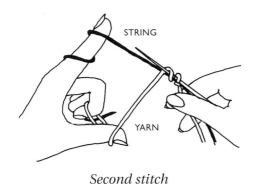

Second stitch

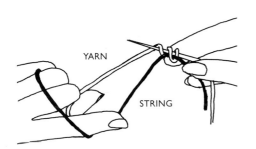

Third stitch

crosses in front of the yarn. Bring the thumb forward, carrying the yarn on it.

5. Put the left forefinger between yarn and string, and open it backward, carrying the string on it. You now have a diamond-shaped opening between yarn and string, with the yarn on the thumb toward you, and the string on the forefinger away from you. The other three fingers of the left hand continue to hold both strands against the palm.

6. Dip the needle point down into the diamond-shaped opening and bring it up toward you, thus picking up a loop of yarn from behind onto the needle. This is the second stitch.

7. Without changing the position of the left hand, turn it over so that the back of the hand comes toward you. This reverses the positions of yarn and string; now the yarn, on the thumb, is at the back of the diamond, and the string, on the forefinger, is at the front. As you turn the left hand over, the yarn wraps itself under the string beneath the needle.

8. Dip the needle point down behind the yarn, on the far side of the diamond, and bring it up through the diamond to put another yarn loop on the needle. This is the third stitch.

9. Still keeping the left hand in its position, turn it over away from you again, so that the yarn and string return to their original positions—yarn in front, string behind. As you do this, the yarn is brought forward under the string, which is still beneath the needle.

Repeat steps 6, 7, 8, and 9 for every subsequent pair of stitches, ending the cast-on with step 8. There will be an uneven number of stitches because the very first stitch on the needle is an extra one. If an even number of stitches is wanted, you can work K2 tog at the end of each first row.

Now you have a lot of yarn loops over the needle and the string running along beneath the needle with the yarn twisted around it. Be sure the string has not been passed over the needle at any point and the loops on the needle are yarn only.

To work the first row, put the needle into the left hand, carefully holding the last cast-on loop on the needle meanwhile. Take the yarn under the string to the back, and begin the row, knitting all stitches through the front loops in the ordinary way. After 2 or 3 rows, you can see that the string is still holding exactly the same number of loops as the number of stitches cast on. Each of these loops will be a stitch to knit in the opposite direction. Leave the string in place until you are ready to pick up these loops onto a needle.

When you are ready to knit in the opposite direction, hold the work with right side facing, cast-on edge up. From the left, carefully slide the needle through all the loops that are on the string. Then pull out the string. Join the yarn at the right-hand edge, and work the first row as follows: K1, *K1b, K1; repeat from *. The reason for knitting every even-numbered stitch through the back is that each of these stitches is twisted and must be knitted in back to straighten it out again. If you were to knit each of the even-numbered stitches in the front loop, it would be crossed at the base, like a normal "K1b." This might provide a very acute observer with a clue concerning the place where you cast on. But without such a clue, no one in the whole wide world—not even the most expert of experts—can ever see the slightest trace of this cast-on row.

[Thank you, Barbara.]

B. Adding a lace edge as an afterthought. For those of you who do not like to commit yourself to going back and doing something on another end (and with the invisible cast-on you really must), or if you're suddenly inspired to add lace to a sweater already worked with ribbings around its body or sleeves, you may snip one-half stitch in the round, or row, above that existing ribbing and simply drop the ribbing off. This procedure will produce a round, or row, of stitches to which you may add a lace edge. As Lace Cast-Off makes a wider trim than ribbing, put the just-produced stitches on a ribbing-size needle and knit 1 round, decreasing the number of stitches by 10%.

The logic of this process, and the madness of the snipping method, are explained under Afterthought Pocket, coming up a little further on in the Sampler directions.

By whichever means, A or B, you have accumulated a needle full of stitches. Proceed exactly as for Lace Cast-Off, i.e., cast onto the left needle the required number of stitches to work your selected pattern. Work one row of knit over the cast-on stitches first, and then turn your work so that row 1 is worked heading away from the garment edge.

As a last resort, you could, of course, work a lace edge directly onto the cast-on, or, as a matter of fact, onto a previous cast-off. Slide a needle into conforming strands of the finished selvedge to acquire a round, or row, of stitches, and there you are, all set to go. The drawback to this method is that you will have a restricting cast-on or cast-off between the fabric and the lace, and thus lose the fluidity of one to the other. Losing this oneness also diminishes the intrigue, for it will be quite obvious that the lace was worked as an addition. Conversely, a scarf or stole, for instance, with lace worked as a cast-off at each end, will look as if it had no beginning.

(Reflecting on lace edges for sweaters brings to mind an elegant petticoat, so trimmed, that is hidden away in the archives at Old Sturbridge Village in Massachusetts, an authentically restored rural New England village of 1790–1840. Made of handspun, hand-woven fabric, dyed scarlet, and enhanced with a wide lace hem knit of the same yarn, it would be as stylish today as it was when it was created. Weavers, take note: The next time you purchase yarn for a fabric, buy extra; weave a long (or short) skirt, and work a border of handknitted lace. In this instance, the lace could be worked separately and sewn on, unless you are inclined toward a crochet hook and could thereby work a round of loops on the edge of the fabric from which to start.)

(For future reference: The Cable Stitch Cast-Off)

If a lace edge is, well, just too lacy, a border of cable stitch may be more to your liking. From other archives, namely the Franklin D. Roosevelt Library in Hyde Park, New York, comes the cable stitch border. Eleanor is remembered as "knitting, always knitting." Upon her death, her memorabilia joined Franklin's, and it will do your knitting heart good to see that the exhibit organizers recognized her "hobby" for what it was—and is to so many others—part of and inseparable from her daily doings. There, at Hyde Park, an entire wall case displays her knitting paraphernalia.

Behind the scene, in her personal papers, are handwritten directions for this cable stitch border. Sent to her from an unknown admirer, the border was described as being "a marvelous way to attach bands for armholes, round, high necks, or wherever a contrasting band with a professional finish is desired." The writer further admonished that "A double border is lovely for a skirt hem when one is tall."

METHOD: The number of stitches to be cast off must be a multiple of 8. The border may be worked either directly, as a cast-off, or on stitches picked up around a previously cast-off or cast-on edge.

◆ With the outside of the fabric facing you, and with a double-pointed needle in your right hand, insert the tip of the double-pointed needle between the first two stitches on the left needle (the one with the garment) and proceed to:

◆ Cast 12 stitches onto the left needle ahead of the stitches to be cast off. Proceed immediately to:

Row 1: Slip 1, P2, K6, P2, K2 tog (1 of border, 1 of fabric). Turn.

Row 2: Slip 1, K2, P6, K3. Turn.

Row 3: Same as 1.

Row 4: Same as 2.

Row 5: Same as 1.

Row 6: Same as 2.

Row 7: Slip 1, P2, cable 6*, P2, K2 tog (1 of border, 1 of fabric. Turn.

Row 8: Same as Row 2.

To work cable 6: Slip next 3 stitches onto another double-pointed needle or a cable needle and hold in front or back; knit the next 3 stitches on the left needle. Return the 3 stitches on the extra needle to the left needle and knit them.

CASTING OFF IN RIBBING

The only casting off in a sweater knit from the bottom up is the last round, or row, of ribbing at the neck edge. Casting off in your ribbing pattern, knitting the knits, and purling the purls, produces a zig-zag selvedge with a good amount of elasticity. If you tend to work this job tightly, use a larger-size double-pointed needle in your right hand; looseness is vital, especially to a crew neck sweater.

In the Sampler, the ribbing pattern will be K2, P2 worked back and forth over 16 stitches. The ribbing will be less cumbersome to work if you use 2 double-pointed needles. Let the circular needle rest.

Start each row with a slip 1. This slip 1 will take the place of the first K1. Work it slip 1 as if to purl, yarn in back.

Check to be sure you are set up correctly: With the outside facing you, the dark yarn should still be attached at the end of the lace work, ready to be used for the ribbing. Using a double-pointed needle in your right hand, knit the next 16 stitches from the circular needle. (To have started right in with K2, P2 in the dark color would have meant droopy purls).

Turn your work after the knit row, and:

> ***Work K2, P2 over the 16 stitches for an inch.***

To work the cast-off:

METHOD

- ◆ Slip 1, K1, pass the slip over the knit.
- ◆ Purl 1, pass the knit over the purl.
- ◆ Purl 1, pass the purl over the purl.
- ◆ Knit 1, pass the purl over the knit.
- ◆ Knit 1, pass the knit over the knit.
- ◆ Purl 1, etc.

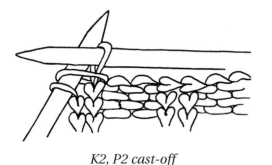

K2, P2 cast-off

> ***Cast off the 16 stitches in K2, P2 ribbing.***

Now that the ribbing section is complete, note the difference in width between the 16 stitches cast off in lace and the 16 stitches cast off in ribbing. The lace produces almost twice the width of the ribbing.

To be prepared for the last "ending," reach down into the Sampler and pull out the original yarn. With a double-pointed needle in your right hand and the inside of the Sampler facing you, purl the remaining stitches. The circular needle is now empty. Put it aside and work the remaining ending with 2 double-pointed needles.

Note: The purl row you have just worked is not the purl row for the turning edge of the hem coming up. It was worked to get you to the outside and onto 2 needles.

A HEM—Amen! You're Almost Through!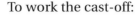

No decent sampler worth its salt should be left unsigned. There-fore, the last 16 stitches will be finished as a hem into which you may knit your initials. Not only is this a perfect ending for your Sweater Sampler, but a hem is also a possibility for the ending of a crew neck or boat neck sweater—another alternative to ribbing. The hem may be worked plain, initialed, in a contrasting color, or with a picot edge. It affords you one last opportunity to personal-ize your sweater.

The initials charted here are 5 stitches high and 3 stitches wide: the smallest possible to knit. Most of the letters are legible; a few, such as N, leave a bit to be desired. Alphabets exist in many other larger, more ornate forms. Search the books and start a collection. And, don't confine initials to a hem; think of sleeves and pockets too. To knit a monogram on a sweater front could be a bit of tricky business; for accurate positioning, Swiss Darning might be best.

> ***Read through the directions for the Plain Hem and the Initialed Hem, and then proceed to the specific directions for working an Initialed Hem in the Sampler.***

The Plain Hem
METHOD (round or flat)

- ◆ Work 1 round or row of purl stitches on the outside for a turning edge. For a picot edge, work a round or row of YO, K2 tog instead. (***Note:*** If the hem will be in a contrasting color, work the purl stitches in the ***2nd round*** of contrast color. For flat knitting, this must be reversed: the 2nd row of the new color will be an inside row, so work it in ***knit***, not purl.)

- ◆ Work 2 rounds or rows in stockinette stitch, decreasing the number of stitches by 10% in the first round/row. These evenly spaced decreases ensure that the hem will lie flat when folded inside.

Decision Point   <<<

If your hem is to be initialed, stop and proceed to the instructions for the Initialed Hem. If the hem will ***not*** have initials, then—

- ◆ Continue working in stockinette stitch for the desired hem depth. Do not cast off the stitches.

- ◆ Break the yarn, leaving enough to stitch the hem to the inside.

- ◆ Thread a Braidkin or a blunt needle and lightly catch each stitch, one by one, to a purl bump on the inside.

- ◆ Work the stitching loosely so as not to constrict the give of the fabric. This stitching may be done with the stitches on the needle easing them off one at a time, or, if you're brave, pull the needle first. That's it.

The Initialed Hem

Graph the desired initials following the examples on p. 68, using 5 squares for height and 3 squares for width. Space the letters one stitch apart. The total width for 3 initials thus equals 11 stitches. Select a likely spot for them to occupy in the hem.

METHOD: Work the initials with a contrasting color. Read the

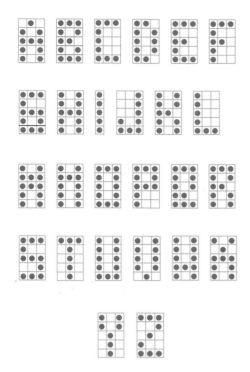

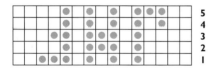

Alphabet graphs

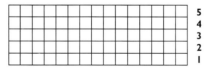

Example—initials for Sampler hem

Blank graph for your initials

graph from the bottom to the top, with the letters turned upside down, as shown in the example graph, so the initials will be legible when the neckline hem is turned to the inside (or when your Sampler is hung by its loop.).

Round: Work each round from right to left.

Flat: Start working the initials on an outside row. Work rows 1, 3, and 5 from right to left (the knit rows), and work rows 2 and 4 from left to right (the purl rows).

With the 5 rounds or rows of initial work complete, return to the directions for the Plain Hem.

> ***Now, for that hem in the Sampler.*** It's flat knitting, so slip the first stitch of every row, for a selvedge.
>
> ***With the outside facing you, and with the Sampler yarn, work a purl row over the remaining 16 stitches for a turning edge.***
>
> ***Purl one more row.***
>
> ***Knit 1 row, decreasing 1 stitch by starting with slip 1, K2 tog.*** (Flat knitters: see note below!!)
>
> ***Purl 1 row.***
>
> ***Set up your initials on the blank graph, or a scrap, as described above (beginning on p. 67).*** The 3 initials, or 11 stitches, are worked in the center of the 15 stitches of your Sampler hem, leaving 2 blank stitches on each end of the needle.
>
> Follow the flat-knitting directions for reading the graph. This is a case of back-and-forth knitting with 2 colors—not as carefree as in the round. Bring the new color from under the old when changing from one to the other, to avoid holes.
>
> ***Work at least 2 rows beyond the initials before tacking down the hem.***

Attention, flat knitters—which is all of you at the present moment. As Elizabeth used to say, it is a GOOD THING that you had to decrease this one stitch. Until now, only brief mention has been made about decreasing at the beginning and/or end of a row. ***Don't.*** If the directions say "decrease 1 stitch at the beginning and/or ending of a row," *never* decrease right on the selvedge; move the decrease in a stitch or two. In other words, start the row with slip 1, *K2 tog*, work across to within 3 stitches of the end, *SSK,* K1. Your decreases have been worked and the selvedge remains intact.

If your selvedge is wider—say, with Cardigan Border or any other such edging—work the decrease immediately after and immediately before the border. For example, with Cardigan Border, start the row with the 6-stitch border, *K2 tog,* work to within 8 stitches of the end, *SSK,* work the 6-stitch border. Moving the decreases in from the edge will still narrow the fabric, and do it in a much more orderly fashion.

AFTERTHOUGHT POCKET

Thanks to the late Elizabeth Zimmermann (*Knitting Without Tears*, p. 37), it's possible to put pockets everywhere: in new sweaters or old favorites, in hand-knits or machine-mades, in plain sweaters or patterned ones—just be sure to position the pocket opening so that the stitch you must snip is in a fairly calm row.

Men love pockets, especially if built to a specific size for whatever their need. (In any case, make them deep enough to be useful.) Children love them in unexpected places; in a mitten, on a hat, or in a sleeve, a pocket becomes a secret hiding place for a special treasure. And, if you truly have a treasure to hide (or simply a little mad money to keep out of sight), don't just graft that sweater underarm; work a "pit pocket" instead. Who would ever think to look there?

In a sweater, the Afterthought Pocket may be worked anywhere. Try on the completed sweater to determine exactly where you want the pocket opening. With a safety pin, mark the stitch that is the center of the opening.

In the Sampler, the pocket will be worked in the open area of the back beside the placket.

With the back of the Sampler facing you, and the placket on your right, count 10 stitches to the left of the last purl stitch of the Cardigan Border. Put a safety pin through the stitch.

Follow the directions for the Afterthought Pocket line by line.

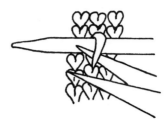

Snip one-half stitch.

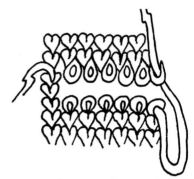

Unravel 5½ stitches to the left and right.

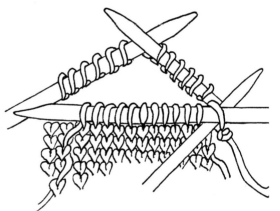

The pocket stitches on 3 double-pointed needles with the yarn connected.

METHOD: Snip one-half of the stitch that marks the *center* of the pocket opening.

◆ With the tip of a double-pointed needle, carefully lift the cut end of the yarn out of 5½ stitches to the right and 5½ stitches to the left of the center opening. (The reason for the half stitch: As you unravel horizontally, you can see that the yarn goes through each stitch twice. It is not necessary to completely free the last stitches. In fact, it is best if you do not. Leaving the yarn half in the last stitch makes the final neatening at the corners of the opening easier).

◆ Do not cut the loosened yarn ends. With a crochet hook tuck them out of your working way at each end of the opening.

◆ The pocket is worked on 4 double-pointed garment-size needles. Pick up the loosened stitches around the opening as follows:

   1. Slide one double-pointed needle through the 12 stitches at the bottom of the opening.

   2. Slide another needle through 6 stitches at the top of the opening.

   3. Slide a third double-pointed needle through the remaining 6 stitches at the top of the opening.

◆ Connect a ball of yarn at the first stitch on the right end of the bottom needle; knot it through, if you wish.

◆ *Purl* across the bottom stitches only for a turning edge. (If you opt to work the pocket in another color, knit the bottom stitches this first time by and purl them on the second pass.) Proceed to the top stitches, and from now on *knit* round and round all the stitches, giving the yarn a good tug from needle to needle, especially at the corners of the opening.

◆ Work the pocket for 2" in the Sampler. In a sweater, work it to the desired depth.

◆ On the last round, combine the top stitches onto one needle.

◆ Break the yarn, leaving about one yard, and thread the end through a Braidkin or a blunt needle.

◆ Turn your work so that when it's facing you the yarn is coming from the first stitch on the right end of the needle farthest away from you. This needle becomes the Back Needle; thus, the needle nearest you is the Front Needle.

You are now in a position to graft the pocket bottom together—in a minute.

GRAFTING

Grafting, also known as Kitchener stitch, is a method of constructing an invisible seam in your work—in this case, in stockinette stitch. This method has fewer steps than other written versions; it achieves the same effect with fewer motions. If grafting has discouraged or confused you before, give this way a try.

In a sweater, the technique comes into play to join the underarm stitches of the body to the sleeves. It is the ultimate touch that preserves the sweater's seamlessness, and therefore allows it to be reversible. The specific set-up for grafting the sweater underarm stitches is detailed at that point in the directions for the Basic Sweater (p. 115); what follow are a few generalities.

The edges to be joined must have an equal number of stitches. The stitches must be on the needle the way you would knit them; a twisted stitch will mar the perfection of the joining. The grafting is worked on the outside of the stockinette stitch fabric with the opening in a horizontal position. To start the grafting process, the yarn must be coming from the first stitch at the right end of the Back Needle. Which is where you are.

> **Follow the directions for grafting line by line.**

Note: Work the grafting loosely, for two reasons.

1. To attempt the proper tension as you work invariably leads to a row of tight stitches that restrict the give of the fabric. At the underarm of a sweater, the fabric must have give. Worked loosely, the new stitches may be adjusted to the tension of the fabric after the grafting is complete.

2. Grafting produces an invisible seam. To work it loosely is your insurance that you can backtrack, if necessary, to correct an error. Otherwise, you won't know what stitches to undo.

METHOD. *Important:* You are slipping the stitches *as if to* knit or purl, not actually knitting or purling them!

◆ *Slip the first stitch on the Front Needle onto the Braidkin as if to knit; let it sit there while you slip the Braidkin through the second stitch as if to purl; pull the yarn through. The first stitch is now off the knitting needle and gone. The second stitch is still on the knitting needle.

◆ Head for the Back Needle, keeping the yarn under the tip of the Front Needle.

◆ Slip the first stitch on the Back Needle onto the Braidkin as if

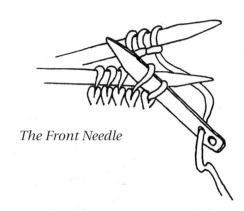

The Front Needle

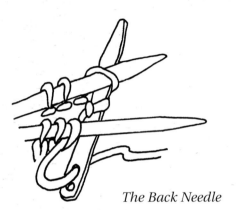

The Back Needle

to purl; let it sit there while you slip the Braidkin through the second stitch on the Back Needle as if to knit; pull the yarn through. The first stitch is now off the knitting needle and gone. The second stitch is still on the knitting needle.

Note: Even though you're making two consecutive moves on each needle, you are doing away with only one stitch.

◆ Head for the Front Needle, keeping the yarn under the tips of the needles.*

◆ Repeat * to * until you have one stitch on each needle.

◆ Slip the stitch on the Front Needle onto the Braidkin as if to knit, slip the stitch on the Back Needle onto the Braidkin as if to purl, pull the yarn through both stitches.

Once you have worked the grafting technique a few times, the mental process will boil down to:

The Front Needle—Knit off, purl through.

The Back Needle—Purl off, knit through.

(Or, you may find a better short thought.)

Worked loosely, the new stitches should be visible. To ensure proper tension, hold your left hand under them, as a darning egg. (Anyone remember how to darn?) With the tip of the Braidkin, lift the stitches one by one to adjust the tension, starting where you started and ending where you ended. Pull the excess yarn through, take the tail to the inside, secure it, and tuck in the end.

Poke the pocket to the inside and neaten the corners of the opening with the unraveled ends. (In retrospect, you can see why the center stitch of the opening was snipped. Otherwise, you would have had a long end on one side and nothing on the other.) There are no rules for this operation, but the less done the better. Circle the yarn around each corner with a crochet hook and gently ease any hole out of existence.

Done, with the exception of the ends.

THE ENDS

To tidy the Sampler, take the assorted yarn ends to the inside and, with a crochet hook, turn them diagonally under a few purl bumps for about an inch. To level the jog in the cast-on round, take the tail of the slip knot through the lower stitch beside it before taking the end to the inside.

In the working of your sweater, always leave 5" or 6" ends, if possible, so they'll be easy to find and handle for the final clean-up. Tuck them in as is with a crochet hook, sharp needle, or Braidkin.

Or, if the sweater is to be reversible, split the plies and head the ends diagonally in opposite directions. In either case, snip the ends no closer than 2" from their point of origin. Ends at crucial points should be even longer; you never know when a pocket corner, a sleeve cuff, or a neckline might need a minor repair, and an extra inch or two could save the day. And lastly, don't hide the ends from yourself; be consistent as to their burrows, and you'll know where to find them if ever an adjustment needs to be made.

Your Sampler is complete. *Give it a good, strong lengthwise tug.* This tug will shape up its stitch combinations, most especially the ribbings, where the purl stitches should hide.

Take a minute now to study your travels with 64 stitches: from wide to narrow, and wide to narrow again, sometimes with your help—increases and decreases—and sometimes without your help—ribbings and garter stitch simply acting to their own inclinations. Now it's time to act to yours. With the Sampler's options at your fingertips, it's on to the sweater. Your choice of yarn, the proper tools, and some straight thinking will guarantee its success.

As colorful and varied as lobster buoys hanging on an old gray-shingled shack, these few Samplers show off their individuality, yet the techniques each knitter mastered are the same. What will yours look like, and where will it hang?

(Samplers courtesy of Shirley Baker, Joan Bruno, Miriam Chesley, Nancy Cook, Jan Fish, Linda Lincoln, Ellen Longo, Cheryl Schenker, Toni Trudell, Louise Vance, and Lindsay and Thea Woodel.)

Equip Yourself

Yarns   The world of yarn is now your oyster. With a free spirit and from a cast of thousands, you may select your sweater yarn. Well, almost a free spirit. Stemming from the premise that the yarn must be worthy of your time, there are two factors that deserve your consideration: content and ply.

Fiber Content. A natural fiber is best. Underground concoctions will never reproduce that which grows or walks above. Wool, cotton, linen, silk, angora, mohair, alpaca, cashmere, camel hair, quiviut, and yes, even dog hair, are the most promising candidates. Wool tops that list on purpose; there is no substitute for its warmth, protection, longevity, color range, and variety of texture. The assortment is tremendous; every country seems to have a specialty—a yarn distinctive to its region. Of all the natural fibers, wool is the most versatile. It may be spun as thin as a cobweb, for a light evening sweater, or as thick as a cord, for a modish bulky jacket. Wool blends with other natural fibers and also with synthetics—how successfully with the latter is difficult to say; word of mouth may be your best reference.

The popularity of wool/synthetic blends (or synthetics alone) is, of course, due to their affinity for the washing machine. Perhaps it is possible to toss in acrylics full-cycle, but what matter? They are what they are, never to be confused with, nor be a replacement for, a wool sweater. They don't wear like wool, act like wool, feel like wool, look like wool, last like wool, or knit like wool.

As opposed to wool, cotton produces a year-round, any-season sweater, cool in summer, warm in winter. (Lacking a down puff, try a cotton sheet or spread over a wool blanket some cold and blustery night—an insulation better than feathers.) Its dual properties are somewhat hampered by the limitations of its colors; available most often in light pastels and vivid brights, it associates with hot-weather wardrobes. Noticeable too, is a difference in the way it handles. Lacking the spring of a wool yarn, cotton is more likely to strain and tire your hands. Once knit, however, the fabric has give; it stretches quickly when worn and shrinks back to shape when washed.

Due to their scarcity, the remaining natural fibers approach the luxury level of knitting yarns, and understandably so. A cashmere sweater, for example, requires an amount of yarn equal to the annual fleece of two or three goats. On the contrary, the fleece of one sheep yields enough yarn for two or three sweaters. Silk, alpaca, cashmere, etc.—expensive and elegant all, but treat yourself to their exclusiveness, if only as a touch here or there.

Novelty yarns are in a class by themselves. Each outdoes the other with whirls and mixes of color, texture, "eyelashes," and content—a sight to behold on the shelves. Irresistible, yes, but often flamboyant, so proceed with caution. Purchase one skein and knit a sample—or even two or three. Then pin them on and face the glass. What promised to be the last word when compacted in a ball may speak too loudly once expanded in a sweater. If so, confine its bid for power to the yoke or a trim, remembering that a little bit of a good thing goes a long way. And if its splendor ends up as decor in a basket, it is still a feast for the eyes.

Handspun Yarns. The ultimate knitting thrill is to work with your own handspun yarn. An attachment develops between you and your offspring through the picking, carding, spinning, and plying. You'll also develop a respect for the tools and the process, not to mention the fiber's origin: the plant, the animal, or the worm. Anyone who holds a needle or deals with yarn should be required to go back to the source, follow the steps, and become familiar with the operation of wheels, hand cards, niddy-noddys, swifts, clock reels, and the like. Avail yourself of the nearest spinning class or head for a live demonstration. Perhaps the time-consuming task is not for you. Fine. At least you will be knowledgeable about that with which you work, and will better understand its properties.

Any natural fiber may be handspun by itself or blended with another. Again, wool is the leader, for all the previous reasons, plus availability. The problem lies not in finding a good fleece, but in resisting the urge to pick up one more. The "black" sheep provides color values ranging through the browns and grays as well as blacks. Whether to card the shades together or work them separately is the first Decision Point for spinners; in effect, the earliest planning of a sweater takes place at that irreversible moment. Either way, the result is a truly unique yarn in the strictest sense of the word. No two fleeces are alike, no two spinners spin alike, and no two handspun yarns are alike; they are originals, not to be duplicated.

The white sheep is indeed indispensable. Each breed has a characteristic staple, and its own interpretation of white—from white-white, through the pearly tones, to cream. Used as is, or naturally dyed, it reflects its individuality as well as yours. Who else besides Carol Conners, of Janesville, Wisconsin, has an off-white cardigan with a yoke of red-clay pink, privet hedge green, and dandelion yellow? Just try to embroider a logo on that one or give it a label; it parts company with the catalog crowd.

And nonspinners, you don't have to sit back and admire these natural beauties from a distance. A commercial white or off-white wool yarn will dye just as nicely. Go—pick flowers, gather nuts and pine cones, collect tree barks and onion skins; borrow or buy a good dyeing book, and set out on your own color adventure. Keep in mind one fact: any stuff that stains the hands, such as beets or berries, will not take fastly to the yarn. The best dyestuffs are the ones that give no hint as to what they will produce. Queen Ann's Lace, green and white, will magically bring forth a clear, sharp yellow. The fun, the suspense, and the mystery of natural dyeing come from the unexpected outcome. Why not surprise your sweater with a stripe or two in hues commercial dyes cannot imitate?

Coned Yarns. Often overlooked as a source of unusual yarns for knitting are so-called weaving yarns. Don't be shy; open the door to a shop with looms on display, and you're certain to find yarns of substance and depth, interesting textures, and a better selection of natural fibers. Though they may look strange, wound as they are on a cone, most are perfectly adaptable for sweaters. Some that seem a bit rough or coarse will become soft and supple if washed first. Incidentally, herein lies the fundamental difference between a woven fabric and a knitted fabric: A woven cloth is not considered finished until it has been washed and fulled. Weavers accept this condition and therefore work directly from cone to loom, allowing not only for the eventual shrinkage of the yarn itself, but for the pull-in of the fabric once released from the tension of the loom. After the finishing, the fabric is cut and sewn to shape. Knitters do not figure a shrinkage allowance; the sweater/fabric must fit right off the needles and remain the same size through washings. In short, then, weavers wash last, knitters wash first, and should do so no matter what the yarn; it's the only guarantee that the sweater will always fit.

Coned yarn, or any yarn, can readily be skeined for washing with the aid of a niddy-noddy, the back of a chair, or even a bent arm. Tie the skein in several spots with figure-eights of cotton string to prevent tangling in the process. Wash the skeins in cool water with a mild soap, and rinse twice in water of the same temperature as the wash water. Put to spin in the washing machine for one minute to remove the excess water, and hang to dry. (The procedure for washing a sweater is the same, except lay it flat to dry.)

Ply. The second factor to consider before your yarn decision is ply. Plying is the twisting of two or more spun strands ("singles") into one yarn; a 4-ply yarn is made up of four singles twisted together, a 2-ply is two singles, and so forth. Ply has nothing to do with the diameter of yarn; a 2-ply yarn may be very fine or very thick, depending on the diameter of its individual strands. Yarn is plied to make it stronger; it goes without saying that a 2-ply yarn is stronger than either of its individual strands. Yarn is also plied so that it will knit a straight fabric, for plying is usually done in the opposite direction from that in which the individual strands were spun. Reversing the twist helps to correct any overspin in the singles, yielding a "balanced" yarn that will not cause your knit-in-the-round fabric to skew. To knit with a single, overspun or not, can often result in a permanent bias slant to the fabric. Conversely, if the single strand is underspun (too lightly spun), the yarn will pull apart as you knit, and the finished sweater will keep growing and stretching as it is worn.

Contrary to popular opinion, a thick, lightly spun single does not produce a rugged sweater; it results in one of soft bulkiness. On a scale of 1-ply to 5-ply, it is the 5-ply twisted yarn that is the most sturdy, as attested to by the Scottish Ganseys that were worked from this yarn at nine stitches to the inch and have survived from generation to generation.

For handspinners, plying also results in a more even yarn, if the thick and thin spots in the single strands conveniently meet their opposite in the process—and fortunately they usually do.

How Much to Buy? The next question concerns quantity. How much of that favored yarn is needed for a sweater? The two factors to consider are the size of the sweater and the diameter of the yarn. The first is a simple matter, and the second will be shortly.

There ought to be a law that all yarn be sold in fat and healthy 4-ounce skeins (or, now that grams are in vogue, 100-gram skeins). It is the varying amounts of yarn in a skein and the dual system of weights that cause confusing calculations. Who can cope with grams vs. ounces and deal with yarn in weird amounts? What good is one and five-eighths of whatever? Perhaps a revolt is in

---

Metric Measurements

Pull out the calculator . . .

For the convenience of ounce-minded knitters working with yarn packaged by the gram—and for all the non-U.S. knitters using this book—a few useful conversions are listed below. (For a chart of equivalent needle sizes, see p. 80.)

Metric / English Conversions

ounces = grams ÷ 28.57
grams = ounces x 28.57
inches = centimeters ÷ 2.54
centimeters = inches x 2.54

A Few Equivalents

1 ounce = 28.5 grams
1.5 ounces = 43 grams
1.75 ounces = 50 grams
3.5 ounces = 100 grams
4 ounces = 114 grams

order against all those small balls, some even packaged in plastic.

Handspinners have the definite advantage; they must and they do calculate on their own, and are free to think in ounces or grams at their pleasure. The amount of yarn needed can be determined in a fleeting second—the time it takes to plop a similar sweater on a scale. If it weighs in at 12 ounces, they must spin 12 ounces—easy as pie. As spinners do, so should you. Be brave; devise your own system of weights and measures. Invest in a scale. It needn't be a "legal" measure; it's just for your own private use. An old baby scale, the wicker basket type, is perfect (or a new one, if you also have the proper occupant). Then, weigh your sweaters and weigh the yarns, making notes for future reference.

If a scale is not in your immediate future, you can still estimate yarn amounts on your own—though, granted, it will require a little more thought. Most yarns can be categorized into three weights by their diameter: fine, medium, or heavy. A sweater of a fine yarn requires fewer ounces than an equal size sweater in a medium yarn, for there are more yards to its ounce. Based on that fact, a rough calculation is possible. For instance, as shown in the accompanying chart, a size 40 sweater takes approximately 12 ounces of a fine yarn, 20 ounces of a medium yarn, and 28 ounces of a heavy yarn. As sizes go up and down by twos from 40, add or subtract one ounce for each size change in the proper category.

As stated in the chart, this measure is rough and approximate, but what harm? If you overcalculate, you will have enough left over for a scarf or a cap; if you land under, your creative brain will have a chance to strut its stuff. At least you won't be empty-handed, for using a mental calculation allows you to buy yarn anywhere, any time. If you suddenly find yourself in the midst of a great sale, or make an unexpected stop at a mill, don't hesitate; buy all you can carry. Repeat, repeat, and repeat to yourself: "40 equals 12, 20, 28." (Of course, it doesn't really, for those quantities add up to 60—but you'll know what you mean.) Etch it into your brain (or photocopy this page, cut out the chart, paste it onto a business card, and pop it in your wallet), and may you never have to pass up a yarn bargain again. And, if the yarn obliges by being sold in 4-ounce skeins, you know in a wink that, for a size 40 sweater, you need 3, 5, or 7 skeins, depending on the yarn diameter.

So, let's hear it for yarn in 4-ounce skeins (and that's the loose-hank type, not the pull-from-the-center variety). First, larger skeins make for fewer connections; second, they are ready for washing and/or dyeing; and third, they simplify the math. To be perfectly honest, there is a fourth: They can be hugged.

A Rough & Approximate Guide to Yarn Amounts (in ounces)

SIZE	FINE	MEDIUM	HEAVY
46	15	23	31
44	14	22	30
42	13	21	29
40	12	20	28
38	11	19	27
36	10	18	26
34	9	17	25
32	8	16	24
30	7	15	23
28	6	14	22
26	5	13	21
24	4	12	20
22	3	11	19

Handling Your Yarn. Needless to say, there are some who don't like yarn in loose skeins, for it must be balled before use. But yarn doesn't come on a silver platter or grow on shelves. Wool yarn was alive, it is alive, and it will come alive in your hands. The least you can do is take part in the very last step of its processing. It's your chance to avoid an otherwise sterile approach to its being. Open the skein, shake the strands loose, take a good look at it, squeeze it, feel it, talk to it (sweetly) as it runs through your fingers. Become a part of it. It is nothing short of a miracle.

If you happen to be a nonstop knitter, and time is your biggest objection to working with loose skeins, a swift and a ball winder would pay for themselves in very short order. The swift holds the yarn and is adjustable to any size skein. It replaces the need for another pair of arms or the back of a chair. The yarn is wound around the tubelike projection on the ball winder, thus allowing the yarn to collapse in the middle once the winding is completed. The end result is a soft ball of yarn that will sit in a stationary position beside you. Worked from the center, the yarn will continue to collapse and relax and be under a minimum amount of tension.

Lacking these tools, wind the yarn by hand into a loose, yes, even sloppy-looking ball. Avoid stress and tightness at all costs; keep it soft, soft, soft. Or, use the favored method of Japanese knitters and wind the yarn into a loose cocoon. Under no pressure at all, the yarn is merely transferred from a nonworkable skein into a workable skein-like arrangement. The cocoon lies flat, and the yarn is worked back and forth from the center. As unbelievable as it sounds, it is possible to wind an entire 4-ounce skein around your left hand. (Thank you, Sachiyo Nagasawa, of Tokyo, Japan—a workshop student at the Rhode Island School of Design.)

The Yarn Cocoon

1. Borrow some arms, or place the skein around the back of a chair.
2. Wind one end of the yarn around the tip of the middle finger of the left hand 3 or 4 times. Hold the palm of the left hand facing you, with the yarn behind the middle finger.
3. Take the yarn completely around the outside of the left hand via the base of the thumb, the little finger, and the forefinger.
4. *Take the yarn to the back between the forefinger and the middle finger.
5. Cross the back of the hand and bring the yarn to the front via the heel of the palm and around the outside of the thumb.
6. Cross the palm, heading for the heel.

The yarn cocoon

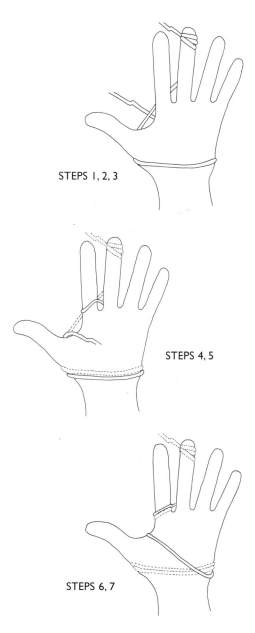

STEPS 1, 2, 3

STEPS 4, 5

STEPS 6, 7

7. Cross the back of the hand and bring the yarn to the outside of the forefinger*; repeat from * to *.

8. When the skein is completely wound around your left hand, tuck the working end under a few strands and secure it.

9. Remove the left hand.

10. Start working with the end that was wrapped around the middle finger.

Needles

Circular needles, in combination with double-points, are all that are needed to knit a sweater, period. This fact will undoubtedly upset your knitting apple cart, especially if you have carefully, and finally, amassed a collection of knobby-ended needles. To be perfectly blunt (and it's about time someone was), long, straight needles are useless. The culprit who first put an end on a knitting needle was most likely an accomplice to whoever began writing sweater directions in pieces. Oh, for the pleasure of stringing them both up with some raveled yarn.

A dead-end, or one-way, needle not only interrupts the rhythm of your knitting, but also the rhythm of your sweater. For just as you are getting up to speed, you must come to a roaring halt, and your pattern is then in need of an interfering seam. Moreover, a knobbed needle hinders creativity. In contrast, a circular needle allows stitches to be slipped or knitted from one to the other, or, to be left "on hold" without a thought as to knitting direction. Other advantages are more obvious: A circular needle is lightweight, easy to use, and in one piece. It confines your work to the boundaries of your lap; no longer are you flapping those long, thin wings.

A well-rounded needle collection includes 16" and 24" circulars and sets of 8" double-points in sizes 3, 4, 5, 6, 7, and 8. Fill in with the smallers and the largers if you are the type for very fine or very thick yarn; you are probably one or the other, not both. The shorter circulars work the sleeves and neck ribbings; the longers are used for the body proper, the body ribbings, and neck ribbings on occasion. When you have too few stitches for the 16" circular, the double-points substitute; working in fours, they act as round. Individually or in twos, they perform the small jobs, and being two-way, they come to the rescue in strange situations. True, sweaters of seamless construction require five or six needle changes, but switching from one to the other becomes automatic by the second sweater, as long as you have the needles on hand. Nothing is more aggravating than not having the correct needle size when you need it, so stock up. The cost is minimal compared to that of weaving supplies; be glad you don't need a loom with all its trappings.

Needle Conversion Chart

U.S.	Metric (mm)	Can./Brit.
0	2	14
1	2.5	13
2	2.75	11
3	3	10
4	3.5	9
5	3.75	8
6	4	7
7	4.5	7
8	5	6
9	5.5	5
10	6	4
10.5	7	3
11	8	2

As for the needles themselves, those of metal are far superior to plastic. They are fast, smooth, and end up where they are aimed. Click they do, but only to announce progress; a quiet needle seems always at a standstill. Purchase needles all of one brand or kind. Working a gauge sample on plastic and the sweater on metal, or vice versa, could affect your stitches-to-the-inch measure, for the plastic ones tend to be a tiny bit larger. Also, steer clear of pre-packaged sets with screw-on ends; the end you want will always be busy on another project. Who has the patience for that performance in the middle of a brainstorm? Be particularly fussy about the joinings; a circular needle is only as good as its connection. And be aware that older, or much used, colored circular needles with worn ends may discolor your yarn. A light-color yarn, especially white or off-white, may turn into a fabric streaked with black, and a natural dyed yarn may completely change color.

Miscellany

Braidkin. The handiest little tool of all is the Braidkin (manufactured by Braid-Aid, Route 53, Pembroke, MA 02359). Long familiar to rug-braiding enthusiasts for lacing braided strips together, the Braidkin also belongs in the knitter's basket. Its blunt, angled tip slides around and through stitches without splitting them, thus making a neat job of any task requiring a needle. If at first you don't succeed and have to try again, it's a simple matter to flip the yarn back out, as it will not be hung up in the middle of a strand. The Braidkin has two eyes, only one of which you must thread. If you're handy with a file, the two eyes could become one. Fine to medium-weight yarns pose no threading problem.

Dental Floss Threader. This unusual piece of equipment comes to the rescue for threading heavy-weight or novelty yarns through the Braidkin. Put the yarn through the loop end, and then pull the straight end through an eye of the Braidkin. Threaders also do an excellent job of guiding yarn through button eyes. Keep these in a special place, for they tend to disappear in a knitting bag or basket. (Distributed by John O. Butler Co., Chicago, IL 60611).

Needle Gauge. This measure is an absolute necessity. Once out of their cases, most circular and double-pointed needles are unidentifiable as to size, and without a needle gauge they might very well remain homeless the rest of their lives. Be aware that some foreign-manufactured needles might fit a tiny bit loosely in a U.S. gauge. Some circulars are marked in millimeters on the needle near the joinings at both ends. All you have to do is translate, if millimeters are not your forte. (See conversion chart, p. 80.) Many needle gauges include an opening for counting stitches to the inch.

Tools of the trade

Markers. Markers are another absolute necessity. Yes, they do keep hopping off the needle, but find another and put it right back on again. Invest in the thinnest markers you can find; fat ones tend to distort the seamline. And purchase them in a variety of colors— a green one for "Go" is indispensable. (Yarn markers have their places, but in constant use they fray, and in flat knitting they have to be flipped and flopped from one side of the work to the other. Limit their use to temporary positionings.)

Scissors, Crochet Hooks, Tape Measure. Stow this miscellany in a zippered pouch or in the needle case described below.

The Needle Case

This easy-to-make needle case is designed to hold all your circular and 8" double-pointed needles as well as the above miscellany. When filled, it compactly folds into a case no bigger than a paperback book. Tuck it in a bag or a suitcase, and you're off with all your knitting tools. (Design © 1979 by Alice Beal. Thank you, Alice.)

To keep the needle case open and the needles easily acessible, find a basket about 7 or 8 inches in diameter and 6 inches high. Invert the case and stand it on edge around the inside of the basket, leaving a handy center "hole" for other odds and ends. Then your needles are all visible and ready to grab.

Materials

　¾ yard outer fabric
　¾ yard inner fabric

Both fabrics should be firmly woven cottons (denim, calico, kettle-cloth), wools, or corduroys in coordinating colors/patterns.

Cut 6 Pieces:

　(A) one 19" x 18½" piece of outer fabric for case
　(B) one 19" x 18½" piece of inner fabric for case
　(C) two 19" x 8½" pieces of inner fabric for pockets
　(D) two 1½" x 15" pieces of outer fabric for ties

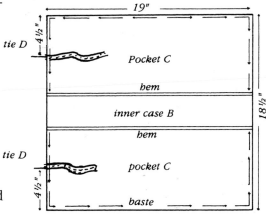

Sewing Instructions

(For sewers only: You may revert back to thinking "right" and "wrong" to describe the sides of the fabric. See Definitions, p. 92.)

Pockets

　1. Hem one 19" edge of each pocket piece (C).
　2. Place pocket pieces (C) right side up on right side of inner fabric piece (B).
　3. Machine baste raw edges of pockets to inner fabric with a ⅜" seam.

Ties

　4. Fold in ends and sides of tie pieces (D) ¼". Press.
　5. Fold each tie in half lengthwise, and press again.
　6. Topstitch the ends and sides of ties.
　7. Pin ties to the right side of the left edge of inner fabric 4½" from top and bottom with their ends heading into the case.

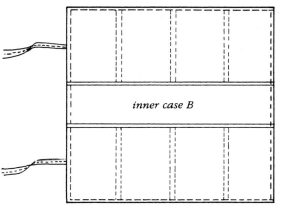

Case

　8. Lay outer piece (A) on top of inner piece (B), right sides together.
　9. Stitch around all sides using a ½" seam, leaving a 3" opening on one 19" side for turning.
　10. Turn right side out, and press.
　11. Topstitch around all edges.

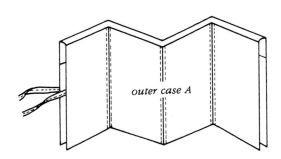

Divide Pockets

　12. Divide each pocket piece (C) into four equal sections by drawing chalk lines from the hemmed edge to the top and bottom of the case.
　13. Sew a double row of stitches ¼" apart through all layers to form pockets.
　14. Press to finish. Fold in half, top to bottom, and then fold accordion style and tie.

Unravel Your Thinking

The Sweater Construction

Pure, logical, simple, sensible, easy, exciting, and fun—all these words and more can be used to describe the construction of a seamless raglan sweater. Built to principles as ages old as any other form of shelter, the sweater is worked from the bottom up. It rises from a firm foundation, is worked round and round to the top, and is finished in the process, the same as an igloo of ice, a cabin of logs, or an adobe of bricks.

The logic of the method is amazing, and the question nags, who took the garment/sweater apart and why? Not that we will ever

A 14th-century depiction of seamless circular knitting on double-pointed needles—the Virgin working on a vest-like garment for her infant son. Detail from "The Visit of the Angels," by Meister Bertram.

know for certain, but it is interesting to speculate. The more one delves into the matter, the more it appears that construction methods have come and gone, and gone and come full circle. The clues are derived from early fragments, illustrations, paintings, and patterns.

When it all began, this means of creating a fabric with sticks and fiber, survival was foremost. The motivating factor was need: immediate need for a protective body covering. And what could be simpler or quicker than a seamless garment instantly wearable immediately off the needles? Apparently nothing, for there is proof that knitting had seamless beginnings.

A painting called "The Visit of the Angels," by Meister Bertram, c. 1390 (formerly part of the altar at Buxtehude Abbey and now in the Hamburger Kunsthalle in Hamburg, Germany) depicts the Madonna working with four straight needles around the neck of what appears to be a seamless garment. Some might argue that she is only picking up the neck stitches to work them in the round, but the needles look to be of adequate length to have worked the entire garment in that manner. And, as an aside, if four straight needles were not long enough to work the desired article, five, six, or more double-points would be placed into action. Today we are conditioned by the fact that needles are usually marketed in sets of four. (Look around, however; some brands do come in sets of five, which is an extremely useful and often "knit-saving" factor when one needle manages to slither between the sofa cushions, disappear forever in the street, or escape aboard the bus or on the train.)

Back to the subject at hand, within its textile collection, The Museum of London[1] has two knitted garments, an undershirt and a tunic. The undershirt is knitted from a two-ply handspun white wool yarn and worked from the bottom up. It is very tiny, infant size, measuring 23 inches around the bottom, 16.5 inches around the chest, and 13.5 inches in length. Though tattered and torn, it is a valued example of 17th-century (or possibly even earlier) hand knitting.

The other article belonged to Charles I and is the beautiful pale blue silk tunic he wore to his very unpleasant death, having been executed (beheaded, actually) while wearing this extraordinary garment. The tunic also was worked from the bottom up; however, the sleeves were worked from the cuff to the shoulder and were sewn in. It is patterned throughout and measures 36 inches around the chest and is 32.5 inches in length.

1. Information provided on May 10, 1983, by Joanna Marschner, Museum Assistant, Department of Costumes and Textiles, The Museum of London.

A Tudor infant's vest or undershirt excavated in London, probably from the mid-16th to mid-17th century. Made from a soft, 2-ply handspun white wool, the garment is of seamless construction, worked on several needles from the bottom up. The photo shows it in its pre-conservation condition.

This slim-waisted golfer is wearing a sweater that is knitted up the back, over the shoulder, and down the front. From Whitney's Treatise on Crocheting and Knitting in Yarns and Worsteds.

Of the same vintage as the Golf Sweater, the Newport Jacket is started at the edge of one front and worked around to the other front edge. From Latest Novelties in Fancy Work, with Directions for Making.

The practice of piecemeal construction dates from the birth of the cottage industries. For production purposes, each family member or neighboring knitter was responsible for one section of a garment, the whole being made from the parts. (Do you suppose they drew straws for the job at the end of the line?)

The machinery of the Industrial Revolution perpetuated the piecework construction of garments. Knitted fabric was loomed flat, then cut to shape and sewn together. Or, it was loomed full-fashioned—that is, loomed in pre-shaped pieces—and seamed together at the selvedges. Circular knitting frames produced tubular fabrics of various diameters, but this fabric, too, was cut and stitched for undergarments. Hosiery was the only exception.

Though many of the ethnic sweaters in Europe and Scandinavia, and most particularly the traditional fisherman sweaters, or Ganseys, of Scotland were then, and still are, constructed in the round, in many instances there were no written directions to follow. Designs were passed along from generation to generation without benefit of the written word. But even if the upper-class ladies of this country knew of these garments, most likely they would have considered the styles too primitive and/or ill-fitting, as the trend at the time was for very fitted styles.

When printed sweater directions made an appearance in the mid- to late 1800s, construction was flat. The Misses Golf Sweater found in *Whitney's Treatise on Crocheting and Knitting in Yarns and Worsteds,* from the T. D. Whitney Company in Boston, is a good example of one-piece body construction, for the back is worked to the shoulder and then work is continued over the shoulder and down the front. The sleeves are worked separately, starting from the top, and are increased to shape the cap, then worked down to the cuff, which is decreased and ribbed. The sleeves and body seams are crocheted together. And, apparently, the inane practice of facing the front edges with ribbon dates back this far. The buttonhole (only one?) seems to be cut into the fabric and stitched around its edges.

The Ladies "Newport Jacket" (not to be worn at Absecon) in another 19th-century pattern book[2] works its way around the body. It starts at the center edge of one front; stitches are added and bound off as needed for neck, shoulder, and underarm shaping; and the garment ends up at the other front edge. The shoulders are joined, and the sleeves worked separately and sewn in. The neck, waist, and sleeves are ribbed with K2, P2 and then finished with a

2. *Latest Novelties in Fancy Work, with Directions for Making,* Isaac D. Allen Company, 21 Winter Street, Boston, est. 1871.

picot edge, probably crocheted. It is made entirely of garter stitch, except for collar, cuffs, and waistband.

It's interesting to note that each of the sweaters in these Victorian-era pattern books had a very specific purpose. Heaven forbid that one would attempt to play tennis in a "golf sweater," or go motoring in a "country club sweater," or wear a "porch sweater" in the boudoir or a "polo sweater" when playing football. Who do you suppose was brave enough to start mingling the times when, and the places where, a particularly titled sweater could be worn?

The most obvious feature of both the Newport sweater and the golf sweater is the fit; it looks as if there is nary an inch to spare. They hug the body as second skin. If this "fit factor" was of paramount importance, perhaps that explains the practice of piecemeal construction; sweaters could be "made to measure," constructed as dresses were, of stitched-together components.

In 1979, the Smithsonian Institution published a fascinating history of dressmaker's drafting tools in use from 1838 to the early 1900s, entitled *Cutting a Fashionable Fit*. This comprehensive study by Claudia B. Kidwell explains the drafting systems once used for making the close-fitting attire of the mid- to late 19th century and shows how construction methods changed in the days of more relaxed styles and with the advent of paper patterns and ready-mades. The W. B. Pollock device (at right) was a frame that measured almost every inch of the torso. Spring clips held the pieces in place, and the device could be removed, then laid out flat as a template for making a paper pattern. As fitteth the dress, so fitteth the sweater?

Can you imagine donning this frame? Lordy, lordy, when these ladies went for a fitting, they went for A FITTING! It must have taken all day. The contraption would have been worse to get out of than into, and once it was off, what a nightmare it would have been to figure which bands measured what areas of the body. It could have been a device such as this that decreed that sweater shoulders had to be bound off in those horrid steps—steps that would never sew up to look neat. If, after all this time, that idea still exists in your mind, have the courage to think knitting and ignore it; bind off straight across, and your shoulders will be just fine.

The Impression System (shown on the next page) was a bit less formidable, as it limited itself mainly to the measurement of the bust, waist, hips, and the length from neck to hip. At least it doesn't look as if one had to be Houdini to escape its confines, though the "Indicator" and the "Curve Scale" look a little daunting to fathom. But with such measures the fashions of the time were created.

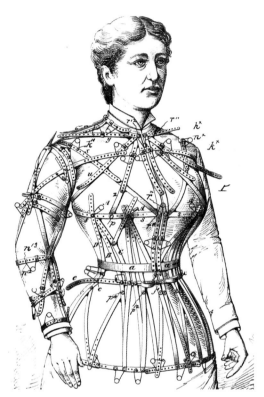

It's no wonder garments in the late 1800s fit like a second skin—every inch of the body was measured. Hail to the hero who reduced the process to one tape measure! Illustration from the cover page of the U.S. Patent Office documents for William Bloomer Pollock's elaborate garment fitting device (1885).

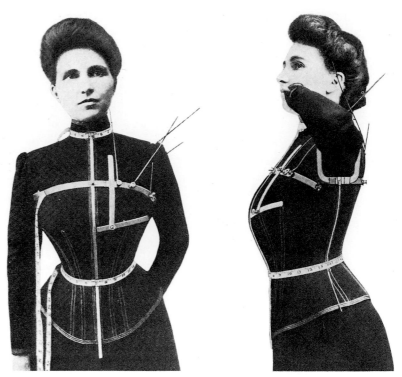

Zenith Manufacturing Company's "Impression System," published 1904, cut down on the number of measurements taken and concentrated on the body curves—the back, neck, shoulder, and bust.

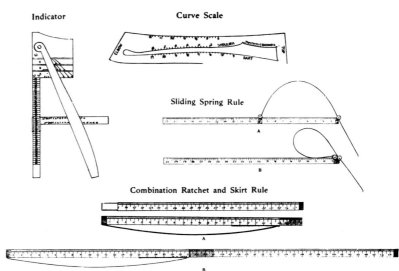

For evidence that knit garments were created with the same thought processes as sewn garments, you have only to look at the illustrations in a 1917 booklet, *Good Shepherd Fingering Yarns and Their Use—Being a Modern Treatise on the Art of Hand Knitting and Crocheting and Containing the Most Advanced Designs.*[3] The photos of the shaped pieces before the sewing-up show the precision of the work required to mesh and match the parts: the tiny pockets, the button bands, the collars, the belts and even the little

3. Published by Shepherd Worsted Mills, Newton, Massachusetts, in 1917, it originally sold for twenty-five cents. Thanks go to Mary Anne Hadwen, of Berwick, Maine, for the discovery and loan of this booklet.

sleeve cuffs. Note, too, the different styles of body construction. Isn't it intriguing that, with all the working of disconnected pieces, the body proper never completely came apart? It stayed joined at the sides when it was worked from front edge to front edge; it stayed joined at the shoulder when it was worked up the back, over the shoulder, and down the front (or the reverse—up the front,

Both the Porch Sweater (top) and the Sweater Coat with Pointed Sailor Collar (bottom) look like cut-and-sew projects, with sleeve cuffs, facings, and pockets worked as separate pieces. From Good Shepherd Fingering Yarns and Their Use.

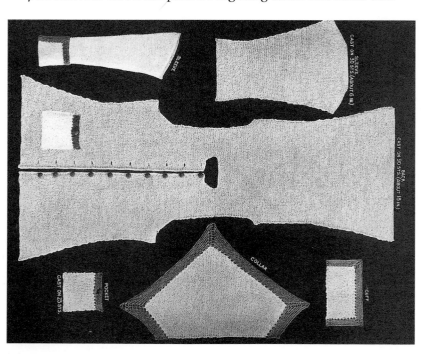

over the shoulder, and down the back); and it stayed joined when worked as a T shape with stitches cast off for the neck opening.

However, at this same time the inevitable happened. The "Roberta" design in a 1918 *Fleisher's Knitting and Crochet Manual*[4] shows the front and the back sections of the sweater finally disconnected altogether. For the most part, they have remained as separate entities to this day. Often the result is dismaying: The vision of the perfect sweater vanishes with the reality of the finished garment— too long, too short, too loose, too tight. Or the sweater is never finished at all, and the pieces forever remain in a basket awaiting the sewing needle. For some, the enjoyment of knitting is gone.

The seamless raglan sweater presented in *The Sweater Workshop* brings back that lost pleasure. Its construction is such that it grows and develops the way you will wear it; try it on as you go. Work the body to the underarm, the sleeves to the underarm, then join the three tubes and head for the top. And who's to know at the start how it will end? Options galore will pop into your head, a procrastinator's delight, until Decision Points are reached.

The firm foundation welcomes patterns; they originate from a given number of stitches and travel completely around, with nothing to break their rhythm. The simplicity of the sweater's shape leaves it wide open for design. Think color, contrast, line—or take the easy way out and rely on nothing more than the texture of the yarn itself for interest. Whatever, you will acquire a taste for thinking and knitting on your own, for the sweater will be you, and it will fit.

Gauge, coming up.

Analyzing Gauge

The importance of gauge, or tension, is stressed in every knitting book, magazine, pamphlet, and individual sweater pattern. You, the knitter, are warned and cautioned to work to the gauge of the sweater's designer. Some of you heed the advice, and some of you don't, but it's often a no-win situation in either case. Those who dutifully keep changing needles until the correct gauge is achieved may end up suffering through the sweater by either cramping their natural knitting style, or being constantly on the alert to "think loose." Those who barge ahead using the suggested numbers and needles may suffer the consequences of an ill-fitting sweater of a fabric that is either too stiff or too frail.

4. *Fleisher's Knitting and Crochet Manual,* The Fleisher Yarns, S. B. & B. W. Fleisher, Philadelphia, 1918.

The variable lies in your hands. For as your fingerprint and signature prove, your hands are like no others; you each have your own knitting rhythm and tension. But you often knit in isolation, filling quiet, solitary hours with the comfort of yarn and needles. This aloneness conceals the fact that the same yarn and needles in the hands of another result in a different gauge. If you were to knit in a room with twenty others, the fact would be obvious; twenty knitters could equal twenty sweater sizes. Find a friend. Knit together, and the need for a gauge sample will become self-evident.

To knit on your own, you have no choice but to knit the gauge sample, for your gauge sample is the source of your numbers to calculate the dimensions of the sweater. It is also your assurance that you, your yarn, and the resulting fabric will be content. You may knit to your normal tension, your yarn will sit in its most comfortable position on whatever size needle best fits its contours, and the fabric may be as dense or as airy as you choose. In addition, the sweater this fabric becomes will be the intended size, which is the heart of the matter. Yes, you are knitting a sweater, but you are, more precisely, knitting a fabric in the shape of a sweater. You are a

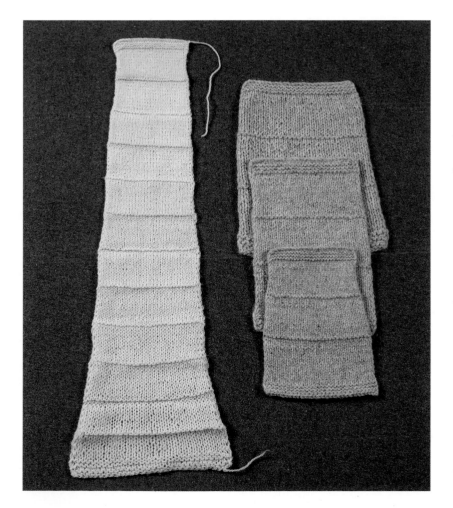

Left: You certainly do not have to work a gauge sample such as this one, on 11 different-size needles—usually a range of 3 sizes is sufficient to achieve the fabric you want. What this sample shows is that there is no "correct" or "incorrect" fabric anywhere along its length. If you want a firm, tight fabric in a fine yarn, you have it on size 0 or 1 needles. If you prefer a light, lacy effect, needle size 10 or 10½ will do the job—and then there are all those gradations in between. The choice is yours, and yours alone.

Right: This trio of gauge samples clearly illustrates the need to work to your own gauge. They were all worked with the same yarn, on the same size needles, over the same number of stitches, for the same number of rows. The obvious difference in their widths and lengths—and thus in stitches-to-the-inch—is attributable only to the three sets of hands working to their owner's individual knitting tensions— tight, loose, and somewhere in between. From top to bottom, Anne Pompeo, the author, and the late Nancy Sladen.

production line of one, for the finished fabric is a ready-to-wear garment requiring no further cutting or sewing. For this reason the fabric must be appropriate to the sweater, and at the same time, the completed sweater must fit the body.

The purpose of a gauge sample is to see to it that you achieve both goals in one operation. Primarily, it produces a sample piece of fabric, and secondarily, it serves as an accurate count of stitches to the inch, the measure upon which the size of the sweater depends.

Here, in this one little bit of knitting that takes about ten or fifteen minutes of your time, is the key to a perfectly fitting sweater. It is not a boring procedure; it is a preview of the delightful sweater to come. You may even become addicted to sampling. Sample everything.

Definitions

All that remains between you and the Basic Sweater are a few definitions. Though they constitute a glossary, they are not presented in alphabetical order; they are grouped in sensible order. Read these terms and definitions in the order they're printed, as you would any page, and digest the terminology before you start; the meanings are paramount to the working of the sweater.

The fabric of your sweater, as any fabric, may be described as having a right side and a wrong side, a front side and a back side, or an outside and an inside. If these terms are used interchangeably in knitting directions, confusion arises, for *right* is not only the opposite of *wrong*, it is also the opposite of *left*. *Front* and *back* are not only the sides of a fabric, but are also used to identify the sections of a sweater.

With that as food for thought, the following definitions are gospel for all the directions that follow.

> **Fabric.** The material of a sweater.
>
> **Gauge sample**. A sample piece of fabric.
>
> **Right.** As opposed to left.
>
> **Left.** As opposed to right.
>
> **Front**. The front section of a sweater.
>
> **Back.** The back section of a sweater.
>
> **Outside.** The side of the fabric other people will see.
>
> **Inside**. The side of the fabric other people won't see—unless you wear the sweater inside-out.

Right-hand knitters. Those who hold the yarn in their right hand.

Left-hand knitters. Those who hold the yarn in their left hand.

Round knitters. Those who are working in rounds on a circular needle, or four or more double points.

Flat knitters. Those who are working in rows on a circular needle or two straight needles.

Seamline. For sweaters knit in the round, this is not a seamline to be sewn, but an identification point for the right and left sides of the sweater body, for the raglan decreases in the yoke, and for the increases on the inner side of the sleeves.

One round. Once around the needle, or needles, from a starting point back to it.

One row. Once across the needle.

Outside round or row. As you work, the outside of the sweater faces you.

Inside round or row. As you work, the inside of the sweater faces you.

Straight round or row. A round or row without increases or decreases.

Decrease round or row. A round or row with decreases.

Increase round or row. A round or row with increases.

Plain round or row. As opposed to one with pattern.

Pattern round or row. As opposed to one that's plain.

Work. Keep on with whatever you are doing.

Stop. Stop working at a specified point to go off and do something else.

Secure. Break the yarn; take the end to the inside; knot by taking the yarn under a handy stitch to form a loop and pulling the end through the loop.

Knit into. Knit under both strands of the chain selvedge to produce a stitch.

Unknit. Undo the stitches on the right-hand needle and put them back on the left-hand needle.

Checkpoint. To thine own gauge be true.

Decision point. Do you want a V neck, or don't you?

To the underarm. Assumes a position 2" below the actual body underarm.

The Basic Sweater, *a.k.a. the Five-Skeiner Sweater. This example was made with Bartlettyarns' Fisherman 2-ply yarn. Five 4-ounce skeins of yarn usually are enough for a sweater up to size 40 or 42, with a 15" body length. One skein of Color A is used for the body ribbing and lower body until it is gone. One skein of Color B is used for the midsection of the body to the underarm (you may or may not use it all). The final 3 skeins, Color C, are used for the sleeves and yoke.*

This particular example is worked with K2, P2 ribbing, full sleeves, Raglan Seamline B, and a Crew Neck. It features an Afterthought Pocket and a decorative heart added with Swiss Darning.

The Basic Sweater

Adapted from an original by Elizabeth Zimmermann

Select your yarn. Take it to your needles. (For your first sweater, any medium-weight yarn is best, as the aim is for you to acquire the rhythm of working a seam-free sweater, preferably in plain stockinette stitch—two evenings for the body, one for each sleeve, three for the yoke. On the eighth day you can wear it—even if just to rake leaves—and you will have mastered the method.)

Work a gauge sample on a range of needles appropriate to the yarn—or inappropriate, for a special effect. Work a 3" section with each size needle, unless you see immediately that a particular size needle is not producing the fabric you want. In that case, don't bother with the full 3 inches.

The following are suggestions only:

Fine yarn	#1 through #4
Medium yarn	#4 through #8
Heavy yarn	#8 through #10½

Note: Work a purl row on the outside of the fabric sample to serve as a dividing line between needle sizes. Because the needle size used in the final stitches-to-the-inch count is the body-size needle for the sweater proper, you MUST know what size needle you used in that section of your gauge sample. Don't trust your memory to keep track of the needle sizes; jot them down, in order, on a hang tag. (Or, for a built-in record, work a corresponding number of purl stitches into a corner of the 3" area. Separate the purl stitches with a few knits rather than working them side by side; it's quicker to count them that way.)

METHOD

- ◆ Cast on 30 stitches using two 8" double-points.
- ◆ Work 6 rows of garter stitch.
- ◆ *Work 3" of stockinette stitch, or your selected pattern.

Stop after a purl row.

- ◆ Change to the next size needle, and purl a row *.

The Gauge Sample

◆ Repeat * to * until you, the yarn, and the fabric are content.

◆ To end: Work 6 rows of garter stitch. Cast off. (Or keep the stitches on the needle for an ongoing sample.)

Counting Stitches to the Inch. Place the gauge sample flat on a table, not on your lap. Zero in on the area where the fabric looks and feels its best to you, and where it was comfortable for you to knit. For this measuring operation, a stitch gauge is best. Press its opening onto the sample, and with your finger carefully count the number of stitches within. Repeat in one or two more spots for accuracy. Do not ignore any half or quarter stitches in this count. Then divide the number of counted stitches by the length of the opening (most are 2"). The answer is your number of stitches to the inch.

Before entering this number on the Gauge Page (coming up on p. 98), double-check the count; measure the width of the sample. Its width in inches should equal the gauge over 30 stitches. For example: with a gauge of 5 stitches to the inch, 30 stitches should produce a fabric sample 6" wide. (Would that for all gauges the math were this simple, but you do relish a challenge, don't you?)

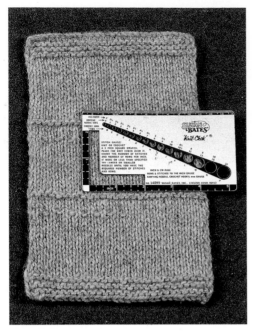

The Gauge Sample. *To count the number of stitches to the inch, center the opening of a stitch gauge over the section of the sample where the fabric looks and feels its best to you, and where it was comfortable for you to knit. Carefully, with your finger, count the stitches inside the opening and divide the number of stitches by the length of the opening to achieve your stitches-to-the-inch count.*

If the stitches of a sample worked with handspun or novelty yarn are too ill-defined to count individually, you will have to average the stitches to the inch. In this case, measure the width of the sample and divide the number of inches into 30 stitches. For example: if the fabric measures 6", divide 30 stitches by 6. The gauge is 5 stitches to the inch.

Enter the number of stitches to the inch on the Gauge Page along with the corresponding needle size.

The Sweater Measurement

The fit of a sweater is indeed the most personal of matters. Some who measure a 34 are happy in a size 32, where others might prefer a 40. For this reason, a body measurement alone is useless; it tells you nothing. Instead, measure your favorite-fitting sweater. This is your only assurance that your new creation will fit "as you like it." But, before you go grabbing for any old sweater, herewith a few words of warning.

The sweater you measure must be of a similar weight yarn to the one you are about to knit. It may surprise you to find that all your sweaters are not the same size; though you remain constant, they don't. The diameter of the yarn makes the difference. A sweater of a heavy yarn has a wider outside measurement than a sweater of fine yarn. This is because of the sheer bulk of the yarn itself, and you must take this bulk into account. Inside, where you are, the sweater is smaller, but you must knit to the outside measurement. No more will you be knitting your sweaters all to one size. A size 36 sweater in a fine yarn may be perfect, but in a heavy yarn, too tight. So, be sure to measure a similar weight sweater.

If you don't have a sweater that is a close match to your intended yarn, run to the nearest store with a tape measure. It matters not whether you measure a hand-knit or a machine-made. In the case of the latter, don't jump to conclusions. Though a commercial sweater may have a label that clearly states it is a certain size, don't trust your sweater's fate to others. Measure it yourself with a tape.

Measure it from underarm to underarm with the sweater smoothed on a flat surface, not on your body. Don't forget to double the number of inches; the sweater does have another side.

Enter the sweater measurement on the Gauge Page.

Now, the figuring begins. But first, a round of applause for the late Elizabeth Zimmermann. That you are able to turn two simple measurements into a sweater of any size is due to her EPS, otherwise known as "Elizabeth's Percentage System." With her very kind permission, her EPS is presented here for you in the form of my Gauge Page. Once you multiply your number of stitches to the inch by the number of inches around your sweater, you will be in proud possession of your Key Number and on the road to knitting on your own.

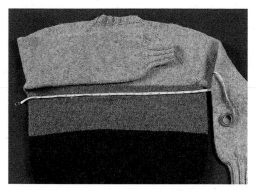

Determining the Sweater Measurement. *In order that your new creation will fit "as you like it," measure your favorite-fitting sweater of a similar weight yarn from underarm to underarm and double the number of inches. (Make sure that* you *align your tape with the edge of* your *sweater better than in this example!)*

The Key Number of Stitches

Multiply the number of stitches to the inch by the number of inches required for your sweater. The answer is your Key Number of stitches. The ultimate shape of the sweater depends on this number and the percentages derived from it. Complete your arithmetic and check it for accuracy.

In order to emphasize the importance of one-half or one-quarter of a stitch per inch, and to point out how quickly these fractions disappear, here is an example:

Gauge:	5 stitches	5¼ stitches	5½ stitches
Sweater:	36 inches	36 inches	36 inches
Key #:	180 stitches	189 stitches	198 stitches

Figuring:	36	36	36
	x 5	x 5¼	x 5½
	180	9	18
		180	180
		189	198

Or, by calculator: 5 x 36 = 180; 5.25 x 36 = 189; or 5.5 x 36 = 198.

THE GAUGE PAGE

Gauge = _____ stitches to the inch/cm (#_____ needle)

Sweater Measurement = _____ inches/cm around

Body

Stitches x Inches = _____ KEY NUMBER OF STITCHES

Body Ribbing

10% of KEY # = _____

Cast On = KEY # minus 10% = _____ stitches (#_____ needle)

Sleeves

Cuff (Ribbing) = 20% of KEY # = _____ stitches

Upper Arm = 33.3% of KEY # + 1 inch (2.5 cm) = _____ stitches

Increase = upper arm minus cuff = _____ stitches

Underarm = 8% of KEY # = _____ stitches

FIGURING

Yarn Type: _____

Sweater Style: _____

Finished Weight of Garment: _____ ounces/grams

Body Ribbing. The body ribbing is worked on the Key Number of stitches minus 10%. For example:

Key Number: 180 stitches	180
10% of 180 = 18	$\underline{-\ 18}$
	162

(As a shortcut, you can multiply the Key Number by .9 and get the same result, but do make a note of the 10% number; you'll need to use it later on.)

Therefore, the number of stitches to cast on for the ribbing is 162. However, this number may have to be adjusted to accommodate the multiple of your selected ribbing pattern. For instance, if you want to work a K2, P2 ribbing, the number must be divisible by 4. Since 162 isn't, it must be changed to 160 or 164. Up or down is up to you.

METHOD: Using a 24" circular needle, two sizes smaller than the body-size needle, cast on your ribbing number of stitches. Select a ribbing pattern with its pull-in tendencies in mind.

◆ Work the ribbing to within 1 round of the desired depth.

◆ On the last round of ribbing, increase the number of stitches by 10% of the Key Number—or more or less, if you adjusted the ribbing number of stitches. Space these increases evenly throughout the round.

Stop at the right seamline (above the tail of the slip knot). Count the number of stitches on the needle to be certain you have increased to the Key Number for the body of the sweater. If you are going to work a pattern into the body, be certain that the number of stitches on the needle is a correct multiple.

The Body. The body is worked on your Key Number of stitches using the 24" body-size needle. To change from the ribbing-size needle to the larger needle, simply work from one to the other.

METHOD: With the outside of the sweater facing you, tuck the right end of the ribbing needle down into your work. With the body-size needle in your right hand, insert the tip of it into the first stitch on the ribbing-size needle in your left hand.

◆ Work one round.

Stop at the right seamline. The ribbing needle is now empty. Before starting the next round, slip a marker on the right needle. This marker identifies the right seamline when the sweater is on you. It is the starting point of all rounds.

◆ As you work the next round, count the stitches. At the halfway point, put a marker on the needle to identify the left seamline. Though you may not use these markers in a plain sweater

The Body

until you reach the underarm, they will be there for reference and provide a feeling of security.

◆ Work round and round until your sweater measures about 3" above the ribbing.

Stop at the right seamline.

>>> **Checkpoint:** At this point your sweater may look too small. Keep in mind the three legitimate reasons for its appearance:

1. It is on a 24" needle.

2. The ribbing has been worked on a needle two sizes smaller, and on 10% fewer stitches.

3. You have worked a decent ribbing with good pull-in tendencies.

Though the sweater may look too small at the Checkpoint—3 inches above the ribbing—it will be the right size when it gets where it's going, which is to the underarm, if your gauge is correct.

Now for the illegitimate reason (and why you must check the fit at this point): Your gauge sample was worked back and forth on two needles. Once you start zipping around on a circular needle, your tension could change; a few knitters tighten up, a few loosen up. So, to check your gauge and to check the fit, slip (as if to purl) approximately half the stitches onto the empty ribbing needle. This move will allow your sweater to open up to its full width. With the sweater thus released from the confines of a single 24" needle, count the number of stitches to the inch—again, over more than one inch, and in two or three spots.

If all is in order as far as gauge is concerned, wrap elastics around the needle ends to secure the stitches and slip what there is of the sweater onto your body. Check the width of the ribbing in the desired position, and then hike the body part of the sweater up. If the fit is satisfactory, put all the stitches back on the body-size needle and continue working.

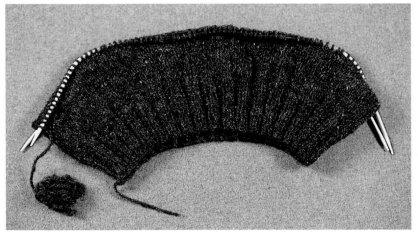

Checkpoint. *With half its body stitches slipped onto a spare 24" circular needle, what there is of the sweater is ready for a gauge check and a try-on.* **Note:** *To hold the markers on the needle, work one stitch beyond them, and to hold the stitches on the needle for the try-on, tightly wrap elastics around their individual ends.*

If you detect a change in gauge, *start again*. Use the gauge achieved on the round needle for setting up a new Gauge Page. Take note of the words "start again," a more pleasant concept than "rip out," and a more exact assessment of the situation. The thought, and the job, of ripping is demoralizing; it can ruin an otherwise beautiful day. In addition, it is not wise—not all at once, anyway—for how are you to know whether the second attempt is an improvement over the first, if the first is gone? The psychological and sensible solution is to knit as you rip, and you are in a perfect position to do so, starting again, as you are, with a ribbing. Ribbings are the best home for ripped yarn, as any loss of bulk is less noticeable because the ribbing is worked on smaller needles than the body proper.

So, to start again, pull the needle, break the yarn, and place the reject beside you. Then rip an old round, and rib a new round. When the new ribbing is complete, check its new size against what is left of the reject. In the same manner, use the remainder of the original ribbing later for the ribbing on sleeves and neck. Before you know it, the distasteful task of ripping is done, and the reject is gone. The best part is that you never had to look at a horrid ball of kinky yarn.

Apply the same philosophy to other situations. Don't rip immediately; wait until you must use the yarn, and aim for ribbings. To change in mid-sweater from new yarn to used might be detectable. The alternative is to restore the yarn's fullness by washing, but in that case, you may be committed to washing all the yarn for the project, if you didn't take that previous step; washing only the ripped yarn could make a bad situation worse.

Or, don't rip at all. You have the ready-made start of another sweater (or, if small enough, a cap or a turtle-to-go). If the reject ribbing was to be a cardigan, bind it off for a matching scarf.

Lastly, many small errors are easily corrected with a crochet hook. Dropped stitches, forgotten decreases, reversed stitches, and knits that should be purls (or vice versa) are instances that may not require ripping. Try anything else first, and treat ripping as a last resort. And remember, everything hand-done is entitled to one tiny mistake.

Now, back to the business at hand. If you had to start again, knit faster to catch up.

As you work to the underarm, consider these two Decision Points:

>>> **Decision Point for short rows**—3" above the ribbing.

>>> **Decision Point for sweatshirt pocket**—5" or 6" above the ribbing for an adult; 3" or 4" for a child.

Stripes, patterns, designs, or other decorations may be added anywhere you like. For a pattern or a design, select one with a multiple that works in with a minimal change to your Key Number of stitches. An adjustment of one or two stitches is tolerable, but be forewarned: any more than that would affect the size of the sweater (a dilemma you may encounter at some point in your sweater knitting).

◆ Work the body until you are about 2" shy of your actual underarm.

Stop at the right seamline.

◆ Once more, to be absolutely certain of the correct body length, slip half the stitches onto another needle, and try on the body. With the ribbing where you want it, check the position of the top of the body in relation to the underarm. Then slip the stitches back on the body needle. (Be sure they are on the body-size needle.) If you must adjust up or down for length, do so, but be absolutely sure that when you stop, you . . .

Stop at the right seamline. Do not break the body yarn. Start the sleeve with a new ball.

The Sleeve

Sleeve Ribbing. The sleeve ribbing is worked on 20% of the Key Number of stitches. Calculate as Key Number x .2. For example:

Key Number: 180 stitches	180
20% of 180 = 36	.20
	36.00

Therefore, the number of stitches to cast on for the sleeve ribbing is 36. If the number must be adjusted to work your ribbing pattern, consider the size of your wrist. By now you must know whether it is a little smaller, or larger, than "normal." Adjust the number up or down accordingly.

The ribbing is worked on four double-pointed ribbing-size needles.

METHOD: Cast your ribbing number of stitches all onto one needle, loosely.

♦ Starting with the last cast-on stitch, divide the stitches evenly among three needles by slipping some of them (as if to purl) from the first needle to the other two. Each needle does not have to have exactly the same number of stitches; your tension will be better if each needle starts with a knit stitch as opposed to a purl.

♦ Hold the needle with the tail in your left hand.

♦ Hold the needle with the last cast-on stitch and the working yarn in your right hand.

♦ Be certain all the stitches are straight on the needles, with their bottoms under the needles.

♦ Carefully transfer all three needles to your left hand and, using the fourth needle in your right hand, insert the tip of it into the slip-knot stitch, and work the stitches, in ribbing pattern, from the first needle onto the fourth needle.

♦ Insert the now-empty first needle into the first stitch on the second needle and, continuing in ribbing pattern, work the stitches from the second needle onto the first. Insert the now-empty second needle into the first stitch on the third needle, and continuing in ribbing pattern, work the stitches from the third needle onto the second. You are now back where you started, and the now-empty third needle starts the next round.

♦ Continue using needles in rotation as they empty. Be sure your work is on three needles at all times. The sleeve ribbing grows toward your lap, hanging below (on the outside of) the needles, with the tail of the slip knot marking the seamline.

♦ Work the sleeve ribbing to desired depth, adding extra length if it is to be folded back.

Stop at the seamline, knowing there is one last round of ribbing to be worked.

Decision Point for Sleeve Style. Select one of the following six sleeve styles. (For your first sweater, the fitted, the semi-fitted, or the full sleeve would be a good choice.) After that, you may be as fancy as you wish, as long as you end up at the upper arm with the correct number of stitches.

<<<

The upper arm is one-third of the Key Number of stitches, plus one inch's worth of additional stitches. For example, again assuming that your Key Number is 180 and the gauge is 5 stitches per inch:

$$180 \div 3 = 60 \quad \text{or} \quad 3\overline{)180}^{\,60} \qquad 60 + 5 = 65$$

Six Sleeve Styles. *Sleeves may vary from fitted to very full, depending on where and how many increases are worked.*

Fitted

Semi-fitted

Full

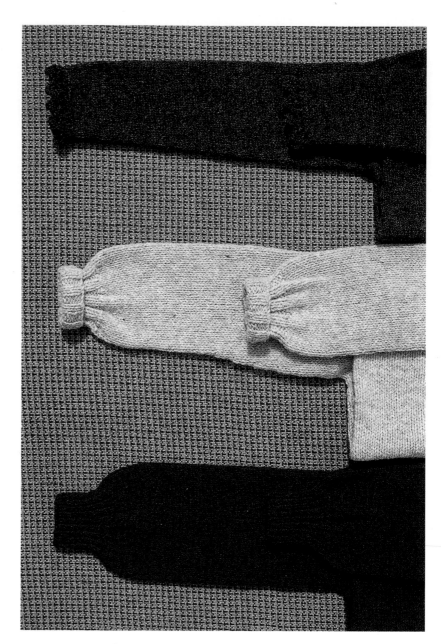

After determining the number of stitches needed at the upper arm, subtract the number of stitches you already have on the needle for the ribbing. Continuing with our example:

Upper arm = 66 (rounded up from 65 for an even number)

Ribbing = 36

66 – 36 = 30

Therefore, the number of stitches to be increased somewhere, somehow, as you work your way up the sleeve is 30.

Working the Sleeve Increases and Decreases

◆ To increase "in the ribbing" means to work the Bar Increase (p. 37) evenly spaced as many times as necessary in the last round of rib while on the ribbing-size needles. Keep the other

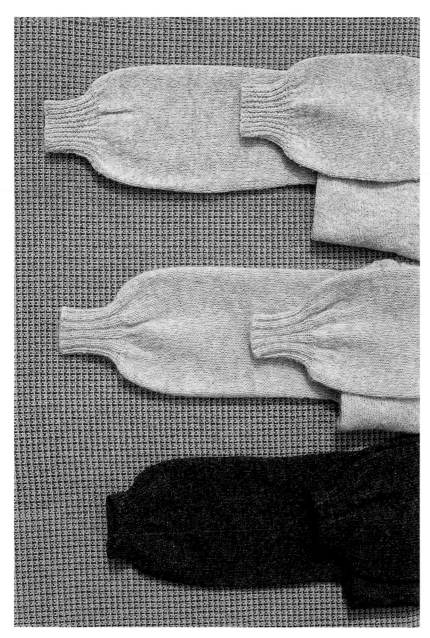

Fuller

Fullest

Even fuller fullest

stitches in the ribbing pattern. If the stitch that must be in-creased is a purl, treat it as a knit and work the increase into it.

◆ To increase "at the seamline" means to work the Bar Increase on each side of the seamline marker about every inch or so: Work to within 2 stitches of the marker, increase K1, slip marker, K1, increase.

◆ To decrease "at the seamline" means to decrease a stitch on each side of the seamline marker about every inch: Work to within 3 stitches of the marker, K2 tog, K1, slip marker, K1, SSK.

◆ To decrease "in the yoke" means to decrease an extra stitch on the **sleeve side** of the normal raglan decrease every third or fourth decrease round: Work the normal K2 tog as a K3 tog, or the SSK as an SSSK.

METHOD

The Fitted Sleeve. Increase one inch's worth of stitches in the last round of ribbing; increase the remainder by pairs at the seamline, starting one inch above the ribbing and every inch thereafter. For the inch's worth of stitches, refer to your gauge. In the example sweater, the gauge is 5 to the inch. Round this number off to 6, as 36 divided by 6 equals 6; therefore, you'll increase in every sixth stitch in the last round of ribbing, and then increase 12 pairs of 2 at the seamline for the remaining 24, to achieve the additional 30 stitches.

The Semi-Fitted Sleeve. Increase one-half (more or less) of the needed stitches in the last round of ribbing; increase the other half, (more or less) by pairs at the seamline between the elbow and the upper arm. The "more or less" is noted to call your attention to the fact that the needed number does not have to be divided exactly in half. To simplify the math and make the increases more convenient, you may split the number off-center. Example: Rather than splitting the 30 needed stitches into 15 and 15, you might want to split them into 18 and 12. Why? With 36 on the needle, to increase 18, you simply would increase into every other stitch of the ribbing, and then increase the 12 as 6 pairs of 2 at the seamline between the elbow and the upper arm. Let the numbers dictate the split.

The Full Sleeve. Increase all the needed stitches in the last round of ribbing. In the example sweater with 36 ribbing stitches, you would be increasing into all but 6—say, 2 on each needle.

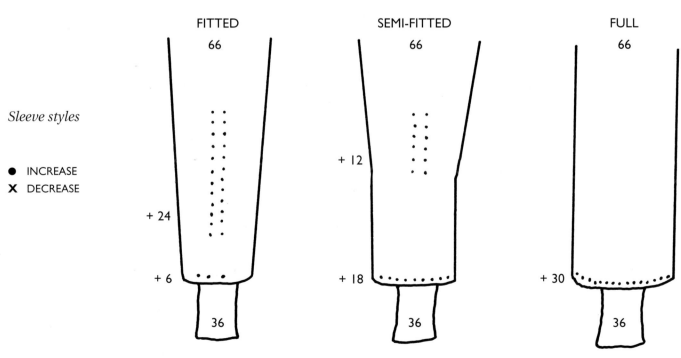

Sleeve styles

● INCREASE
X DECREASE

FITTED
66
+ 24
+ 6
36

SEMI-FITTED
66
+ 12
+ 18
36

FULL
66
+ 30
36

The Fuller Sleeve. Increase into every stitch in the ribbing. Since 36 and 36 equal 72, now you have 6 stitches more than the needed number of 66. Decrease the excess 6 stitches at the seamline as 3 pairs of 2, starting above the elbow. (We can thank Connie Pearlstein for this graceful sleeve with knit-in fullness above the cuff. As she says, "It does away with the 'fiddle factor' of constantly pushing the sleeve up to achieve the same effect." Amen.)

The Fullest Sleeve. Increase into every stitch in the ribbing. Since 36 and 36 equal 72, now you have 6 stitches more than the needed number of 66. For this sleeve, work straight to the upper arm and decrease the excess 6 stitches ***in the yoke, on the sleeve side of the raglan seamlines.***

The Even Fuller Fullest Sleeve. Again, increase into every stitch in the ribbing. Since 36 and 36 equal 72, now you have 6 stitches more than the needed number of 66, and for the added fullness, in the next round increase 8 more evenly spaced—72 divided by 8 equals 9, so increase into every ninth stitch, for a total of 80 stitches, or 14 more than the needed number. Decrease 8 of those extra 14 as 4 pairs of 2 at the seamline above the elbow, and the other 6 ***in the yoke, on the sleeve side of the raglan seamlines.***

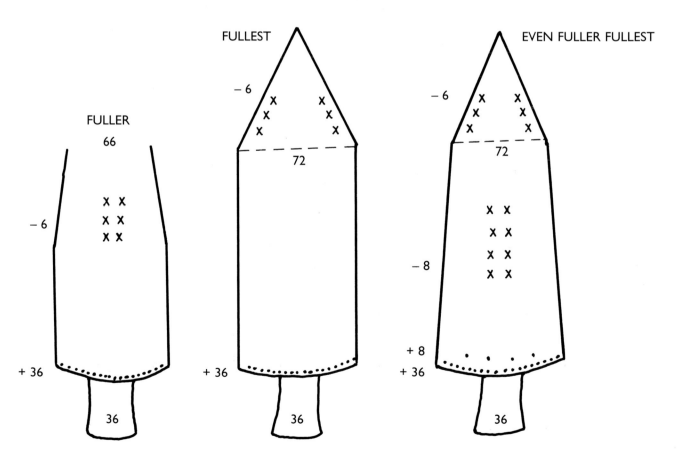

◆ Make a decision on sleeve style and work the last round of ribbing, increasing the appropriate number of stitches.

The Sleeve Proper. The sleeve is worked on four double-pointed body-size needles, unless or until you have enough stitches to comfortably fit around a 16" circular needle. (Even if you have selected the full sleeve and numberwise now have enough stitches to fit around the 16" needle, the stitches have not yet had a chance to blossom to their full width.)

Therefore, one by one, as you work the next round, change from the four ribbing-size double-pointed needles to four body-size double-pointed needles.

If you are working the fitted sleeve, the paired increases are made at the seamline. As the seamline is now between two needles, a marker would not stay put. So, on the next round, slip the stitches around on the needles and position the seamline in the center of one. This move makes the increase track more visible.

Work the sleeve until you are about 2" shy of your actual underarm. Try the sleeve on as you work, with the ribbing folded up or down according to how you intend to wear it.

Stop at the seamline when the length is correct. Break the yarn, leaving a good yard for future grafting of the underarm stitches, and tuck it down into the sleeve. Work the other sleeve to match.

If you must use the same needles for the other sleeve, slip the stitches from the finished sleeve onto anything from which they may be worked—a good job for the old plastic needles with which you now do not know what to do. In any case, do not put the stitches of the finished sleeve onto a stitch holder or a scrap of yarn; that move will only slow down the joining round and add an unnecessary step to the proceedings.

Joining the Sleeves and Body

The Preparation for Joining

The number of stitches for each underarm section of the body and the sleeves is 8% of the Key Number of stitches. For example:

Key Number = 180 stitches

$$180 \times .08 = 14.4 \qquad \text{or} \qquad \begin{array}{r} 180 \\ \times\, .08 \\ \hline 14.40 \end{array}$$

Disregard any figures beyond the decimal point and round off to the nearest even number. In this example, the number of stitches to be left behind for the underarm grafting is 14.

◆ Thread the Braidkin with a yard of scrap yarn.

Sleeve Preparation

METHOD: The seamline is the center of the underarm stitches; one-half are to the right, one-half are to the left. The sleeve knitting stopped at the seamline, and the sleeve yarn is in the center of the underarm stitches. If your sleeve is still on double-points, slip the stitches until the center of the seamline is back between needles.

- ◆ Unknit the right half of the underarm stitches, which automatically transfers them to the left needle.
- ◆ Slip the underarm stitches (as if to purl) from the left needle onto the Braidkin. Pull the scrap yarn through the underarm stitches, break it, and tie the ends loosely. The rest of the sleeve stitches remain on the knitting needle, or needles, for the moment.
- ◆ Repeat on the other sleeve.

Body Preparation: The Right Seamline

METHOD: The right seamline is the center of the underarm stitches; one-half are to the right, one-half are to the left. The body knitting stopped at the seamline, so the body yarn is in the center of the underarm stitches.

- ◆ Unknit the right half of the underarm stitches, which automatically transfers them to the left needle.
- ◆ Slip the underarm stitches (as if to purl) from the left needle onto the Braidkin.
- ◆ Pull the scrap yarn through the stitches, break it, and tie the ends loosely.

In order that the underarm stitches at the left seamline are prepared for your arrival as you work the joining round, they also are to be put on a scrap. However—do not knit your way over to them. Just pick up your Braidkin and go to . . .

Body Preparation: The Left Seamline

METHOD: The left seamline is the center of the underarm stitches; one-half are to the right; one-half are to the left.

- ◆ Run the Braidkin with the scrap yarn through the underarm stitches, detouring around the marker at the left seamline.
- ◆ Break the yarn and tie the ends loosely. The left underarm stitches stay on the yarn and on the circular needle for the moment.

The three pieces of knitting are now prepared for the joining round.

The Joining Round. *With the body and sleeves worked to the underarms, the sweater is ready to be joined together. One at a time, the sleeves are connected to the body; all the stitches are thus united on the body needle—except for the underarm stitches, which hang by their scraps until they are grafted later on.*

The Joining Round. One at a time, the sleeves will be joined to the body as you work this round. All the body and sleeve stitches will end up on the body needle except for the underarm stitches. They will hang by their scraps until the sweater is done and then be grafted together. Think sewing. (You're not actually going to; just think it.)

METHOD

- Pick up the body and hold it just as you would to continue knitting, with the outside facing you and the right seamline to your left.

- Tuck the end of the left body needle that is now at the back out of the way. At the moment, it is separated from its mate by the underarm stitches, but soon they will be together again clicking away in perfect harmony. Now . . .

- Pick up a sleeve, either one. They are both the same—unless you have done something strange to one, such as adding a monogram or an asymmetrical design, and therefore have a particular arm in mind.

- Holding the sleeve outside the body at the right underarm, match the underarm stitches of the sleeve to the underarm stitches of the body.

- *With the right end of body needle and body yarn in your right hand and the sleeve needle in your left hand, insert the right tip of the body needle into the first stitch on the sleeve needle. (This first stitch on the sleeve needle is the first stitch to the left of the underarm stitches.) Work the sleeve stitches from the sleeve needle, or needles, onto the right end of the body needle. Find the left end of the body needle.*

- Using the body needle only, work across the back of the sweater until you come to the left underarm stitches that are on the needle as well as the scrap.
- Remove the left needle from these stitches and let them hang loosely on their scrap.
- Pick up the other sleeve.
- Hold it outside the body at the left underarm, matching the underarm stitches of the sleeve to the underarm stitches of the body.
- Repeat * to *.
- Using the body needle, work across the front of the sweater.

Stop where you started the joining round.

Important: Two Must-Do's

1. Put a large safety pin somewhere in the sweater near this point to quickly identify the front of the sweater.
2. Put a marker (green for "go," if you have one) on the needle between the last body stitch and the first sleeve stitch. This marker will forevermore be referred to as the marker at the *right front seamline*. The raglan seamline decreases, the neckline set-ups, and anything else in the yoke of the sweater depend on it as a reference point.

The Marker Round. Work the next round, putting markers at the other 3 points where the sleeves join the body. If you are working a pattern, check to be sure it joined correctly. If you must adjust, do so near the joining points on this round.

Stop. Read. Rejoice. Feed the cat. Walk the dog. Your knitting is all *together*, and you are on the home stretch.

You are now approaching the yoke of the sweater. The yoke is defined as the upper part of the sweater from the joining round to the neck ribbing. It develops four raglan seamlines as you decrease at the four marked joining points, and somewhere along the way it also develops a neckline. The former remain consistent for any sweater; the latter varies as to its starting point and set-up depending on the style.

The Basic Sweater directions take you through the Crew Neck. By so doing, come the next sweater, you will have the decreases at the raglan seamlines down pat and can concentrate on constructing a different neckline.

- Work around all the stitches for 1½".

Stop at the right front seamline. **Read.**

The Raglan Decreases

The raglan decreases start 1½" above the joining round, which is where you are. Make a quick check of the following: (1) Count to be sure the front stitches equal the back stitches. (2) Count to be sure the sleeve stitches equal each other. (The sleeve stitches are not equal to the back and front stitches.) If you find an error, mark the section it is in and correct it on the next round by knitting two together near a joining point.

Refer to The Raglan Seamline Decreases in the Sampler directions (p. 42) and refresh your memory as to their various characteristics. Select A, B, B-Reverse, C, D, or E. The decrease rounds start at the marker at the right front seamline—actually 2 or 3 stitches before this marker, depending on the decrease you have chosen.

To shape the yoke, you will work a paired decrease at each of the raglan seamline markers every fourth round three times, and then every other round until the sleeves are gone. Though the neck shaping starts before the sleeves are gone, it in no way interferes with this rate of decrease at the raglan seamlines.

To keep track of your first few decrease rounds, check off the accompanying chart as you work up the yoke from the joining round. The chart is simply to get you started in proper order. If you find it helpful, continue it on a scrap of paper (or in the book itself—feel free to scratch below.) However, don't go racing all the way to the top of the sweater. Once you've accomplished a few decrease rounds and are accustomed to working them, take a break and check in on Decision Point for the Crew Neck (next page). If you go too far, you'll have to rip back.

Raglan Decrease Chart

To begin the yoke and the raglan seamline decreases, follow this chart *from the bottom up*, checking off the rounds as you work the yoke from the joining round.

_____ straight

_____ decrease

_____ straight

_____ decrease

_____ straight

_____ decrease

_____ straight

_____ straight

_____ straight

_____ decrease

_____ straight

_____ straight

_____ straight

_____ decrease

_____ straight

_____ straight

_____ straight

_____ decrease <**You are here.**

____✔____ 1½ straight inches

____✔____ marker round

____✔____ joining round

Decision Point. The Crew Neck shaping starts when 20 or 21 stitches remain to be decreased on each sleeve. (*Note:* This Decision Point assumes you are working with a medium- or heavy-weight yarn. If you are using a fine yarn, see The Mathematics of the Neck Shaping, p. 118.)

<<<

The Crew Neck

Your count of the number of stitches remaining to be decreased must be done correctly; it is vital to the neckline shaping. *Do not count between the markers;* to do so would be to include the raglan seamline stitches with the sleeve stitches. The raglan seamline stitches—two, three, or four of them—sit, one or two on one side of the marker and one or two on the other. *These seamline stitches are unto themselves, and are not counted anywhere for anything.* By now, they should be very visible. Hold them out of the way and count only the number of stitches between the seamlines. *Take this count on a straight round.*

The same rules apply when counting the number of stitches in the front of the sweater to set up the neckline shaping. *Do not count from the marker.* Do not include any seamline stitches in the count. Count from the seamline.

Set-Up: Work until 20 or 21 stitches remain to be decreased on each sleeve. (If the sleeve had an even number of stitches as you started to decrease, you will have 20. If the sleeve had an uneven number of stitches as you started to decrease, you will have 21.)

METHOD

Stop at the right front seamline after a straight round.

◆ Thread a Braidkin with a scrap of yarn.

◆ Run the scrap through all the front stitches except for 14 on each side next to the sleeves. Tie the scrap loosely.

◆ These center front stitches remain on the scrap and on the needle for a moment.

◆ Work a decrease round until you come to the center stitches.

◆ Remove the needle from these stitches.

Stop. Read.

The center front stitches will remain behind, hanging on the scrap until the neck shaping is complete. Because they have interrupted your immediate round of knitting, you were unable to complete a full round back to the right front seamline. If it bothers you or your pattern that the stitches in the section to the left of the center front stitches will be minus a row of work in the final accounting, you may need to work them separately, just this once. This step is known as the catch-up row. It can usually be omitted in a one-color sweater without a pattern. For those of you who need it:

The Catch-Up Row. With the outside facing, and using a separate length of yarn, take a double-pointed body-size needle in your right hand and work the unworked stitches from the right-side neck up to the decrease at the right front seamline. (Do not work a decrease here—you did at the start of the round.) Slip the caught-up stitches back on the body needle. The round is now complete. Secure both ends of the Catch-Up Row yarn to get them out of your working way. Return to the body yarn.

Working the Neck Back and Forth. You will now be working back and forth on the needle. If you are working in a pattern, you may have to reverse your knits and purls on the inside rows. You will no longer be working in rounds that start at the right front seamline. You will be working in rows that start with the first stitches on the needle at the right and left side neck edges. This in no way affects your decreases at the raglan seamlines. If anything, it makes it easier to keep track of your decrease rounds vs. your straight rounds, because the outside rows are the decrease rows, and the inside rows are the straight rows.

From now on, start all rows with a slip stitch for a chain selvedge:

> *Outside rows*—Slip as if to purl, yarn in back.

> *Inside Rows*—Slip as if to purl, yarn in front.

METHOD

- ◆ *Turn your work.* With the inside facing you, and the right end of the body needle in your right hand, *work the inside row.*

- ◆ On the next 4 outside rows only, decrease 1 stitch at the neck edges and continue to decrease at the raglan seamlines. Start and end these next 4 outside rows as: slip 1, K2 tog, work to the last 3 stitches, SSK, K1.

- ◆ Then, continue *only* the decreases at the raglan seamlines until the seamlines come together and the sleeve is gone.

Stop at the end of an outside row.

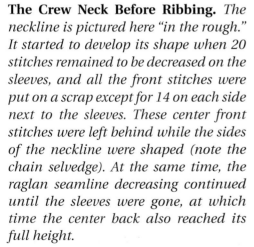

The Crew Neck Before Ribbing. *The neckline is pictured here "in the rough." It started to develop its shape when 20 stitches remained to be decreased on the sleeves, and all the front stitches were put on a scrap except for 14 on each side next to the sleeves. These center front stitches were left behind while the sides of the neckline were shaped (note the chain selvedge). At the same time, the raglan seamline decreasing continued until the sleeves were gone, at which time the center back also reached its full height.*

Note how few stitches will need to be knit up for the neck ribbing; most are already in existence on the scrap and body needle.

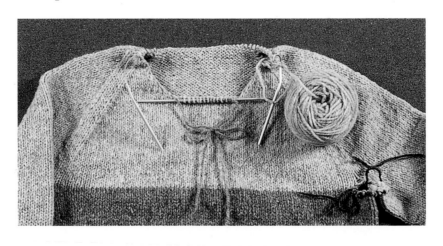

(*Note:* "Left-side neck" refers to the left side as the sweater is worn. "Right-side neck" refers to the right side as the sweater is worn.)

METHOD: Using a 16" circular ribbing-size needle in your right hand:

- Knit into the left-side neck chain selvedge.
- Knit the stitches on the scrap (slip them onto a double-point).
- Knit into the right-side neck chain selvedge, and,
- Knit the back neck stitches from the body needle. **Stop.**
- Count the number of stitches on the needle. If the number must be adjusted for the ribbing pattern, do so in the first round of ribbing near a raglan seamline.
- Put a marker on the right needle and work the ribbing pattern loosely for an inch. Neck ribbing should not pull in; the purl stitches are open and visible, not hidden as in the ribbing on the body and the sleeves.
- Cast off *loosely* in ribbing, leaving a yard of yarn.

The Neck Ribbing

METHOD

- Slip a double-pointed needle through the body stitches at the left underarm. Remove the scrap.
- Slip a double-pointed needle through the sleeve stitches at the left underarm. Remove the scrap.
- Now, insert the tip of each end of each needle into the sweater itself and pick up the stitch adjacent to the opening.
- Reach into the sleeve and pull out the reserved yard of yarn.

The Underarm Opening

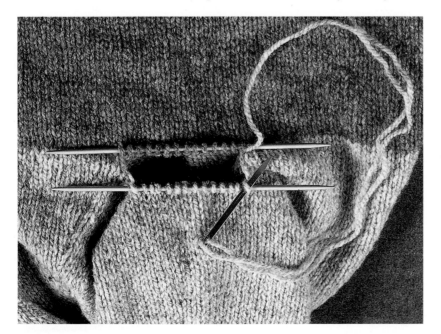

Underarm Grafting—Getting Ready. *Double-pointed needles are inserted through sleeve and body stitches, the scraps are removed, and one additional stitch is added from the sweater itself to each end of both needles to minimize any holes at the joining points.*

The yarn is coming from the first stitch on the right end of the Back Needle (you have just moved it there from the middle of the right end of the opening), and the Braidkin is inserted into the first stitch on the right end of the Front Needle as if to knit.

◆ Thread the end through the Braidkin. With the outside of the sweater facing you, and the opening in a horizontal position, the attached yarn should be at the right end of the opening. Notice that the yarn is in the middle of the right side of the opening. To begin grafting, it must be coming from the first stitch on the right end of the Back Needle (The Back Needle is the needle farthest away from you; the Front Needle is the one nearest you.) To position the yarn correctly, a preliminary step is necessary:

◆ Slip the Braidkin through the first stitch on the right end of the Back Needle as if to knit; pull the yarn through the stitch, leaving the stitch on the needle.

◆ The yarn is now where it should be to begin grafting.

Refer to Grafting in the Sampler directions, p. 71. When the grafting row is complete, adjust the new stitches to match the tension of the sweater fabric.

Underarm Grafting—Completed.
Kitchener stitch produces an invisible "seam" even when the two sections to be grafted are of different colors. However, more important than its looks is its comfort, for the "seam" has the same tension and give as the sweater fabric.

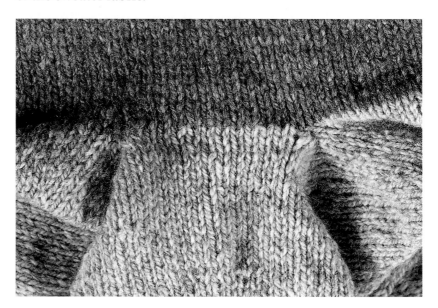

Thanks are due to Carol McClennen for the clever idea of grafting the one extra stitch from the sweater itself at each end of each needle, a move that tends to minimize the likelihood of holes at the corners of the opening. However, if you have been left with one, treat it gently. Using the yarn in the Braidkin, or a separate length with a crochet hook, circle around the hole and ease it out of existence. The less done the better.

Repeat the grafting process at the right underarm opening.

Finis. Wear proudly. (P.S. If you can't get your sweater over your head, you have cast off the neck ribbing too tightly. Think ***loose***, and try again with the reserved yard of yarn.)

Understanding the Yoke

The following explanation of the mathematics of the yoke shaping is not mandatory reading unless you are interested in the whys and wherefores of what you have just accomplished. You should, however, acquaint yourself with it if you intend to add an all-over precision-type stripe, pattern, or design, for in that case, you must know the number of rounds from the joining to the neck ribbing.

The Mathematics of the Yoke Shaping. The number of rounds in the yoke (from the joining round to the neck ribbing) approximately equals the number of stitches on one sleeve after the joining round, for the sleeve is decreased until it is gone at the approximate rate of 2 stitches every other round. This is the equivalent of 1 stitch to 1 round. Therefore:

1 sleeve stitch equals 1 round, and

_____ sleeve stitches equal _____ rounds.

To figure the full number of rounds in the yoke, you must take into consideration the number of rounds in the straight 1½", the number of additional straight rounds worked while you are decreasing every fourth round rather than every other round, and the number of stitches lost to the seamline itself. Therefore:

The stitches on one sleeve plus the number of additional

straight rounds equal _____ .

Subtract the number of stitches lost to the seamline _____ .

The number of rounds in the yoke then equals _____ .

Two-Color Knitting in the Yoke. For those not attuned to precise math, hit-or-miss stripes will liven up the yoke with less mental effort. Though worked in the round, stripes take a right-angle turn at the raglan seamlines—a departure from the expected and a fillip for geometric souls. Always change from one color to the next at the right front seamline. If you happen to change on a decrease round, work the first half of the decrease in the new color.

A bird's-eye view of the stripes in the yoke of a sweater worked in the Ringing the Changes pattern exemplifies the fact that, though you are working in the round, the yoke is being decreased in an ever-diminishing rectangle because the rounds of knitting make a right-angle turn at each raglan seamline decrease.

A small band of two-color knitting is almost as carefree an addition as stripes. A good guess will more than likely land it in a logical position. However, limit the two-color work to a 3-, 4- or 5-round design. To keep its multiple intact, you may interrupt the normal sequence of raglan decreases, but you should work a decrease round immediately before and immediately after the pattern rounds. Be aware that by omitting a decrease round or two, the yoke will be a few rounds deeper. If you plan far enough in advance, you can shorten up on the "decrease round, three straight rounds" sequence to compensate. And, of course, before you start, count all stitches to be certain you have the correct multiple.

To work a two-color pattern throughout a raglan yoke is not a good idea. For some reason, even though the waiting yarn is loosely carried on the inside, two-color yokes have a tendency to become funnel-shaped, and the comfort of the raglan style is compromised. Further, the raglan seamline decreasing tends to interrupt the design sequence.

If you insist on working two-color knitting in the yoke, it is probably best to find a Fair Isle yoke pattern that is an approximate multiple of the stitches on your needle. The decreases for a Fair Isle yoke are "built into" the pattern and are scattered throughout the yoke rather than being concentrated in four raglan seamlines. To lessen the customary "rolling fold" one sees in the center front of a Fair Isle yoke, try to select a design with at least five or six decrease rounds. Better still, if you are not allergic to two-color knitting in the flat, work the Fair Isle yoke with a placket neck; the slash alleviates the folds.

Each style seems to have its drawbacks. The easiest solution is to put two-color knitting everywhere but the yoke—the sleeves and body are just sitting there waiting to be fancied up—and limit the yoke to a few rounds of complementary patterns.

The Mathematics of the Neck Shaping. This section on the mathematics of the neck shaping *is mandatory reading*. It explains the reasoning of the Crew Neck shaping, which is the basis for the U-Neck, the Slit Neck, the Placket Neck, and the Cardigan, as well as adjustments for neckline depth and for yarn diameter.

The set-up and the decreasing for every neckline depends on the number of stitches remaining to be decreased on the sleeve, for when the sleeve is gone, the neckline must be complete. To better understand this close relationship of sleeve to neckline, concentrate on the right front seamline of your Crew Neck for a moment.

As you worked the paired decrease at this seamline, one of the front stitches and one of the sleeve stitches were devoured each time. Keep in mind that only half of the sleeve stitches were decreased at the right front seamline; the other half were decreased at the back seamline. To grasp the principle of the Crew Neck shaping, you need only consider the half that are decreased on the right front seamline; the back takes care of itself.

The Crew Neck shaping started when 20 stitches remained to be decreased on the sleeve. Of the 20 stitches, 10, or one-half, were decreased at the right front seamline. In order to work a paired decrease at this seamline, 10 of the front stitches had to be there on the needle, available as partners. To round the corner for the neckline shaping required 4 stitches. As 10 plus 4 equals 14, you may now see why and from where cometh:

> When 20 stitches remain to be decreased on each sleeve, run a scrap yarn through all the front stitches except for 14 on each side next to the sleeves.

Matched stitch for stitch, the 10 stitches of the sleeve disappeared with the 10 stitches of the front, and the 4 stitches vanished at the neck edge. Thus, when the sleeve was gone, the neck shaping was complete.

On that same basis, you may start the neck shaping wherever you wish. If 20 seemed too high up on a sweater worked in a medium-weight yarn, start the set-up when 26 stitches remain to be decreased on the sleeve. One-half of 26 is 13, so 13 sleeve stitches are to be decreased at the right front seamline. Therefore, leave 13 plus 4 (17 stitches) on the needle at each side next to the sleeve, and put the rest on a scrap.

The Crew Neck shaping for a sweater worked in a fine yarn should begin back when 30 stitches remain to be decreased on the sleeve, for the stitches are smaller and the rounds to the inch are less. In that case, with one-half of 30 being 15, you would leave 15 plus 4 (19 stitches) on the needle at each side next to the sleeves, and put the rest on a scrap. In fact, in a fine yarn, it might take 6 stitches to round the corner; if so, leave 15 plus 6 (21 stitches) on the needle at each side next to the sleeves and work 6 decreases at the neck edge.

To sum up: You may start the Crew Neck shaping wherever you wish. If it's low enough, it will become the U-Neck. The formula is: count the number of stitches remaining to be decreased on one sleeve; divide by 2; add 4. The answer is the number of stitches to leave on the needle at each side front next to the sleeves. Put the remaining center stitches on a scrap.

To add a decorative heart motif like the one shown in the p. 94 photo, work the chart below with Swiss Darning (p. 52).

II STITCHES × 12 ROUNDS

Minor Adjustments

The Basic Sweater is constructed on principles and percentages to fit the average figure. The following adjustments may be made, if necessary.

The sleeves and/or the body may be lengthened or shortened by working more, or fewer, rounds to the underarm. No suggested lengths were given for these measures, as individuals and sweater styles vary so. A short-waisted knitter might find that an 11" body is perfect; but that would never do for someone taller. Take advantage of the fact that the construction is such that the sweater pieces may be tried on as you work.

To knit a sweater for someone other than yourself, it will be necessary to know the body length and sleeve length to the underarm as well as the sweater measurement itself at the underarm. Again, take these measurements from the recipient's favorite-fitting sweater, if possible.

The yoke may be made deeper by decreasing every fourth round a few more times than prescribed. For a Crew Neck style, an alternative would be to decrease every third round all the way to the top.

For a shorter yoke, cut down on the number of times you decrease every fourth round. However, don't cut it out entirely. Work the first decrease round followed by three straight rounds at least once. To start decreasing every other round immediately brings the seamlines together too rapidly, and the fabric will pucker at the base of each seamline.

The sleeves and/or the shoulders may be made wider by adding two inches' worth of stitches to the 33% for the upper arm. The Crew Neck shaping would then start when you had 20 plus the additional stitches remaining to be decreased on each sleeve. Once the neck shaping is complete and the 14 stitches at each side neck have been worked, the sleeves will not be gone; the added stitches will remain between the seamlines for extra shoulder width and the neck opening will also be larger.

To narrow the sleeve at the upper arm, do not add the prescribed inch's worth of stitches to the 33% for the upper arm. Keep trying on the sleeve as you work it. If it is wide enough without the added inch's worth of stitches, don't bother with them. Stop increasing when you reach the 33% figure.

The more sweaters you knit, the cannier you will become. Once you realize you are in control of your own sweater, you will gain the confidence to rely on your own good common sense—not only for fit, but for fashion. Experiment and adventure are yours for the knitting.

The Sweater Variations

Plain and fancy sweaters. *About the only things these two pullovers have in common are their kempy Harris Tweed yarns and their rolled crew necklines. The plain model could be worn anywhere with anything, while its tricolor mate requires a bit more coordination, with its random stripes and nonmatching sleeves.*

Both of these are variations of the Basic Sweater. Instead of working ribbing for a Crew Neck, simply work knit or purl rounds on the knit-up neck stitches. If you want the roll neck to curl to the outside, work knit rounds; if you want it to curl to the inside, work purl rounds. In either case, it will roll as purl stitches. Stop when the amount of roll is pleasing to you and bind off in either knit or purl, as the case may be.

Inspiration Abounds All Around

If not during, then certainly after, the first sweater you work "on your own," you'll find yourself translating ideas from everywhere into sweater designs. Jot them down, cut them out, or simply stash them in your subconscious for future reference. Just brushing the surface, here are a few ideas to add to yours:

1. Museums. Where else to go for such an abundance of color and design? Study your best-loved paintings for color ideas and check the old textiles.

2. Your old or very old pattern books. Stylewise, history has a way of repeating itself.

3. Current fashion magazines. Better yet, get your name on the right list and you'll be on the receiving end of the best in catalogs.

4. Other sweaters. Check out examples in stores, or on your friends, neighbors, fellow travelers, coworkers, or complete strangers. When they ask you what you're doing up that close, just tell them: counting stitches.

5. Spinners—"Think mink." Once off the farm, the woolly black fleece is as fine as anything in the fur department. Its rich natural shadings are every bit as wondrous as those of an expensive skin. Check out the latest styles and give your handspun the fur-coat treatment. Or, if you can find it, spin mink!

6. Weavers—Knit your weaving patterns.

7. Braiders—Think color as for a rug: one in, one out.

8. Nature. How about a goldenrod sweater with a million pockets for tissues?

9. Your yarn may have ideas of its own, perhaps. Pick it up and get started.

10. Last, but not least, visit the library and venture out of 746.43. Wander through the math, music, antiques, and art/design shelves.

Herewith a few examples:

Fibonacci Sequence.[1] Leonardo Fibonacci was a 13th-century mathematician who speculated on the following question, "How many pairs of rabbits can be produced from a single pair in a year, if each pair begets a new pair every month, and each new pair reproduces from the second month on, and no rabbit dies?" His answer works well in a sweater: **1** and **1** are **2**; **1** and **2** are **3**; **2** and **3** are **5**; **3** and **5** are **8**; **5** and **8** are **13**; **8** and **13** are **21**; **13** and **21** are

1. From William Karush, *The Crescent Dictionary of Mathematics.* Thank you, Connie Pearlstein, for applying "Fibonacci" to the knitted fabric.

34; etc., etc. The sequence is arrived at by starting with 1 and 1, then continually adding the two previous numbers. In short: 1, 1, 2, 3, 5, 8, 13, 21, 34, and on, for as many rabbits as you'd care to knit.

Work the sequence in two colors, or as many as will fit into a sweater. Work a purl round, leaving the sequence in between as stockinette. Work the sequence in reverse for a yoke.

For a more random stripe or sequence, try:

Ringing the Changes.[2] The pealing of church bells, tuned to the major scale and rung in succession, will add rhythm to a sweater. The first series of five bells ring in this order (read the rows left to right from top to bottom.):

Color Translation

(start) 1, 2, 3, 4, 5,	#1 bell: _____ color
2, 1, 4, 3, 5,	#2 bell: _____ color
2, 4, 1, 5, 3,	#3 bell: _____ color
4, 2, 5, 1, 3,	#4 bell: _____ color
4, 5, 2, 3, 1 (end)	#5 bell: _____ color

Select five colors, or even five yarns. Assign each color or yarn to a bell number. Starting with the round above the ribbing, work one round of #1, two rounds of #2, three rounds of #3, four rounds of #4, five rounds of #5. That completes the first sequence (top row, reading left to right). Now start the second row, which begins to mix the colors and/or yarns up a bit: work two rounds of #2, one round of #1, etc., etc. Complete the series and start again.

The number of bells that ring in a series can vary from five to twelve, and the number of changes possible with twelve bells (or twelve colors) is 479,001,600. That ought to keep you in striped sweaters forever.

And, while you're in a musical mood, why not knit your favorite song? On a scale of 1 to 8, you might complete a bar or two.

The Dedham Bunny.[3] An alternative to the overabundance of whales and alligators is the famous rabbit pattern of the Dedham Pottery Company. This distinct New England pottery dates from the late 1800s and was the creation of Hugh Robertson. The off-white rabbits in a cobalt blue border ran around plates, mugs,

---

2. *The New Grove Dictionary of Music*, Vol. 4, p. 134.
3. From Heinz Edgar Kiewe, *History of Folk Cross-Stitch*, p. 76.

bowls, and pitchers. They are equally engaging running around sweaters in the same or reverse color treatment.

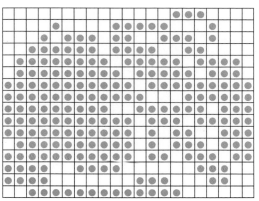

MOTIF: 21 STITCHES x 16 ROUNDS

The Dedham Bunny. In this graph, the traditional color scheme is reversed, with the bunny being worked in blue on a white background.

Color Study Sources. *The Color Source Book,* by Margaret Walch, is an arrangement of palettes, not only of famous artists and craftsmen, but of cultures and times. A glance through its pages will set you to knitting a Williamsburg sweater, a Wedgwood sweater, a Paul Gaugin sweater—a sweater with meaning.

Even better, locate a course in Color Theory based on the book by Josef Albers. Class exercises with silkscreened papers (or any colored papers, paint chips for that matter) point out the action and interaction of colors and how they influence and change each other through illusion. Apply these theories to your yarn.

To experiment for possible stripe sequences, select four colors. Cut the colored paper into strips of the same length, but vary the widths from wide to narrow. Move and switch the strips until they are in an arrangement that is pleasing to you. Take note of the fact that the same color may speak softly, yell loudly, or completely change face due to its width and the influence exerted on it by its neighbors. Having achieved a persuasive arrangement, paste the strips to a piece of cardboard and translate the colors and widths to a sample with yarn. The sequence may be repeated throughout the whole sweater, or worked only once in the body, the yoke, or the sleeves.

Play the Odds. Buy the odd dye lot, trade a leftover skein, or splurge on an ounce or two of handspun yarn—odd unto themselves, not enough for a complete project, but the heart and soul of creativity. Think back to the old patchwork quilt created with what was on hand; the clever quilter turned her scraps into an original, and now treasured, heirloom. So, seek out the odds. Don't pass up a sale or a bargain. A marked-down dusty skein of white can be dyed (to go through that process it doesn't have to be pristine). And don't worry about "having enough"; running out could be the best thing that ever happened to you and your sweater.

In the planning stage, take a tip from nature. Count the petals on a flower: an odd number—which is why "he (always) loves me" and you're still searching for that four-leaf clover. Design your sweater with odd numbers in mind—three colors, five stripes, seven-row patterns. If you have only two colors, use one in three places. Your sweater will balance and be pleasing to the eye. Odd numbers hold true for buttons and buttonholes too. The placket neck is best with three and a cardigan with seven or nine.

Rely on Nature. For your sweater to stand head and shoulders above the crowd, dye the yarn, all or enough for stripes, with nature's colors. The unusual, unmatchable, and often unpredictable shades may be tossed together or used alone to create your very own impressive effects. To be dyed, the yarn must be in skeins tied in four spots with figure-eights of cotton string. Use white, off-white, or even a natural light gray wool yarn for the best results.

Natural dyeing has become a much more popular craft in the past decade or so, and more and more excellent how-to books are now available. One of the earliest is still one of the best, however: Rita J. Adrosko's *Natural Dyes and Home Dyeing*.

Patterns

Most any pattern stitch may be worked into the Basic Sweater, from a simple double moss stitch to an intricate Aran Isle. Except for the Aran Isle and other sweaters with large varying patterns, work the gauge sample in your chosen pattern stitch to see whether it is appropriate for your choice of yarn. Beyond that, by working a swatch you will discover whether or not you enjoy working the selected pattern. Some are tedious and not worth the effort, and it's best to find this out before embarking on a whole sweater. You may decide to confine a fussy pattern to a few inches in the body, and /or the sleeves.

Pattern Selection Hints. Keep the following points in mind when *selecting* an all-over pattern stitch:

1. Select a pattern with a multiple of stitches that closely fits into your Key Number of stitches. Adding, or subtracting one or two stitches is fine, but above that, you may be dealing with an inch or more, added to, or subtracted from the final width of the sweater.

2. To contradict all of the above: If you decide on a large pattern, such as the Dedham Bunny, with its multiple of 22 stitches plus one (or two) for separation, you will have to decide whether you want to go larger or smaller by a good amount of stitches in some cases. Or, rather than have them running completely around the sweater, you could settle for just one in a surprising spot. However, to knit just one of any design in the round can be a bit of a nuisance. You certainly don't want to carry the design color around and around to work a few stitches in one spot. One solution is to work the isolated pattern with separate lengths of yarn, though that procedure leaves the inside full of ends. A better method is to use the Patchwork Sweater technique (see p. 215) for the design rounds. Another alternative is to work the motif in Swiss Darning (p. 52).

3. Select a pattern with a plain knit or plain purl round, if possible. This simplifies the joining round. In bottom-up sweaters, the body and the sleeves must stop at the underarm on the same pattern round. Then, when the three pieces are united, all is in order for the yoke. Stopping before a plain knit or a plain purl round and using it for the joining round allows you to concentrate on the joining before you return to the pattern.

4. All-over ribbing patterns fit like a second skin. If you prefer a loose-fitting sweater, avoid them—unless, as in the Crew Neck with Reversible Pattern (p. 157), the rib is accomplished by more knits than purls, or vice versa. Another good choice is the Garter Stitch Rib, p. 155.

5. Select a pattern that is applicable to both round and flat knitting, for you must work it both ways in the sweater: round for the body, sleeves, and some of the yoke; flat once the neck shaping is started. Directions for most patterns are written for flat knitting. For round knitting you may have to reverse the knit and purl stitches of the even-numbered rows—an easy job if those rows are plain knit or plain purl in the original directions.

6. Again, because most patterns are written for flat knitting, there may be an extra stitch added beyond the multiple that is not needed in round knitting.

7. In a gem of a booklet, *Double-Knitting Patterns*,[4] Janetta Dexter compiled a collection of two-color knitting designs written and graphed to be worked in the round. Throughout her native Nova Scotia she traveled with pen in hand, and put

4. Available from Nimbus Publishing Ltd., P.O. Box 9501, Station A, Halifax, NS B3K 5N5 (street address: 3731 Mackintosh St.).

to paper patterns that previously existed in memory—patterns that had been brought to her country from Britain, France, and Germany. These designs, with their quiltlike names, may be worked in commercial yarns, or as they always were, "in homespun wool in natural shades of black, white, and gray, or in yarns dyed in soft colors with natural dyes." Janetta Dexter's Sampler Sweater (p. 207) was inspired by the wonderful designs in her little book. (Thank you, Janetta.)

Pattern Knitting Hints. Keep the following points in mind when *knitting* an all-over pattern stitch:

1. Even when working with a pattern that has a small multiple of stitches—2, 3, 4 (or more!)—and especially if you are working a vertical pattern of cables, ribs, or panels, the multiple must divide into your Key Number, and the quotient must be an even number so that the back and front sections of the sweater have the same number of pattern repeats. See the Reversible Sweater directions for a fuller explanation, p. 157.

2. The first round, or row, of the body after the ribbing (if any) is vitally important because it sets up the pattern for the whole sweater. Place markers at the side seamlines, and count (and recount) to be absolutely certain you have the correct multiple and the same number of pattern repeats in the back and front sections.

3. In round knitting, start the pattern at the right seamline in the body, and at the seamline in the sleeve. The rounds must start and end correctly.

4. In the Cardigan Sweater, the pattern is worked between the front borders. Be sure that whatever is next to the border on one side is next to the border on the other, so the meeting fronts will match.

5. To repeat: the body and the sleeves must stop for the underarm on the same pattern row.

6. When working a vertical pattern, adjust the number of underarm stitches to another, if it is more logical. (See the Reversible Sweater directions for a fuller explanation, p. 160.)

7. When working a horizontal pattern, you may have to adjust a stitch or two after the joining round. Make any necessary adjustment at the joining points.

8. *Most important:* The sleeves of a sweater are sometimes longer than the body. In a sweater with a pattern, or a stripe in sequence, you must take this discrepancy into consideration. Either account for the excess length at the start of the sleeve, or just before the upper arm. The pattern, or the stripe itself,

In a striped sweater where the sleeves are longer than the body (as they usually are), it is a good move to add the needed extra depth of stripes above the sleeve ribbing, then match the sleeve stripes to the stripes that are above the body ribbing, so that the sleeves and body will end on the same stripe for the joining round. The same principle applies to other patterns as well.

will usually dictate the solution. Generally, it is best to put the excess rounds at the start of the sleeve. Then, at the point where the sleeve pattern meets up with the first round of body pattern, repeat the body pattern in the sleeve to the underarm.

Suggested Patterns

Directions are for round knitting; reverse alternate rows once you start working back and forth for the neck shaping. These patterns all include a plain knit or purl round you may use for the joining round. (All patterns are from *Knitting Dictionary, 1300 Stitches and Patterns,* 1970 edition.)

Hurdle Stitch. A multiple of 2.

> **Round 1:** Knit.
>
> **Round 2:** Purl.
>
> **Round 3:** *K1, P1*, repeat * to *.
>
> **Round 4:** *K1, P1*, repeat * to *.

Pebble Stitch. A multiple of 2.

> **Round 1:** Knit.
>
> **Round 2:** Knit.
>
> **Round 3:** *K2 tog *, repeat * to *.
>
> **Round 4:** *P1, P into the horizontal thread before the next stitch. * Repeat * to *.

Waffle Stitch. A multiple of 3.

>**Round 1:** *K2, P1*, repeat * to *.
>
>**Round 2:** *K2, P1*, repeat * to *.
>
>**Round 3:** *K2, P1*, repeat * to *.
>
>**Round 4:** Purl.

Granite Ridges. A multiple of 2.

>**Round 1:** Knit.
>
>**Round 2:** Knit.
>
>**Round 3:** Knit.
>
>**Round 4:** Knit.
>
>**Round 5:** Knit.
>
>**Round 6:** *K2 tog *, repeat * to *.
>
>**Round 7:** *K1, P1, into each stitch*, repeat * to *.
>
>**Round 8:** Knit.

Harris Tweed Stitch. A multiple of 4.

>**Rounds 1 & 2:** Knit.
>
>**Rounds 3 & 4:** K2, P2.
>
>**Rounds 5 & 6:** Purl.
>
>**Rounds 7 & 8:** K2, P2.

Alternating Seed Stitch. A multiple of 2. This looks almost like a true seed stitch but is much quicker due to the alternating all-knit rounds (or, in flat knitting, the all-purl rows).

>**Round 1:** K1, P1.
>
>**Round 2:** Knit.
>
>**Round 3:** P1, K1.
>
>**Round 4:** Knit.

You have now reached the point where you're ready to try some or all of the sweater variations. Assuming that you heeded the admonishment that "this book, as any book, starts on page 1," you have mastered the Sampler techniques and have enjoyed the freedom of completing the Basic Crew Neck Sweater in your choice of yarn. Now it's time to move on to the many sweater-variation ideas that have been running around in your head. There is no prescribed order in which to knit these alternative styles—just go to it!

The following directions for the variations presuppose that you have worked the Basic Sweater (pp. 94–116). Your gauge samples and your numbers on the Gauge Page will vary according to your choice of yarns, but ***the construction remains constant*** except for the neckline set-ups; check the Decision Points for each style.

CREW NECK WITH ARAN BRAID

Answering to three different names in three different pattern books, this wide cable pattern entwines itself nicely up the center front of a crew neck sweater. Whether it is known as Interwoven Cables, Celtic Plait, or Aran Braid, the directions are basically the same, but the number of stitches varies a bit. This choice is worked over 18 stitches, which most likely will be close in number to the stitches to be put on a length of scrap yarn or piece of string once the crew neck shaping starts. It is taken from *The Complete Book of Traditional Aran Knitting,* by Shelagh Hollingsworth.

Since all these cable crossings tend to pull in the front of the sweater, you'll add 6 stitches at the center front to compensate. First, work a plain knit round above the ribbing (after the normal increase round), putting markers at the right- and left-side seamlines and isolating the 12 stitches in the center front of the sweater with markers—remembering that in round knitting you work across the back of the sweater first.

Then, on the next round, increase into every other stitch of the 12 center front stitches, thus adding 6 stitches to make the 18 stitches needed to work the cable pattern. The additional stitches will compensate for any width lost by working the cables.

On the following round, commence the cable pattern with Round 1 and repeat the 8 rounds of pattern up the front of the sweater to the neckline shaping.

Aran braid

Round 1: P2, (K2, P1) 4 times, K2, P2.

Rounds 2, 4, 6, and 8: P2, (K2, P1) 4 times, K2, P2.

Round 3: P2, K2 (P1, slip the next 3 stitches onto a cable needle, hold in front, K2, then slip the P stitch from the cable needle to the left needle and P it, then K2 from the cable needle) 2 times, P2.

Round 5: Same as Round 1.

Round 7: P2, (slip the next 3 stitches onto a cable needle, hold in back, K2, then slip the P stitch from the cable needle to the left needle and P it, then K2 from the cable needle, P1) 2 times, K2, P2.

Top: ***Crew Neck with Aran Braid.*** *Worked in a yarn handspun by the author from a combination of wool and mohair carded together and then dyed a luscious emerald green by Pauline Boyce of Deer Isle, Maine, this Crew Neck is well deserving of its center panel of Aran Braid. The ribbings are K2, P2, and Raglan Seamline C is used for the yoke decreases.*

Bottom: ***Crew Neck with Lace and Cable Patterns*** *(p. 132). A jewel-tone Harrisville Designs weaving yarn, skeined and washed, makes the soft, classic sweater with a 21-stitch center panel of lace and cable. The ribbings are K1b, P1 (the Twisted Rib), and feathery Raglan Seamline D defines the yoke decreases.*

CREW NECK WITH LACE AND CABLE PATTERNS

Shown on page 131

This Lace and Cable Pattern is less chunky than the Aran Braid on the previous pages and would be a better choice for the center panel of a sweater worked in finer wool, silk, cotton, or linen yarn. It is taken from *The Harmony Guide to Knitting Stitches*. The panel consists of lace (yarn-overs) centered between cables of twisted knit stitches, and it shows up most effectively on a background of stockinette stitch.

Since the pattern panel is worked over the center front 21 stitches, it will most likely end as the stitches to be put on a length of scrap yarn as you work the neck shaping. It is a flatter panel than the Aran Braid, so does not require any added front stitches to compensate for any drawing-in of the pattern. If you like, the panel could be centered up the sleeve stitches as well. To accent the detail of the cables' twisted knit stitches, a Twisted Rib might be a good choice for the body, sleeve cuff, and neck ribbing.

Work to the round above the body ribbing, placing markers at the right and left seamlines—remember that you are working across the back of the sweater first—and also isolating the center front 21 stitches with markers. The directions are arranged in columns to separate the components of the panel, and the necessary "decipherings" follow the directions on p. 133.

Lace and Cable Pattern
An 8-round repeat worked over 21 stitches

Round 1	P2	K4B	K1, YO, K2 tog B, K3, K2 tog, YO, K1	K4B	P2
Round 2	P2	K4	P1, K7, P1	K4	P2
Round 3	P2	K4B	K2, YO, K2 tog B, K1, K2 tog, YO, K2	K4B	P2
Round 4	P2	K4	P1, K7, P1	K4	P2
Round 5	P2	CF4B	K3, YO, slip 1, K2 tog, PSSO, YO, K3	CB4B	P2
Round 6	P2	K4	P1, K7, P1	K4	P2
Round 7	P2	K4B	K9	K4B	P2
Round 8	P2	K4	P1, K7, P1	K4	P2

Note: Rounds 2, 4, 6, and 8 are the same, so the only real busy work is on rounds 1, 3, 5, and 7.

Decipherings for Lace and Cable Pattern

K4B	Knit the 4 knit stitches through the back.
YO	Yarn forward in a purl position.
K2 tog B	Knit 2 sts together through the back.
CF4B	Slip next 2 sts to cable needle, hold *in front* of work, K2B (knit 2 sts. through the back), then K2B from the cable needle.
Sl 1	Slip the stitch as if to purl.
K2 tog	Knit 2 stitches together as 1.
PSSO	Pass the slipped stitch over the K2 tog stitch just worked.
CB4B	Slip next 2 sts to cable needle, hold *in back* of work, K2B, then K2B from cable needle.

CREW NECK WITH STEPS AND MOSS PATTERN

The Filey Pattern IV consists of steps and moss panels bordered with cables. (It is taken from *Patterns for Guernseys, Jerseys and Arans*, by Gladys Thompson.) This panel is traditionally worked in a Guernsey sweater with a very strong 5-ply yarn at 11 stitches to the inch. With thicker yarn and larger needles, it takes on a more contemporary air at 4 stitches to the inch. The 60 stitches of this pattern fit particularly well into the front of a sleeved sweater or a sleeveless vest (p. 135). The mathematical example given here uses 160 stitches as a Key Number—80 front, 80 back—and the 60-stitch panel is centered on the front, leaving 10 "blank" stitches on each side next to the right and left seamlines.

The sweater has a plain stockinette stitch back, but the steps and cables climb up the sleeves. This layout means *thinking ahead*. Using the same example, with a Key Number of 160, centering the panel on the front again leaves 10 "blank" stitches on each side next to the right and left seamlines. The number of these blank stitches is important when adding steps and cables to the sleeves. The 10 blank stitches on each side of the front panel abut 10 blank stitches on each side of the back (whether or not you have put the panel there.) That amounts to 20 blank stitches centered at the underarm. In order that the sleeve and body patterns meet precisely for the joining round and subsequent raglan seamline

Crew Neck with Steps and Moss Pattern and Matching Cap. The 60-stitch panel of Steps and Moss is worked only on the front of this sweater knit of Briggs and Little lavender 2-ply wool yarn. The sleeves are a variation of the pattern—the steps are widened between the cables and the moss is omitted. The ribbings are K2, P2, and the "disappearing" Raglan Seamline A is used in the yoke.

The matching cap makes use of all 3 components: steps, moss, and cables. It is decreased to 9 stitches—3 on each double-pointed needle—and 3 separate lengths of Knitted Cord are worked for about 2" and knotted singly to decorate the peak.

decreasing, you must also have 20 blank stitches centered at the sleeve seamline.

With a Key Number of 160 stitches, the sleeves in our example must have 58 stitches (54 + 4) at the upper arm. Plan on working the full sleeve (p. 106) so that any increasing will not interfere with the design. Subtract 20 for the blank stitches to match the blank stitches at the body underarm. That leaves 38, from which 16 are subtracted for the cables (8 on each side of the steps), which leaves 22 stitches over which to work the steps pattern. The steps are easy to widen from the original 7 stitches.

At the underarm, the center 12 stitches (8% of 160) are put on a scrap, leaving 4 knits of the body to meet up with 4 knits on the sleeves at the base of the raglan seamlines. As the decreasing gets underway, cables and steps will come together in order, a successful joining, as long as you ***think ahead*** when dealing with panels.

Follow the directions for the Basic Crew Neck, beginning on p. 95. The pattern directions are written in columns to separate the components of the panel, and the necessary "decipherings" are explained below the directions.

Steps and Moss (Filey Pattern IV)
An 8-round repeat worked over 60 stitches

Round	Cable	Steps	Cable	Moss	Cable	Steps	Cable
1	P2, K4, P2	K7	P2, K4, P2	K2, M10, K2	P2, K4, P2	K7	P2, K4, P2
2	P2, K4, P2	K7	P2, K4, P2	K2, M10, K2	P2, K4, P2	K7	P2, K4, P2
3	P2, K4, P2	K7	P2, K4, P2	K2, M10, K2	P2, K4, P2	K7	P2, K4, P2
4	P2, K4, P2	K7	P2, K4, P2	K2, M10, K2	P2, K4, P2	K7	P2, K4, P2
5	P2, K4, P2	P7	P2, K4, P2	K2, M10, K2	P2, K4, P2	P7	P2, K4, P2
6	P2, K4, P2	P7	P2, K4, P2	K2, M10, K2	P2, K4, P2	P7	P2, K4, P2
7	P2, CB4, P2	K7	P2, CB4, P2	K2, M10, K2	P2, CF4, P2	K7	P2, CF4, P2
8	P2, K4, P2	K7	P2, K4, P2	K2, M10, K2	P2, K4, P2	K7	P2, K4, P2

Note: If the patterns continue through the flat knitting for the neck shaping, the even rounds must be reversed, i.e., knits are purls and purls are knits. As you can see, rounds 2, 3, 4, and 8 are the same as round 1, and round 6 is the same as round 5, so minimal thinking is required once you are underway. You really only have to be alert for round 7.

Decipherings for Steps and Moss Pattern

M10 All odd rounds: *K1, P1* 5 times. All even rounds: *P1, K1* 5 times.

CB4 Slip next 2 stitches to cable needle and hold in back of work, K2, then K2 from cable needle.

CF4 Slip next 2 stitches to cable needle and hold in front of work, K2, then K2 from cable needle.

For the sleeve panel, use only the Cable and Steps columns of the chart. Work the first column of 8 cable stitches, then as many step stitches as necessary, and then the last column of 8 cable stitches.

SLEEVELESS U-NECK WITH STEPS AND MOSS

Shown on page 195

The Steps and Moss pattern is the ideal front for a sleeveless sweater as it peeks out from under a blazer or jacket. The panel disappears nicely, with the outer cables the first to go as you work the underarm shaping. The steps might continue to the shoulder, and the inner cables and moss will be left behind at the neckline shaping. Depending on your choice of yarn, needles, gauge, and size of sweater, the patterns may not end in this stated manner, but don't worry about it until you get there; something just as orderly is bound to happen. Also, it is perfectly all right to work the back of the sweater in plain stockinette. Many times a sleeveless sweater is worn under a jacket, so only the front is on display.

Follow the directions for the Basic Sweater (p. 95), centering the 60-stitch Steps and Moss panel (p. 135) on the front of the body. Work proceeds in the round to the underarm, then the back and front are worked flat, separately, with the plain back stitches worked first. Slip the front stitches to a holding needle.

Armhole Shaping. Decrease 4% of the Key Number of stitches (half of 8%) one at a time at each end of the outside rows as follows: Start slip 1, K2 tog, work to within 3 stitches of the end, SSK, K1.

Work the back to the top of the shoulder. Leave the back stitches on hold and work the front, decreasing at the front underarm in the same manner as for the back.

Shaping the U-Neck. Start the neck shaping after the underarm stitches have been decreased. Put one-third of the center front stitches, less 4 stitches on each side, on a scrap. Work each side front separately, decreasing the 4 stitches at the neck edges one at a time on every outside row, as for the Basic Crew Neck sweater, to round the corners of the neckline.

Work the side fronts to the top of the shoulder.

With Kitchener stitch, graft the front shoulder stitches to a corresponding number of back shoulder stitches, working in from the shoulder edges to the neck.

With a 24" circular needle, starting at the left shoulder, knit into the chain selvedge of the left front neck stitches, knit the center front neck stitches from the scrap, knit into the right front neck stitches, and knit the back neck stitches from the holding needle. Rib around for about an inch and cast off in ribbing pattern.

Knit into the chain selvedge around the armhole edges, work an inch of ribbing, and bind off in ribbing pattern.

STEPS AND MOSS CAP

Using the same combination of steps, moss, and cables as on the Steps and Moss sweater, you might like to use your excess yarn for a matching cap.

Shown on page 134

> ***Yarn:*** A bit less than 4 ounces of a medium weight.
>
> ***Needles:*** 16" circular #7 or #8 and a set of double-points of the same size.
>
> ***Size:*** For an average adult head. To enlarge, increase the number of stitches in steps or moss stitch columns. To make smaller, decrease the number of stitches in steps or moss stitch columns.

Cast on 92 stitches using the circular needle. Join your work, being careful not to twist the stitches. Place a marker at the starting point after the first round of ribbing.

Work an inch of K1, P1 or K2, P2 ribbing, decreasing one stitch in the last round (91 stitches).

Referring to the table at right, work the 8 rounds of pattern for about 5 inches above the ribbing in the following order, starting at the marker and making sure to also work the single K1 stitches that separate the columns of cable and moss patterns: Cable (8), K1, Step (7), K1, Cable (8), K1, Moss (10), K1, Cable (8), K1, Step (7), K1, Cable (8), K1, Moss (10), K1, Cable (8), K1, Step (7), K1 (91 stitches).

	Cable	Step	Moss
Round 1:	P2, K4, P2	K7	M10
Round 2:	P2, K4, P2	K7	M10
Round 3:	P2, K4, P2	K7	M10
Round 4:	P2, K4, P2	K7	M10
Round 5:	P2, K4, P2	P7	M10
Round 6:	P2, K4, P2	P7	M10
Round 7:	P2, CB4, P2	K7	M10
Round 8:	P2, K4, P2	K7	M10

At 5 inches (or desired length), decrease 1 stitch, then work the decrease rounds as follows, changing to double-pointed needles at round 9:

> **Round 1:** *K8, K2 tog* around.
>
> **Round 2 and all even-numbered rounds:** Knit.
>
> **Round 3:** *K7, K2 tog* around.
>
> **Round 5:** *K6, K2 tog* around.
>
> **Round 7:** *K5, K2 tog* around.
>
> **Round 9:** *K4, K2 tog* around.
>
> **Round 11:** *K3, K2 tog* around.
>
> **Round 13:** *K2, K2 tog* around.
>
> **Round 15:** *K1, K2 tog* around.

Continue knitting 2 together until 3 stitches remain on each needle.

On each needle, work about 2 inches of Knitted Cord (see Sampler p. 53). Knot the three cords individually at the top of the cap and close up the center hole with yarn ends.

CREW NECK WITH ARAN PATTERNS

Whereas Guernsey sweaters rely on patterns of knit and purl stitches with an occasional cable or two for their decoration, Aran sweaters have cables that boggle the imagination, and more intricate detail achieved with stitches that are crossed, twisted, slanted, slipped, and bobbled. Knitters who wish to work Aran motifs in the round most likely will have to adapt flat-knitting directions to round knitting.

Even though Aran patterns have distinctive names and form definite vertical panels, the directions written for flat knitting often do not clearly distinguish the transition from one panel to the next. Rather, they overlap the panels, if the end stitch of one panel (i.e., a knit or a purl) is the same as the first stitch of the next—a practice that makes their working more confusing than need be. Granted, cardigan styles must be written for flat knitting, but still the directions would be easier to comprehend if the individual patterns were isolated. Add to that confusion the necessity of reversing the knit and purl stitches on the even-numbered rows, and it's enough to forever keep some knitters away from the beauty of an Aran sweater.

In circular knitting for a pullover style, it is an easy matter to translate your choice of patterns to columns as long as you have been careful to select patterns with even-numbered rows that are "calm" (i.e., with just knit and purl stitches—no busy work). Then, for the most part, the even-numbered rows (the inside of the sweater) will become the same as the odd (the outside of the sweater). So, grab a shirt cardboard and go to it; rewrite your pattern choices in columns for circular knitting. (The cardboard will outlast a flimsy sheet of paper.)

Another smart idea is to select patterns with an 8-row repeat (or less). Then, in circular knitting, it is very easy to keep track of these short repeats. There's no need to keep 37-row repeats under control unless your heart is set on a particular motif.

The four 8-round repeat patterns presented here are a pleasing mix and are simple to follow once underway: Wishbone, Popcorn, Tree of Life, and Plait. Notice, in the column for the Wishbone pattern, that rounds 2, 3, 4, 5, and 6 are the same—you just knit the knits and purl the purls as they roll by—but you do have to pay attention to rounds 1, 7, and 8. For Popcorn, you must snap to only for round 3; conversely, Tree of Life will keep you alert on

every round. Finally, the center Plait has busy work only in rounds 3 and 7. Again, immediately under each column are specific instructions for whatever it is that makes that panel unique.

The tricky part of an Aran Isle sweater is figuring gauge, i.e., stitches to the inch, to come up with a Key Number. It is very difficult to judge the specific amount of pull-in for each different pattern. Even working a cap first is not foolproof; when the various patterns all get together in a sweater, you can't trust them to behave the same way. One solution is to simply work your gauge sample in stockinette stitch and add 8 or 10 inches' worth of stitches to the Key Number—experience has borne out this solution. Arans are most often outdoor garments and can hardly be too big—the more you can wear underneath, the better.

Although it goes against my grain to even suggest specific working numbers, the **Crew Neck with Aran Patterns** *is included to show the simplicity of working an Aran pullover in the round. It is constructed as are all the other sweaters, from the bottom up, and its firm foundation of Twisted Rib gives way to 4 Aran patterns, each with an 8-round repeat. The patterns were selected for the easy rhythm they provide once memorized, and with the outside of the patterns always facing you, the possibility of errors is minimal.*

Planning the Body Patterns

Once your Key Number of stitches has been calculated, then it is time to decide on the order of your selected patterns.

For a size 44 sweater at a gauge of 4 stitches to the inch in stockinette stitch, the Key Number would be 176 stitches: 88 stitches each for front and back. The set-up for the four 8-round patterns used here adds up to 206 stitches (103 stitches each for front and back)—an increase of 30 stitches above the Key Number for a size 44 sweater, which is almost an additional 8 inches' worth of stitches.

This sweater has Plait (9 stitches) in the center, Wishbone (12 stitches) to each side of it, then Popcorn (5 stitches) to each side of Wishbone, then Tree of Life (13 stitches) to each side of Popcorn, another Popcorn (5 stitches) to each side of Tree of Life, and finally another Wishbone (12 stitches) to each side of Popcorn.

To wit, the patterns for the front (and identically, the back) add up:

WISHBONE		POPCORN		TREE OF LIFE		POPCORN		WISHBONE		PLAIT		WISHBONE		POPCORN		TREE OF LIFE		POPCORN		WISHBONE
12	+	5	+	13	+	5	+	12	+	9	+	12	+	5	+	13	+	5	+	12

Total for front = 103. Total for the size 44 sweater = 206 stitches.

For sizes larger than 44, panels of seed stitch may be worked to each side of Wishbone at the body and sleeve seamlines.

Planning the Sleeve Patterns

As the number of patterns used for the body would be too many for the sleeves, the sleeve set-up is: Plait in the center with Tree of Life on each side of it, then Popcorn on each side of Tree of Life, and Wishbone on each side of Popcorn. To make up for the missing Wishbone and Popcorn next to the center panel of Plait, a P2 is added on each side of the Plait, followed by a K1 to separate the P2 from the purls in Tree of Life.

To wit, the patterns for the sleeve add up to 75:

WISHBONE		POPCORN		TREE OF LIFE		K1	P2		PLAIT		P2	K1		TREE OF LIFE		POPCORN		WISHBONE
12	+	5	+	13	+	1	+ 2	+	9	+	2	+ 1	+	13	+	5	+	12

For a sleeve with a Key Number of 206 stitches, the sleeve should be 72 stitches, or one-third (206 ÷ 3) = 68, rounded off, plus an inch's worth of stitches (at 4 to the inch) = 72 stitches, plus or minus a few—in this case, plus. And, if you have added panels of seed stitch to the body at the side seams, be sure to add the same number of seed stitches to the sleeve on each side of Wishbone, so that the underarm stitches of the body and the sleeve will match.

Aran Patterns for Crew Neck Sweater

Round	WISHBONE (12 stitches)	POPCORN (5 stitches)	TREE OF LIFE (13 stitches)	PLAIT (9 stitches)
1	P2, WB, P2	K1, P3, K1	P1, FC, P3, Sl1, P3, BC, P1	K9
2	P2, K1, P6, K1, P2	K1, P3, K1	P2, Sl1, P3, K1, P3, Sl1, P2	K9
3	P2, K1, P6, K1, P2	K1, P1, POP, P1, K1	P2, FC, P2, Sl1, P2, BC, P2	CF3, K3
4	P2, K1, P6, K1, P2	K1, P3, K1	P3, Sl1, P2, K1, P2, Sl1, P3	K9
5	P2, K1, P6, K1, P2	K1, P3, K1	P3, FC, P1, Sl1, P1, BC, P3	K9
6	P2, K1, P6, K1, P2	K1, P3, K1	P4, Sl1, P1, K1, P1, Sl1, P4	K9
7	P2, K1, P2, K2, P2, K1, P2	K1, P3, K1	P1, K1, P2, FC, Sl1, BC, P2, K1, P1	K3, CB3
8	P2, K1, P2, K2, P2, K1, P2	K1, P3, K1	P1, Sl1, P4, K1, P4, Sl1, P1	K9

WB: Wishbone. Slip next 3 stitches to cable needle, hold in back, K1, then P3 from cable needle; slip next stitch to cable needle, hold in front, P3, then K1 from cable needle.

POP: Popcorn. Knit into the front, back, front, back, and front of next stitch, then slip the 2nd, 3rd, 4th, and 5th stitches over the 1st stitch.

FC: Front cross. Slip next stitch to a cable needle, hold in front, P1, then K1 from cable needle.

Sl 1: Slip 1 stitch as if to purl, yarn in back.

BC: Back cross. Slip next stitch to a cable needle, hold in back, K1, then P1 from cable needle.

CF3: Cable front. Slip next 3 stitches to cable needle, hold in front, K3, then K3 from cable needle.

CB3: Cable back. Slip next 3 stitches to cable needle, hold in back, K3, then K3 from cable needle.

Ribbing and Body

As for the Basic Sweater, work the ribbing—Twisted Rib is a good choice–on needles two sizes smaller than those on which you achieved your gauge and on 10% fewer stitches (186) if you want a snugger bottom. Then, in the last round of ribbing, increase into every ninth stitch to yield the needed 206 stitches for the body.

Change to body-size needles in the next round and work the patterns in the proper order, following the directions for each in the chart on p. 141 *and* using markers to isolate each pattern as well as to indicate the right and left seamlines.

Work the body and sleeves to the underarm, stopping each section on the same round of pattern. Round 2 or 3 is a good choice, as then the outer knit stitches of Wishbone have been crossed and brought together in round 1.

Underarm

Though 16 stitches (.08 x 206) normally would be the number of underarm stitches for a sweater with a Key Number of 206 stitches, getting rid of all the Wishbone panel is a good idea in this case, so run a piece of scrap yarn through 10 stitches to the right and left of the seamline marker—20 stitches total. This move will put Wishbone on the scrap and leave 4 purl stitches in the center of the underarm.

Yoke Shaping

Now, the yoke of an Aran sweater is different from that of the Basic Sweater due to the stitches added to compensate for the pull-in of the patterns. Using the "normal" rate of decrease (i.e., work around straight for an inch and a half, then work one decrease round followed by 3 straight rounds, three times, before decreasing every other round) tends to make the yoke too deep and funnel shaped. These excess stitches are the culprit, since in "normal" raglan shaping the yoke is worked until the stitches are gone.

So for an Aran yoke, you need to either consider rounds to the inch—something you do not ordinarily have to bother with—or, after joining body and sleeves, simply work around straight for about 3 rounds, then immediately start decreasing every other round.

If you do want a more precise idea of where you are headed as you work up the yoke, measure the depth of the yoke on a plain sweater (in inches), count the number of stitches to be decreased on the sleeve, and that number will be the number of rounds to the top of the sweater (see The Mathematics of Yoke Shaping, p. 117).

The 8-round Wishbone pattern used in this Aran sweater is easy to measure; use it as your rounds-to-the-inch guide and you will have a better idea of the depth of the finished yoke. To repeat, loose is better than snug, to leave room for a turtleneck, or whatever, underneath.

(If, perchance, you did add seed stitches at the seamline for additional width, those stitches will be the center of the underarm stitches to put on the scrap yarn. In this case, simply put the normal number of stitches on a scrap for the underarm—8% of the Key Number—and let the Wishbone pattern disappear as the raglan decreases are worked.)

For this sweater, with Tree of Life (and its purl background) coming together at the raglan seamlines, a decrease of purl 2 together on each side of the raglan markers is a logical choice to blend in with the Aran patterns.

When the sleeve has been decreased until 20 or so stitches remain, **think ahead** and plan for the crew neck shaping. Once you are working back and forth, you want the simpler even-numbered rows to be **inside** rows, where you will work the knits as purls and purls as knits. In the Tree of Life pattern, should any of it still remain, the "slip 1" in the even-numbered rows must be reversed to "slip 1 as if to purl, **yarn in front**."

You also will have to work a catch-up row after putting the center neck stitches on a scrap yarn (see p. 114).

Once the sleeves are gone, proceed with knitting up the crew neck stitches as for the Basic Sweater (p. 115) and work the ribbing for about an inch. **Finis!**

The Wishbone pattern, with its purl background, comes together at the raglan seamlines. To minimize pattern interruption, a P2 tog decrease was worked on each side of the seamline markers.

Mini-Samplers for Aran Designs

*Although neither popcorns/bobbles nor twists/slants were in-
cluded in the Sweater Sampler, why not practice a few and then
make your own choices? A generous selection of both techniques are presented here (pp. 144–47) for you to try in an Aran
mini-sampler.*

*In fact, you'll find it's time-saving and wise to keep a "sampler
in progress." After practicing a new stitch or technique, don't
bind off. Instead, keep the mini-sampler stitches on a spare 16"
needle—at the ready for another "try-out."*

Popcorns/Bobbles

As there is, so they say, more than one way to skin a cat (what a
dreadful expression!), there is also more than one way to work
a popcorn or, if you prefer, a bobble. Does the different terminology relate to size? Depending on how they are executed,
popcorns/bobbles may be either large or small, "innies" or
"outies," neat or sloppy, yet when following sweater directions,
knitters most often work the prescribed method without a
thought as to how they want the finished bobble to look. Ten
different bobble-making techniques from various sources are
listed below for you to try.

Onto a 16-inch circular needle, cast 64 stitches in a worsted-
weight yarn. Work 6 rounds of garter stitch, putting a marker at
the seamline. Knit three rounds of stockinette, and you're all set
to try the different variations to see how they look and how
easy/clumsy they are to work.

Knit 10 stitches and try the first variation, then knit 10 more
stitches and try the second. In this way, you can work 5 variations into the one round, leaving 10 stitches between them.
Then knit 4 or 5 more rounds of stockinette and try the next 5
variations in the same manner. You might want to label them
with hang tags for future reference.

1. *Bernat Book of Irish Knits*
     Knit in the front, back, front of next stitch.
     Turn, K3, turn, K3, turn, K3.
     Slip the 2nd and 3rd stitch over the 1st. Turn.
     Slip bobble stitch to right needle.

2. *Reader's Digest Book of Needlework* **(A)**

Knit in front, back, front, back of next stitch.

Turn, P4, turn, K4, turn, P4, turn, K4.

Slip the 2nd, 3rd, 4th stitch over the 1st.

3. *Reader's Digest Book of Needlework* **(B)**

Knit in front, back, front, back, front of next stitch.

Slip the 2nd, 3rd, 4th, 5th stitch over the 1st.

4. Gladys Thompson, *Guernseys, Jerseys, and Arans*

Knit in front, back, front, back, front of next stitch.

K next stitch. Turn, P5, turn, K5, turn, P5.

Slip 2nd, 3rd, 4th, 5th stitches over the 1st.

Turn. K into the back of the bobble stitch.

5. Shelagh Hollingsworth, *The Complete Book of Traditional Aran Knitting* **(A)**

K1, yarn forward, K1, yarn forward, K1.

Turn, K5, turn, P5.

Turn, K1, slip 1, K2 tog, PSSO, K1.

Turn, P3 tog.

6. Shelagh Hollingsworth, *The Complete Book of Traditional Aran Knitting* **(B)**

Purl, knit, purl, knit, purl in next stitch.

Turn, K5, turn, P5.

Slip 2nd, 3rd, 4th, 5th stitches over 1st stitch.

7. Shelagh Hollingsworth, *The Complete Book of Traditional Aran Knitting* **(C)**

K1, yarn forward, K1, yarn forward, K1.

Turn, P5, turn, K5.

Turn, P2 tog, purl 1, P2 tog.

Turn, slip 1, K2 tog, PSSO.

8. James Norbury, *Traditional Knitting Patterns*

Purl in front, back, front, back of next stitch.

Turn, K4, turn, P4, turn, K4.

Slip 2nd, 3rd, 4th stitches over 1st stitch.

Turn, slip bobble to right needle.

9. Lesley Price, *Kids' Knits*

Knit in front, back, front, back of next stitch.

Turn, K4, turn, P4, turn, K4.

Turn, P4 tog.

10. Lardinia Garland (Fletcher Farm Craft School)

Knit into front, back, front, back, front, back, front, back, front of next stitch (9 times).

Slip all 8 stitches, one by one, over the 1st stitch.

Twists/Slants

Twists, or slants, are another common feature of Aran style sweaters, and there are many different methods of achieving the desired end result. Some are quite awkward to work, so you'll find it very helpful to test different techniques in your Aran mini-sampler.

The best trial is to work a right slant immediately followed by a left slant, then work one round of knit, and repeat the same version again. It might help to use different-color markers for the different versions. Also, some twists/slants are worked on a purl background, so you might want to experiment with that variation too.

Here are 6 versions to try:

1. **Shelagh Hollingsworth,** *The Complete Book of Traditional Aran Knitting*
   Right: "RTw"
   > Knit 2nd stitch on left needle.
   > Knit 1st stitch, slip both off.
   Left: "LTw"
   > Knit through back loop of 2nd stitch on left needle.
   > Knit 1st and 2nd stitches tog through back loop. Slip both off.

2. *Reader's Digest Book of Needlework*
   Right: "Cross 2 RK"
   > Knit into front of 2nd stitch, do not drop off.
   > Knit into front of 1st stitch, drop both off needle.
   Left: "Cross 2 LK"
   > Knit into back of 2nd stitch, do not drop off.
   > Knit into back of 1st stitch, drop both off.

3. **Rae Compton,** *Traditional Knitting*
   Right: "Tw2R"
   > Pass needle in front of 1st stitch. Knit 2nd stitch, do not drop off.
   > Knit 1st stitch, drop both off.
   Left: "Tw2L"
   > Pass needle behind 1st stitch. Knit 2nd stitch, do not drop off.
   > Knit 1st stitch, drop both off.

Your first Sweater Workshop *Sampler had a beginning and an ending—four endings, in fact. But that does not mean you should be forever finished with samplers! As this one shows, a sampler is the perfect way to practice whatever new (or old) techniques you come across. You might even want to keep an ongoing sampler with the stitches held on an extra needle, immediately available for your next inspiration.*

There are no precise directions for its working, other than to cast another 64 stitches onto a 16" circular needle. Yours could include, as this one does, a little patchwork practice, and you could experience the enjoyment of creating just one of something—in this case, a sheep—while working back and forth in the round. Then there are stripes, bobbles, slants, and hundreds of other ideas to keep this sampler ongoing for years.

4. *Bernat Book of Irish Knits*

Right: "Right Slant"

Skip next stitch.

Knit next stitch.

Purl skipped stitch.

Left: "Left Slant"

Skip next stitch.

Purl in back of next stitch.

Knit skipped stitch.

5. Gwyn Morgan, *Traditional Knitting*

Right: "t2R"

Knit 2nd stitch on left needle.

Purl 1st stitch, slip both off.

Left: "t2L"

Pull out 2nd stitch on left needle to back of work and purl it.

Knit 1st stitch, slip both off.

6. Jackie Fee

Right slant

Knit the 2nd stitch.

Purl the 1st stitch, drop both off.

Left slant

Knit through the back of 2nd stitch.

Knit 1st stitch, drop both off.

CREW NECK WITH TWO-COLOR SLEEVE DESIGNS

For a sweater you plan on wearing under a down vest, why bother with body patterns that only you know are there? Confine the pattern of two-color knitting to the sleeves, and you'll be wearing your creation in no time.

There are two options presented here: one design will take up a whole sleeve, and the other version comprises five smaller designs to fit in as you wish.

Whole-Sleeve Design

The whole-sleeve design combines a larger pattern and a smaller pattern. (Adapted from *Needlework and Alphabet Designs*, Dover Publications, Inc., 1975.)

The large pattern is 66 stitches wide and 41 rounds deep and is bordered by the small 5-round pattern above the cuff and before the joining, thus increasing the total number of pattern rounds to 41 plus 10 (5 + 5), plus 3 rounds of plain knit before and after the smaller design for separation (6 more rounds), for a grand total of 57 rounds. If these numbers work for you, the two patterns are both graphed and written out below, whichever you prefer.

- ◆ Work the sleeve ribbing, then increase to a multiple of 9 to work the border pattern.
- ◆ Work 3 plain rounds of knit.
- ◆ Work the 5 rounds of border pattern.
- ◆ Work 3 plain rounds of knit, increasing 3 stitches in last round.
- ◆ Work the 41 rounds of the larger pattern.
- ◆ Work 3 rounds of plain knit, decreasing 3 stitches in the last round.
- ◆ Work the 5 rounds of border pattern.
- ◆ Work 3 rounds of plain knit, or however many you need before the joining.

Patterns

Border Pattern: A multiple of 9. Repeat * to *. The background color is dark (D) and the pattern is light (L).

Round 1: *4D, 2L, 1D, 2L*.

Round 2: *1L, 2D, 2L, 3D, 1L*.

Round 3: *1L, 2D, 3L, 1D, 2L*.

Round 4: *4D, 5L*.

Round 5: *6D, 1L, 2D*.

Border Pattern

9-STITCH REPEAT

Crew Neck with Two-Color Sleeve Designs. *The black sweater has a large 41-round continuous design bordered with a small motif. The gold sweater has a tricolored neckline ribbing and a series of 5 small designs in various colors—scrap basket sleeves?! Both of these examples are knitted in Bartlettyarns' 2-ply Fisherman wool yarn.*

Smaller Sleeve Designs

If the whole-sleeve design, with its 41 rounds of pattern, is a bit more than you want to do, here are five smaller two-color designs that will brighten a sleeve (or two) with a bit less concentration.

Two of the designs are a multiple of 10, two are a multiple of 4, and one is a multiple of 16. That may seem an odd combination, but with a few stitches juggled here and there, they do work into a surprising number of sleeves quite easily, with the Semi-fitted Sleeve or the Full Sleeve being the best candidates (p. 106). With a sleeve number of 60, the 10-stitch and the 4-stitch designs would fit in from the ribbing up, and the addition of 4 stitches toward the upper arm would accommodate the 16-stitch motif. A sleeve of 80 stitches would be ideal for all five designs.

(It's a challenge to *think ahead,* and a great satisfaction when the numbers click. Eureka!!)

REPEAT: 4 x 4

REPEAT: 10 x 10

REPEAT: 4 x 18

REPEAT: 10 x 8

REPEAT: 16 x 8

CREW NECK WITH TWO-COLOR POSY DESIGN

The small Posy pattern enhances the yoke and sleeves (and matching cap) of this sweater knit in a muted burgundy tweed wool yarn. Being only 10 rounds high, the Posy design does not distort, or "funnel," the shape of the yoke. The posies are placed so that the decreases (Raglan Seamline C) do not cut off their petals. Ribbings are K2, P2, and in addition, the neckline ribbing ends with a few rounds of stockinette stitch for a roll edge.

The matching cap is a variation of the Mushroom Cap (p. 223) with a rolled edge and a crown full of posies.

Assuming you are working a sweater of Garter Stitch Rib in the round, here's the way to achieve simple perfection: The pattern is a multiple of 8, but as in the Reversible Sweater (next page), when you divide 8 into your Key Number, the *quotient* must be an even number so that you have the same number of pattern repeats across the front of the sweater as across the back. That may mean you have to adjust your Key Number up or down by quite a few stitches. Whether to go up or down is up to you.

That done, work the body ribbing, increase to your Key Number, change to body-size needles, and work one round of plain knit, placing markers at the right and left seamlines, then STOP.

Although the pattern is called K4, P4, that's not the way to start it. So, *thinking ahead* in order to have the underarm stitches of the body and sleeves match up with each other, start at the right seamline marker with K2, then *P4, K4, P4*, repeat * to * until 2 stitches remain before left seamline marker, K2. Slip the left seamline marker and start K2, *P4, K4, P4*, repeat * to * until 2 stitches remain before right-hand marker, K2. Now you have 4 knit stitches centered at the underarm seamline.

Work the body of the sweater to the underarm.

Figure the Full Sleeve (p. 106), being sure the number of stitches is a multiple of 8—the quotient does not have to be an even number. Work the sleeve ribbing, increase to the number of underarm stitches, change needles, and knit one round. Then start at the marker, with K2, *P4, K4, P4*, repeat * to * until 2 stitches remain before marker, K2. Work the sleeves to the underarm.

Rather than using 8% for the underarm number of stitches, use 16: 8 to the right of the markers and 8 to the left—the line-up would be: K2, P4, K2, marker, K2, P4, K2.

Work the joining round. On the next round, you will have 2 knit stitches on each side of the raglan seamline markers. Keep working these 4 stitches as knits for the straight inch and a half, and then use Raglan Seamline Decrease C (p. 42), which is the 4-stitch seamline. It will look as if it is part of the pattern—a raglan seamline in disguise. It's a remarkable construction, *if* started correctly. Don't hesitate to point out the flawless construction to anyone you think would be interested!

CREW NECK WITH REVERSIBLE PATTERN

Pattern Stitch: K7, P1, or P7, K1. The sweater may be worked, and worn, on either side. The directions are for P7, K1. Reverse the knits and purls if you go the K7, P1 route.

Shown on pp. 158 and 159

Work a gauge sample in the pattern stitch.

Determine the Key Number of stitches. The Key Number will most likely have to be adjusted. Follow closely: The pattern is a multiple of 8 stitches, **but** you must have an equal number of "8s" in the front and back sections of the sweater in order that the P1 (or, K1) is positioned at the side seams. Therefore, divide the Key Number by 8 and adjust until the quotient is an **even** number.

For example, if your Key Number is 220:

$$
\begin{array}{r}
27 \\
8\overline{)220} \\
\underline{16} \\
60 \\
\underline{56} \\
4
\end{array}
$$

So, your answer is 27 with a remainder of 4, meaning that you need to adjust up to a total of 224 stitches for an even multiple of 8.

(This is better done in long division than on a calculator. A calculator will give you a result of 27.5, but that .5 could be misleading. You don't want to misread it to mean "five **stitches** over"; rather, it means one half—one half of the divisor. Half of 8 is 4.)

You might be tempted to adjust down by 4 stitches to 216, rather than up to 224. Yes, 8 divides into 216, 27 times, **but** 27 is not an even number. You would end up with either 13 pattern repeats in the front of the sweater and 14 in the back, or vice versa. This is why the quotient figure must be an even number. Adding 4 stitches to 220 sums up to 224, which, divided by 8, gives a quotient of 28— an **even** number. The front and the back will each have 14 "8s."

This is a large multiple with which to deal. Use your own best judgment whether to add or subtract to adjust your Key Number.

Use the adjusted Key Number for all subsequent figuring.

The Body Ribbing

Determine your number of ribbing stitches: Key Number minus 10%. Adjust, if necessary, for your ribbing pattern.

- ◆ Using a 24" circular ribbing-size needle, work the body ribbing to the desired depth—minus one round.
- ◆ On the last round of ribbing, increase to the Key Number of body stitches. Stop at the right seamline.
- ◆ Count to be sure you have increased to the correct multiple.

The Body

- ◆ Change to a 24" body-size needle and, starting at the right seamline marker, commence the pattern—either K7, P1, or P7, K1, adding a marker at the left seamline.
- ◆ Work the body to the underarm. Do not break the body yarn.

Crew Neck with Reversible Pattern. *This example of the reversible sweater is worked in a lavender heather Bartlett-yarns 2-ply Fisherman wool yarn. It may be worked and worn on either its K7, P1 side (facing page) or its P7, K1 side (this page). The key to its perfect construction is having the same number of 8-stitch repeats in the front of the sweater as in the back.*

After the joining round, if the sweater is worked on the P7, K1 side, the single knit stitch is continued up the yoke, becoming part of the pattern, and a P2 tog decrease is worked in purl sections for the raglan shaping. The ribbings shown here are K2, P2.

You do have to make a decision as to which side to work the sweater, and (when it is completed) another decision in the morning as to which side to show to the world.

The Sleeve Ribbing

♦ Determine the number of ribbing stitches: 20% of the Key Number. Adjust, if necessary, for your ribbing pattern.

♦ Using 4 double-points in ribbing size, work the sleeve ribbing to the desired depth—minus 1 round.

Stop at the seamline. **Read.**

The Sleeves

Determine the number of upper-arm stitches: 33% of the Key Number, plus 1". Adjust, if necessary, to a multiple of 8. This math is easier than for the body because the quotient does not have to be an even number. Any number that 8 will go into without a remainder will do. Subtract the number of stitches on the needles for the ribbing from the number you eventually need for the upper

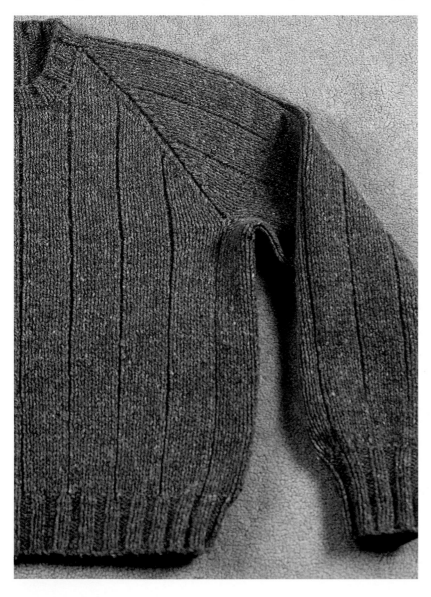

arm. The difference is the number of stitches to increase before the upper arm.

For a full sleeve, increase the needed number of stitches evenly spaced in the last round of ribbing. Change to body-size double-points (and then to a 16" circular, if possible) and, starting at the seamline in pattern, work the sleeve to the underarm. Stop at the seamline. Break the yarn, leaving a yard in reserve.

For a less full sleeve, increase all but 8 of the needed number of stitches, evenly spaced, in the last round of ribbing. Change to body-size double-points (and then to a 16" circular needle, if possible) and, starting at the seamline in pattern, work the sleeve to the elbow.

Stop at the seamline.

◆ Work the next "7 purl" section as follows: P3, K1, P3, and work to the end of the round.

Stop at the seamline, and remove the marker.

◆ On the next round, put the marker back after the "new" knit stitch in the purl section. You have created a new seamline.

◆ To work the remaining 8 increase stitches: Always keeping the new knit stitch as a knit, increase 1 stitch on each side of it every 6th row, 4 times. As the increased stitches come into existence, purl them. When the increasing of the 8 stitches is complete, the new knit stitch should have 7 purls on each side of it.

◆ Work the sleeve in pattern to the underarm, leaving the marker in place to identify the new seamline.

Stop at the seamline. Break the yarn, leaving a yard in reserve.

The Preparation for Joining

This step requires less figuring than usual. Rather than finding the customary 8% of the Key Number, the underarm stitches for the reversible sweater must be 15. Otherwise, the vertical knit stitches won't come together in an orderly manner for the yoke decreasing.

Sleeve Preparation

Full sleeve: Select a knit stitch near the seamline. Designate it as being the center of the underarm stitches, with 7 purls to its right and 7 to its left. Unknit the 15 stitches involved (plus any others that need to be unknit to get to the 15 underarm stitches). Run a scrap through the 15 stitches for the sleeve underarm.

Remove the needle from the underarm stitches.

Repeat on the other sleeve.

Less full sleeve: The new knit stitch is the center of the underarm stitches, with 7 purls to its right and 7 purls to its left. Unknit the 15 stitches involved (plus any others that need to be unknit to get to the 15 underarm stitches). Run a scrap through the 15 stitches for the sleeve underarm.

Remove the needle from the underarm stitches.

Repeat on the other sleeve.

Body Preparation

Locate the K1 at the left seamline. It is the center of the underarm stitches, with 7 purls to its right and 7 purls to its left. Run a scrap yarn through the 15 stitches for the left underarm. Tie loosely. These stitches remain on both the scrap and the needle for the moment.

Locate the K1 at the right seamline. It is the center of the underarm stitches with 7 purls to the right of it and 7 purls to the left of it. Unknit the knit stitch and the 7 purls to the right of it. Run a scrap through the 15 stitches for the right underarm. Remove the needle from these stitches.

The Joining Round

Refer to the Basic Crew Neck Sweater directions (p. 110).

At each of the 4 joining points there are 2 knit stitches side by side. On the round after the joining, knit the 2 knit stitches together. The remaining knit stitch is the center of the raglan seamline decrease. It will remain intact; ***work it as a knit from now on.*** On the next round, put a marker before or after it.

The Yoke

- ◆ Work to the start of the raglan seamline decreases.
  Stop at the right front seamline.

The raglan seamlines are a combination of the purl decreases P2 tog and P1S1:

P2 tog—Purl 2 stitches together as one. Leans right on the knit side.

P1S1 — Purl 1 stitch. Return the new stitch to the left needle. Insert the right needle into the stitch behind it, and lift this stitch over the purl stitch. Return the resulting stitch to the right needle. Leans left on the knit side.

- ◆ On the next outside row, start the raglan seamline decreases. Work to within 2 stitches of the K1 seamline stitch, P2 tog, K1, P1S1.

◆ ***The Crew Neck:*** Work until 20 or 21 stitches remain to be decreased on the sleeves, and follow the Basic Crew Neck Sweater instructions beginning on p. 113. Since this is a plain vertical pattern (without cables, etc.), a catch-up row is not absolutely necessary.

◆ Work back and forth on the needle, working a neck edge decrease 4 times and working the raglan seamline decreases in their proper order.

Stop at the end of an outside row when the seamlines come together and the sleeves are gone.

The Neck Ribbing

◆ Using a 24" ribbing-size circular needle in your right hand, purl into the left-side neck chain selvedge, purl the stitches from the scrap (slip them onto a double-point), purl into the right-side neck chain selvedge and purl the back-neck stitches from the body needle.

◆ Count the number of stitches on the needle. Adjust, if necessary, in the first round of ribbing near a seamline.

◆ Work the ribbing loosely for about 1".

◆ Bind off in ribbing loosely.

The Underarm Opening

◆ Work the grafting on the knit side of the sweater (see p. 115). The center purl stitch will have to be happy grafted as a knit. Other than this one stitch that is a misfit on either side, the sweater is reversible.

◆ Tuck in all ends carefully—split the plies and head the ends in opposite directions.

TURTLENECK (AND TURTLE-TO-GO)

Left: ***The Turtleneck Pullover.*** *For a built-in turtleneck, the normal number of neckline stitches is increased by one-fourth and the neck ribbing is worked for 9 inches so it can be rolled over twice. The yarn in this example is Bartlettyarns' 2-ply Fisherman wool: bracken, denim, and light sheep's gray, with a scrap of purple heather introduced as a purl stripe at the color changes. Ribbings are K2, P2, and the Raglan Seamline Decrease is version C.*

Right: *A **Basic Crew Neck** worked in the Ringing the Changes pattern (p. 123) with coordinating **Turtles-to-Go**. A Turtle-to-Go can also substitute as an "open-air" cap if one's ears get cold during a long wait for the bus.*

The Turtleneck is one of the easiest and simplest neck variations. The established neck stitches are increased in number for both comfort and looks; there is nothing sadder than a scrawny Turtle. The neck ribbing is then extended for 9". (For these reasons, this sweater just misses being a five-skeiner, as you must dip into an additional skein for the turtleneck.) The best ribbing pattern is K2, P2, as it retains its shape and elasticity.

>>> **Decision Point:** Work the Basic Sweater, the Crew Neck, through the round establishing the neck ribbing stitches.

> **Stop** after you have worked the back neck stitches from the body needle.

◆ Put a marker on the right end of the ribbing-size needle.

The Set-Up

◆ Work a knit round, increasing the number of stitches by one-fourth. (Increase into every 4th stitch.)

The Neck Ribbing

◆ Count the number of stitches on the needle. Adjust, if necessary, to the correct multiple on the first round of ribbing near a seamline. (A multiple of 4 needed for K2, P2.)

◆ Work the first 2" or 3" on the ribbing-size needle, then switch to a 16" body-size needle.

◆ Work in ribbing for the desired depth: about 6" to roll over once, or about 9" to roll over twice.

◆ Cast off in ribbing loosely.

Turtle-to-Go

Or, try a Turtle-to-Go. Worked separately, this Turtle keeps you snug at the bus but can be doffed easily in the heat of your destination. Work several Turtles-to-Go in colors to match a striped crew neck sweater, then change your accent color to suit the mood of the day. (Thank you, Connie Pearlstein, for this original idea.)

◆ Count the number of neck ribbing stitches on the matching sweater.

◆ Increase the number by one-fourth.

◆ Adjust, if necessary, to the correct multiple for your ribbing pattern.

◆ Cast the required number of stitches onto a circular 16" body-size needle. Work 3". Switch to a 16" ribbing-size needle and work 3" more. Then return to the 16" body size needle for the final 3".

◆ Bind off in ribbing loosely.

THE U-NECK

Shown on p. 166

The U-Neck is a most comfortable sweater. It affords more room than the Crew Neck when worn over a coordinating blouse or turtleneck jersey—and, of course, it shows off more of that coordinating effort.

The neckline shaping may be started anywhere in the yoke of the sweater. Remember that it will have an inch of ribbing added to it, so start the opening an inch lower than you want it.

Decision Point: Work the Basic Sweater, the Crew Neck, through the joining round.   <<<

> **Stop** at the right front seamline anywhere in the straight 1½"—
> or, for a higher U-neck, at the start of a decrease round.

The Set-Up

- ◆ Count the number of stitches on one sleeve. Take this count between the markers if you have stopped in the straight 1½" section. Count between the seamlines if you stopped higher up and the raglan decreases have already started.
- ◆ Divide the number of stitches on one sleeve by 2 and add 4. The answer is the number of stitches to leave on the needle at each side front next to the sleeves.
- ◆ Run a scrap through the remaining center front stitches.
- ◆ Starting at the right front seamline, work to the center front stitches.
- ◆ Remove the needle from these stitches. *Turn.*

Stop. Read.

You will now be working back and forth on the needle. If you are working in a pattern, you may have to reverse your knits and purls on the inside rows, and, before this next inside row, you may have to work a catch-up row (p. 114) over the stitches from the right neck edge to the decrease at the right front seamline. If you have started the raglan decreases, or when you do:

> The *outside rows* are the decrease rows.

> The *inside rows* are the straight rows.

From now on, start all rows with a slip stitch for a chain selvedge:

> *Outside rows*—Slip as if to purl, yarn in back.

> *Inside rows*—Slip as if to purl, yarn in front.

- ◆ Work the *inside* row.

The U-Neck Pullover. *This particular version is knit of two colors, with stripes that follow Fibonacci's Sequence (p. 122) from below the Joining Round up to the shoulders—a move that necessitates knowing the approximate number of rounds/rows in the yoke. In this example, the Fibonacci Sequence is worked double and in reverse: 13, 13; 8, 8; 5, 5; 3, 3; 2, 2; 1, 1.*

The yoke shaping shown here was accomplished with Raglan Seamline E, which was perhaps not the best choice, as its "feathers" somewhat vie for attention with the featured stripe sequence.

Initials are worked just above the ribbing (see p. 68 for graphs).

♦ *On the next 4 outside rows only*, decrease 1 stitch at the neck edges, and continue to decrease at the raglan seamlines by starting and ending these next 4 outside rows with:

Slip 1, K2 tog, work to the last 3 stitches, SSK, K1.

♦ Then, continue the decreases at the raglan seamlines until the seamlines come together and the sleeve is gone.

Stop at the end of an outside row.

The Neck Ribbing

♦ Using a 24" circular ribbing-size needle, knit into the left-side neck chain selvedge, knit the stitches from the scrap (slip them onto a double-point), knit into the right neck chain selvedge, and knit the back neck stitches from the body needle.

♦ Count the number of stitches on the needle. If the number must be adjusted for the ribbing pattern, do so in the first round of ribbing near a raglan seamline.

♦ Put a marker on the right needle and work the ribbing pattern loosely for an inch.

♦ Cast off in ribbing loosely.

THE V-NECK

Decision Point: Work the Basic Sweater, the Crew Neck, through <<<
the joining round.

♦ Work a few rounds of the straight 1½".

Stop at the right front seamline 6 rounds before the first raglan seamline decrease.

The Set-Up

♦ Count the number of front stitches between the markers. You must have an uneven number. K2 tog before the marker at the right front seamline if you need to adjust.

♦ Put a safety pin *through* the center front stitch. Check to be sure that you have an equal number of stitches on each side of the pin.

♦ Starting at the right front seamline, work around to the stitch on the pin. Remove the left needle from this stitch. Be sure it is secure on the pin. *Turn.*

Stop. Read. Find a pencil.

The Math

You must figure how many times to work a decrease at the neck edges for the V-shaping. If you decrease too many times, you will run out of front stitches before the sleeve is gone. If you decrease too few times, you will have front stitches remaining after the sleeve is gone. The sleeve stitches and the front stitches must disappear at the same time.

As you decrease at the right and left front raglan seamlines, you are eating up one stitch from each side of the front along with one stitch from each sleeve; equally they go, hand in hand. By finding how many stitches on each side front are "excess" above and beyond the number needed for the raglan seamline decreases, you will know how many times to work a decrease at each neck edge.

As the number of neckline decreases will be the same for both the right and left neck shaping, concentrate on the right front for the figuring.

- ◆ Count the number of stitches in the right half of the front.
- ◆ Count the number of stitches on the right sleeve. Since only half the sleeve stitches are decreased at the front raglan seamline (the other half are decreased at the back raglan seamline), divide the number of stitches on the right sleeve by 2.
- ◆ Subtract the one-half sleeve from the right half of the front.
- ◆ The answer is the number of stitches that are excess to the right half front and are not needed to decrease the right sleeve. Therefore, that is the number of times to work a decrease at each neck edge.
- ◆ Keep this number in the back of your head for a moment, or jot it down here: _____ .

Your math is done. Return to the sweater.

The Neck Shaping

You will now be working back and forth on the needle. If you are working in a pattern, you may have to reverse your knits and purls on the inside rows—and, before this next inside row, you may have to work a catch-up row (p. 114) over the stitches from the right neck edge to the right front seamline.

- ◆ Work the inside row to the end of the needle. From now on, start all rows with a slip stitch for a chain selvedge.

  Outside rows—Slip as if to purl, yarn in back.

  Inside rows—Slip as if to purl, yarn in front.

- ◆ On the next outside row, and every *other* outside row thereafter for as many times as are necessary, work a decrease at the neck edges, starting and ending the neck edge decrease rows with: slip 1, K2 tog, work to the last 3 stitches, SSK, K1.

◆ Work 3 straight rows.

◆ On the next outside row, work a decrease at the neck edges, and start the raglan seamline decreases. (As the raglan seamline decreases are worked every 4th row for a while, and the neck edge decreases are worked every 4th row, combining them in the next row starts you off in orderly fashion, and gives you 3 straight rows to follow. Once the raglan seamline decreases start their every-other-row sequence, this respite of 3 straight rows will end.)

So, working the raglan seamline decreases in their proper order, and the neck edge decreases every fourth row as many times as necessary, head for the top. When you are nearly there, stop for a quick number check:

◆ Count the stitches remaining to be decreased on the right sleeve. (Do *not* count between the markers, and do *not* include the seamline stitches in this count.) Divide by 2.

◆ Count the number of stitches on the right-side front. (Again, do not count from the marker and do not include the seamline in this count.) If you have finished your neck edge decreases, these numbers should be equal, and all is well. If the numbers are not equal, and the front has more stitches than half the sleeve, the difference is the number of times to continue decreasing at the neck edge.

If for any reason half the sleeve is *more* than the front, you're in trouble. If the difference is only a stitch or two, K3 tog at the next sleeve decrease, or work a decrease on a straight row. Check the situation at the left-side front and left sleeve as well.

◆ When the raglan seamlines come together and the fronts and sleeves are gone, **stop** at the end of an outside row.

The Neck Ribbing

Using a 16" or 24" circular needle (depending on the size of the sweater and the number of available stitches) *one size smaller* than the body:

◆ Knit into the left-side neck chain selvedge.

◆ Knit the stitch from the pin.

◆ *Put a marker on the needle.*

◆ Knit into the right-side neck chain selvedge.

◆ Knit the back neck stitches from the body needle.

Stop.

To hold the V-neck flat and open to its proper depth, it is necessary to increase a few stitches along each side of the V. It is also necessary to work the center stitch of the V, the stitch before the marker, as a knit throughout the ribbing, and this center knit stitch must start out with a purl, or purls, on both sides of it.

Being conscious of all of the above, proceed cautiously to the first round of your ribbing pattern.

- ◆ As you work the ribbing down the left side, visually keep backtracking from the center knit stitch, picturing the purl, or purls, beside it, and plan your few increases accordingly. (Usually you'll need 3 to 5 increases on a side, depending on size of sweater and diameter of yarn. A large sweater with a deep V-neck worked in a fine yarn might require 6 or more.)

- ◆ Work the Bar Increase (p. 37) into a knit stitch that will be followed by a purl on the next round; assume the bump of the Bar Increase to be that purl.

- ◆ Knit the stitch before the marker.

- ◆ As you start up the right side, work a purl, or purls, after the center knit stitch, and increase the same number of stitches on this side as you did on the other.

- ◆ Now, look ahead to be certain that your ribbing pattern will end correctly as you finish the first round. Adjust near a seamline if necessary.

- ◆ On the next round, and every other round thereafter, decrease 1 stitch on each side of the center knit stitch to miter the point of the V. Use your discretion as to whether to K2 tog or P2 tog, depending on your ribbing pattern. The P2 tog decrease will serve as a better background for the lone knit stitch and make it more of an accent to the base of the V.

- ◆ Work the ribbing pattern loosely for about an inch.

- ◆ Bind off in ribbing loosely.

V-NECK WITH FLAME STITCH PATTERN

One of the oldest fabric patterns incorporating the use of color is Flame Stitch. Originally, this durable embroidered fabric was used for upholstery and for fine personal accessories such as pin cushions, purses, and book covers. The design is an exceptional eye-catcher, with its undulating rise and fall of colors in a harmonious spectrum. Along the way, weavers adopted its image and adapted its construction to produce yardage on their looms for upholstery and drapery fabrics.

Left: ***V-Neck with Flame Stitch Design.*** *The 6-color Flame Stitch pattern is best confined to the body and lower sleeves. In this example, a variation of the Basket Weave stitch makes up the solid-color background. The yoke is decreased with a combination of Raglan Seamline A (used where knit blocks meet) and P2 tog on each side of the marker (used where purl blocks come together).*

Right: *Another simple neckline option is the Boat Neck. (Directions are on p. 172.) In this sweater of a muted burgundy tweed, the boat neck also boasts an added Knitted Cord cast-off.*

Knitters can achieve a faux Flame Stitch design with this 4-stitch repeat worked for 20 rounds, and the 20 rounds repeated as many times as necessary for the desired depth. Restrict its use to the body and/or sleeves, or let it make an appearance as a lively 20-round border. The pattern calls for six colors and is a worthy way to use up odd balls of complementary colors.

Follow the directions for the basic V-Neck pullover (p. 167), incorporating the Flame Stitch in the body and sleeves as desired. The solid-color background areas may be worked in plain stockinette or a textured pattern—a variant of the Basket Weave stitch is shown in the photograph on p. 171.

Basket Weave Stitch Pattern

Rounds 1, 2, 3, 4: K4, P4.

Rounds 5, 6, 7, 8: P4, K4.

Repeat the 8 rounds as many times as necessary to complete the sleeves and yoke.

Flame Stitch Pattern

Work the chart at left from the bottom up and from right to left.

Color A is in 9 rounds.

Color B is in 7 rounds.

Color C is in 7 rounds.

Color D is in 6 rounds.

Color E is in 4 rounds.

Color F is in 4 rounds.

Flame Stitch Color Sequence

4-St Repeat				Round
C	D	C	C	20
D	D	D	C	19
D	B	D	D	18
B	B	B	D	17
B	F	B	B	16
F	F	F	B	15
F	A	F	F	14
A	A	A	F	13
A	E	A	A	12
E	E	E	A	11
E	C	E	E	10
C	C	C	E	9
C	D	C	C	8
D	D	D	C	7
C	C	C	C	6
A	A	A	A	5
A	B	A	A	4
B	B	B	A	3
A	B	A	A	2
A	A	A	A	1 ← START

Working the Boat Neck Variation

For a Boat Neck style, stop the raglan decreasing 1" shy of where you want the top of the neckline. Since there is no neck shaping—the front is the same height as the back—the remaining stitches may simply be ribbed for about an inch and then bound off at this point, *or*...

To add the decorative edge and tie, as shown on the burgundy sweater on p. 171, a 12" length of Knitted Cord is worked separately with the same color yarn, then the 3 stitches of the cord are used to cast off the sweater neck stitches (see Sampler directions, p. 57), and the cord is continued for another 12" beyond the end of the bound-off neckband. The cord ends are then tied in a bow.

THE V-NECK WITH LACE EDGES

Shown on p. 174

Work the V-Neck (p. 167) through the round establishing the neck stitches. *Note:* It is not necessary to add extra stitches along the sides of the neckline, because the application of the lace will hold the V open and flat. (Check your Sampler's "endings" again and observe the difference in width between the ribbing cast-off and the lace cast-off over 16 stitches.)

Upon completion of this round, the needles are positioned at the left shoulder. To start the lace cast-off, they must be at the base of the V, so,

- ◆ Slip all the stitches for the left side of the neck onto the right needle, including the center stitch.
- ◆ Remove the marker. The needles are now separated at the base of the V. The yarn is still at the left shoulder. Break it and secure it there.
- ◆ For security, tie the yarn into the first stitch on the left needle at the base of the V.
- ◆ Count the number of stitches on the needle.

To work the Sampler lace, you must have a multiple of 4 stitches— or, if you select a different lace, you must have its multiple. Keep in mind the number of stitches you must adjust, if any, and do so while working the lace near a back seamline.

With the outside facing, and with a double-pointed ribbing-size needle in your right hand, insert the tip of the needle between the first two stitches on the left needle, and proceed to:

- ◆ Cast 5 stitches onto the left needle.
- ◆ Knit the 5 stitches
- ◆ Turn your work.
- ◆ You are now in a position to work the lace edging, as in the Sampler, p. 59, starting with row 1.

To refresh your memory; it is only at the end of rows 2, 4, 6, and 8 that you are casting off 1 stitch of the neck by knitting a stitch of the lace together with a stitch of the neck. It therefore takes 2 rows of lace work to cast off 1 neck stitch. In the Sampler, the lace stitches were of a different color and easily discernible, but in your sweater, they may be the same color as the rest of the sweater. Work the lace rows carefully and be sure each row ends on the correct stitch.

- ◆ Work the cast-off up the right side neck, across the back neck,

Front: ***V-Neck with Lace Edges.*** *The neck stitches on this sweater made from dark charcoal gray Ulrika light-weight yarn are cast off in the same lace pattern used as an ending on the Sampler—an ample width for a dress-up touch. For the sleeve cuffs and lower body, the lace was added "after the fact," and the body lace is further laced with a Knitted Cord.*

Back: *A tweedy wine-colored Crew Neck takes on a bit of a Victorian air with a touch of lace around the neckline. Again, the Sampler lace is added, starting at the center back, and the two 5-stitch ends are sewn together.*

and down the left-side neck, ending where you started at the base of the V.

◆ On the last row of lace, when you are to cast off the last neck stitch, bind off all the lace stitches, not just the first 4. At the base of the V, the lace edges overlap and may be either left loose or sewn together.

To add matching lace at the sleeve cuff:

◆ ***If you planned ahead and worked the invisible cast-on,*** remove the auxiliary yarn and put the stitches on 3 double-points.

◆ ***If you did not plan ahead,*** snip one-half stitch in the row above the ribbing, as for the Afterthought Pocket (p. 69). Carefully unravel horizontally and drop the ribbing off. Put the exposed stitches on 3 double-points.

◆ Starting at the seamline, tie in new yarn and cast 5 stitches onto the needle. Proceed as above.

THE SLIT NECK

Shown on p. 176

The Slit Neck is an easier version of the Placket neck, as there is no casting on for an overlap. Start the slit anywhere in the yoke by dividing the front stitches in half and working each side separately while continuing the raglan seamline decreases.

Decision Point   <<<

- ◆ Work the Basic Sweater, the Crew Neck, to within 2 rounds of the start of the raglan seamline decreases.

- **Stop** at the right front seamline. (If you want a shorter slit, stop later on, at the right front seamline at the start of any decrease round.)

The Set-Up

Note: The directions assume a 6-stitch Cardigan Border (p. 32) of K1, P1 rib on each side of the slit. If you want a wider border, work 8 or 10 stitches of K1, P1 instead of 6 stitches.

- ◆ Count the number of front stitches. You must have an even number. K2 tog before the marker at the right front seamline if it is necessary to adjust.

- ◆ Tie a yarn marker around the needle at the center of the front.

- ◆ Check to be sure there is an equal number of stitches in each half of the front sections.

- ◆ Starting at the right front seamline, work to the yarn marker.

- ◆ Turn. You now have the inside of the sweater facing you.

Stop. Read.

You will now be working back and forth on the needle. If you are working in a pattern, you may have to reverse your knits and purls on the inside rows, and, before the next inside row, you may have to work a catch-up row (p. 114) over the stitches from the right neck edge to the right front seamline.

- ◆ Work the inside row.

- ◆ Turn.

- ◆ On the next outside row, work the first 6 stitches and the last 6 stitches as Cardigan Border and start the raglan seamline decreases.

- ◆ Continue to work back and forth on the needle, keeping the first and last 6 stitches in Cardigan Border on both the outside and the inside rows. *At the same time,* work the raglan seamline decreases in their proper order.

Top: **Slit Neck Pullover** with lacing. The edges may be worked with a simple chain selvedge or with the Cardigan Border for added body. Buttonholes are not a necessity; if the fabric is a bit loose, a length of Knitted Cord can simply be laced through the edges and tied at either the top or the bottom.

Bottom: **Crew Neck Laced Cardigan** (p. 198). This sweater, though knit as a cardigan, will most likely go through life worn as a pullover. On this example, the yoke is shaped with Raglan Seamline D for a decorative "feathery" touch.

- ◆ *If you want to add a lacing* to the slit, work a buttonhole at each end of the needle using the substitute beginning *and* ending of row 1 at appropriate intervals (refer to Method for buttonholes, p. 34).
- ◆ Work until 20 or 21 stitches remain to be decreased on each sleeve.

Stop at the beginning of an outside row.

Neck Shaping and Neck Ribbing

Refer to pp. 178–81 of the directions for the Placket Neck sweater.

THE PLACKET NECK

Shown on p. 179

Decision Point   <<<

- ◆ Work the Basic Sweater, the Crew Neck, to within 2 rounds of the start of the raglan seamline decreases.

Stop at the right front seamline.

The Set-Up

Note: This set-up is for a placket neck in a woman's sweater. For a man's, see Placket Neck Variations on p. 181. The directions assume a 6-stitch Cardigan Border for each side of the placket opening. For 8- or 10-stitch borders, see the variation on page 182.

- ◆ Count the number of front stitches between the markers. You must have an even number. K2 tog before the marker at the right front seamline if it is necessary to adjust.
- ◆ Tie a yarn marker around the needle at the center of the front.
- ◆ Check to be sure there is an equal number of stitches in each half of the front sections.
- ◆ Starting at the right front seamline, work to within 3 stitches of the center front yarn marker.
- ◆ *Turn.* You now have the inside of the sweater facing you.
- ◆ Insert the right needle in between the first two stitches on the left needle and proceed to . . .
- ◆ Cast 6 stitches onto the left needle.

Stop. Read.

You will now be working back and forth on the needle. If you are working in a pattern, you may have to reverse your knits and purls on the inside rows, **and**, before the next inside row, you may have to work a catch-up row (p. 114) over the stitches from the right neck edge to the right front seamline.

◆ Purl the 6 cast-on stitches and work the inside row to the end. The end is the point where the opening has been made— 3 stitches beyond the yarn marker. This marker may now be removed.

◆ *Turn.*

◆ On the next outside row, work the first 6 stitches and the last 6 stitches (the cast-ons), in K1, P1 Cardigan Border *and* start the raglan seamline decreases. Refer to the Sampler directions for Cardigan Border on p. 32.

When completed, the 6 cast-on stitches are tacked down inside the sweater. This is the button side of the placket. The 6 stitches at the beginning of the outside rows form the buttonhole side of the placket.

◆ Work the first buttonhole (p. 33) about 1" above the opening, the second about 2" above the first, and the third in the neck ribbing. (The placement of the second buttonhole is a bit tricky. The third one in the neck ribbing is made in a position roughly corresponding to the point at which the neck shaping begins, i.e., when 20 stitches remain to be decreased on each sleeve. Be sure to put in the second buttonhole well before this point.)

◆ Continue to work back and forth on the needle, keeping the first and last 6 stitches in Cardigan Border on both the outside and the inside rows. *At the same time,* work the raglan seamline decreases in their proper order.

◆ Work until 20 or 21 stitches remain to be decreased on each sleeve.

Stop at the beginning of an outside row.

The Neck Shaping

◆ Work the outside row to within 15 stitches of the *seamline.*

◆ Slip the stitches you have just worked onto a holder.

◆ Continue working across the row to the 15th stitch after the last *seamline* decrease.

◆ Slip the remaining stitches onto a holder. If it bothers you, or your pattern, that these stitches you are slipping on the holder will be minus one row of work in the final accounting,

Back: *In this **Placket Neck Pullover**, alternating rounds of gray and off white are used throughout, with the Cardigan Border that edges the placket worked in the lighter color, for contrast. Three button-holes are added at the neck opening—two in the placket itself and one in the neck ribbing. Small wooden buttons pick up the shots of rusty color in the yarns.*

Front: *With its left front raglan seamline opening, the **Open Raglan** (p. 188) takes on an asymmetrical air. Here, an alternating seed stitch adds further interest to the variegated yarn, and the ribbings are K3, P3 for maximum elasticity. **The Beaded Rib Scarf** (p. 227) coordinates, with its seed stitch ribbing pattern.*

work to the end of the row and break the yarn. (To work to the end of the row and head back would result in an extra row of stitches on this side in the final accounting.) Tie the working yarn in 14 stitches from the *seamline*. Slip the stitches that are on the needle before the yarn onto a holder.

◆ Check to be sure that the stitches on the holders are equal in number.

◆ Check to be sure that there are 14 stitches at each end of the needle before the front raglan seamlines.

◆ *Turn* and work the inside row. You will now be working back and forth on the stitches between the holders. Start all rows with a slip stitch for a chain selvedge:

> *Outside rows*—Slip as if to purl, yarn in back.
> *Inside rows*—Slip as if to purl, yarn in front.

◆ On the next 4 outside rows only, decrease 1 stitch at the neck edges and continue to decrease at the raglan seamlines. Start and end these next 4 outside rows with:

> Slip 1, K2 tog, work to the last 3 stitches, SSK, K1.

◆ Then, continue the decreases at the raglan seamlines until the seamlines come together and the sleeve is gone.

Stop at the end of an inside row. Break the yarn, and secure.

The Neck Ribbing

Slip the stitches from the holders to double-points to work them. With the outside facing you, connect the yarn at the beginning of the outside row and, using a 24" circular ribbing-size needle in your right hand:

◆ Work the stitches from the holder, keeping the first 6 in K1, P1 Cardigan Border.

◆ Knit into the right-side neck chain selvedge.

◆ Knit the back neck stitches from the body needle.

◆ Knit into the left-side neck chain selvedge.

◆ Work the stitches from the last holder, keeping the last 6 in Cardigan Border.

Stop.

◆ Count the number of stitches *in between* the borders.

You are going to start the neck ribbing pattern on the next row—an inside row—but do your thinking and planning while looking at the outside. As the Cardigan Border continues on the first and last 6 stitches throughout the ribbing, it must have a knit stitch, or stitches, beside it. Therefore:

For K1, P1 ribbing, you must have an uneven number of stitches.

For K2, P2 ribbing, you must have a number of stitches divisible by 4, plus 2.

Keeping in mind the number of stitches to adjust, if necessary, near a seamline and, *thinking in reverse,*

- ◆ Work the inside row of neck ribbing.
- ◆ *Turn.* Before continuing, check the line-up of the knits and purls.
- ◆ Work the neck ribbing loosely for about an inch, adding one more buttonhole.

Stop at the end of an inside row.

- ◆ Bind off loosely in ribbing.
- ◆ Tack the buttonhole side of the placket to the inside.

For a Placket in a Man's Sweater

- ◆ Follow the preceding directions through the set-up.
- ◆ *Then*, to reverse the opening, starting at the right front seam-line, work 3 stitches *beyond* the center front marker.
- ◆ *Turn,* and work the inside row to the end.
- ◆ *Turn,* and cast 6 stitches onto the left needle.
- ◆ Work the 6 cast-on stitches in K1, P1 Cardigan Border; work across the row to within the last 6 stitches; work these last 6 stitches in Cardigan Border.

The 6 cast-on stitches are the button side of the placket. The 6 stitches at the end of the outside row form the buttonhole side of the placket.

- ◆ Refer back to the preceding directions to complete the neck shaping and ribbing.

For a Shorter Placket Opening: The working of the sweater is the same, except that you will have already started your raglan seamline decreases before beginning the placket opening at the desired height.

Stop at the right front seamline after a straight round. The set-up is the same as for the preceding directions, except you must count the number of stitches between the *seamlines,* not between the markers.

- ◆ Refer back to the preceding directions to complete the neck shaping and ribbing.

Placket Neck Variations

For Wider Cardigan Borders

The set-up is the same as for the 6-stitch border *except*:

> ***For an 8-stitch border,*** work to within 4 stitches of the center front marker, etc., and then, cast 8 stitches onto the left needle.

> ***For a 10-stitch border,*** work to within 5 stitches of the center front marker, etc., and then, cast 10 stitches onto the left needle.

The remaining directions are the same, except substitute your 8 or 10 for the 6s.

For a Placket in a Contrasting Color

- Wind two small balls of contrast-color yarn.

- Work the preceding directions to the point where the 6 stitches are to be cast onto the left needle. (See The Set-Up, p. 177.)

- Connect one ball of yarn to the first stitch on the left needle and, using the contrasting yarn, cast 6 stitches onto the left needle.

- With the contrasting yarn, purl the 6 cast-on stitches.

- With the original yarn, work the inside row to within 6 stitches of the end of the needle.

- Connect the other ball of yarn and work the last 6 stitches in the contrasting color.

- On both the inside and outside rows, work the first and last 6 stitches on the needle in Cardigan Border with the contrasting yarn. (Remember to bring the new color from under the old when switching from one to the other, to avoid holes.)

PLACKET NECK WITH SWEATSHIRT POCKET AND HOOD

Given the good old gray-sweatshirt treatment, this sweater, knit of a medium-weight wool (Bartlettyarns' 2-ply Fisherman), has a hood and a pocket. The former grows out of the neck ribbing and the latter out of the body ribbing. Thus, as involved as it looks, the sweater is still worked in a seamless progression.

The Sweatshirt Pocket

>>> **Decision Point**

- Work the Basic Sweater to 5" or 6" above the ribbing for an adult, 3" or 4" above the ribbing for a child.

Note: You must have markers at both the right and the left seamlines. The pocket is centered in the front of the sweater 3" from the right and left seamlines for most sizes. (For a small child, figure 2" from the seamlines.) Translate stitches into inches according to your gauge:

3" equals _____ stitches.

Stop at the *left* seamline after working to the desired depth for the top of the pocket.

Set-Up

- From the *right* seamline, *count* in toward the front of the sweater the number of stitches needed to equal 3".
- Tie a yarn marker around the needle at this point.
- Trace the next stitch down to the row above the ribbing.
- Tie a yarn marker through that stitch.
- Starting at the *left* seamline, *work* in toward the front of the sweater the number of stitches needed to equal 3".

Stop. Do not break the body yarn.

- Trace the next stitch down to the row above the ribbing.
- Working toward the left, slide a long, fine needle under one-half of each stitch in that row just above the ribbing, ending with the marked stitch.
- Connect a new ball of yarn to the first stitch on the right end of the fine needle.
- With a straight body-size needle, knit the stitches from the fine needle. It may be easier to knit them out through the back (and if the pocket is in a contrasting color, the "legs" of the knit stitches won't slant).
- Put the fine needle aside. It has done its job.

Pocket Flap

- Turn your work.
- Using straight body-size needles, purl back across the row of new stitches.

Stop. Read.

Continue working back and forth on the pocket flap, working the first and last 6 stitches on the needle in K1, P1 Cardigan Border (p. 32). This border provides a neat, firm selvedge for the pocket and will stand up to the wear of hands slipping in and out. Also note the pocket options listed below under Variations.

♦ Work back and forth until the pocket flap is as deep as the body (a row shy is better than a row over—don't give the pocket a head start on sagginess).

Stop at the beginning of an outside row.

♦ Break the flap yarn and secure it.

Joining Pocket Flap to Body

♦ Hold the pocket needle in front of the sweater needle. With the body yarn and the body needle, join the pocket to the sweater by knitting together a stitch from each needle.

♦ Continue working the body of the sweater to the underarm.

Sweatshirt Pocket Variations

The sides of the pocket may be curved instead of straight and may also be buttoned, if you wish.

Curved In to Stay

♦ Work a decrease at each end of the needle inside the Cardigan Border on every other outside row, or more often for a sharper curve. Start and end the decrease rows this way:

♦ Work the first 6 stitches in Cardigan Border, *K2 tog*, work across to within the last 8 stitches, *SSK,* work the last 6 stitches in Cardigan Border.

♦ You *must* keep track of the number of stitches you decrease. Then, before attaching the top of pocket flap to the body, work across the body, toward the center for the same number of stitches that you decreased, in order that the pocket flap will be in alignment with the body for joining.

Curved In and Then Back Out

♦ Work a *decrease* at each end of the needle inside the Cardigan Border on every other outside row, as above, to the halfway point. Keep track of the number of stitches you decrease.

♦ Then, work an *increase* at each end of the needle inside the Cardigan Border on every other outside row an equal number of times in the last half. Start and end these increase rows this way:

♦ Work the first 6 stitches in Cardigan Border, *increase* the next stitch, work across to within the last 7 stitches, *increase* the next stitch, work the last 6 stitches in Cardigan Border.

◆ As you increased out the same number of stitches you decreased in, there should be no problem with the alignment of the flap to the body for the joining.

Buttoned Pocket

◆ When the pocket flap is halfway to the body needle, work a buttonhole (p. 33) in the Cardigan Border at each end of the flap on an outside row.

The Sweatshirt Hood

Follow the Placket Neck Sweater directions (p. 177) up to the neck ribbing. Work the neck ribbing the same as for the regular placket neck *except* put a marker on the needle *after* the stitches are worked from the first holder and before the stitches are worked from the last holder. Carry these markers throughout the neck ribbing.

◆ Work the ribbing for about an inch.

Stop at the end of an inside row.

◆ On the next outside row, bind off the stitches before the first marker; increase into every other stitch across to the second marker; work straight to the end of the row.

◆ *Turn.*

◆ On the next inside row, bind off the stitches before the remaining marker, and purl to the end of the row.

◆ *Turn.*

>>>   **Decision Point:** The attached hood may be made without a drawstring (below) or with a drawstring (next page).

Hood without Drawstring

◆ *Change to a body-size 24" needle* and, on both the outside and the inside rows, work the first and last 6 stitches in K1, P1 Cardigan Border.

◆ Work back and forth on the needle until the hood is about 5" above the ribbing, or halfway to the top of your head. On the next outside row, put a marker on the needle before the center stitch.

◆ On the next outside row, and *every other outside row,* work Raglan Seamline B (p. 42) at this marker to refine the point of the hood. (Omit this step if you want a pointed hood.)

◆ Work to the top of the hood, usually 10" above the ribbing. Or, try on the sweater and stop working when the sides of the hood meet at the top of your head—comfortably.

◆ Work the next outside row to the marker.

Stop. Break the yarn, leaving a very good yard.

◆ Thread the end through a Braidkin.

◆ Slip the remaining unworked stitches onto another needle.

The top of the hood is grafted together to produce an invisible seam. Hold the needle with the unworked stitches nearest to you—the Front Needle. Hold the needle with the worked stitches farthest from you—the Back Needle. The yarn is coming from the first stitch from the Back Needle, so you are all set to begin grafting. Refer to Grafting on p. 71.

Note: Treat the last 6 stitches on each needle—those in Cardigan Border—as 3 stitches; in other words, graft those 6 stitches two at a time, scooping a purl with a knit. True, this double-dip grafting will not look perfect, but it will keep the border stitches from widening, and they will be hidden from view once the border rolls to the inside.

Hood with Drawstring

◆ Cast 6 stitches onto the left needle.

◆ Work the 6 cast-on stitches in K1, P1 Cardigan Border, and work to the end of the row.

◆ Turn.

◆ Cast 6 stitches onto the left needle.

◆ Work the 6 cast-on stitches in Cardigan Border; work across the row to within 6 stitches of the end; work the last 6 stitches in Cardigan Border.

◆ Turn.

◆ Change to a 24" body-size needle and continue working back and forth, keeping the first and last 6 stitches of each row in Cardigan Border. One inch above the ribbing, on an outside row, work a buttonhole in the border at each end of the needle (refer to Method in the buttonholes section, p. 34).

◆ Proceed as for the hood without drawstring, beginning with the second step, "Work back and forth on the needle until the hood is about 5" above the ribbing. . . " and continuing up through the directions for grafting the top of the hood.

◆ Fold the border stitches to the inside and tack down lightly around the edge of the hood to form a casing.

◆ Run a drawstring through the casing. Either the Knitted Cord or the Twisted Cord will work (p. 53).

THE OPEN RAGLAN

Shown on p. 179

Trimmed with functional buttons and loops, the raglan seamline opening in this sweater makes for easier ons and offs—a feature that is much appreciated by occupants of all ages.

>>> **Decision Point**

◆ Work the Basic Sweater, the Crew Neck, to the first raglan seamline decrease round. To prepare for the upcoming raglan opening, plan to work Raglan Seamline C (p. 42) at the decrease seamlines. As this decrease creates a wide seamline, you might want to work another decrease style at the other three seamlines, depending on the pattern of your sweater.

◆ Work the yoke to the fourth raglan seamline decrease round.

Stop at the right front seamline.

The Set-Up

◆ Work a normal decrease round through the first half of the decrease at the left front seamline.

Stop. Read.

You will now be working back and forth on the needle. If you are working in a pattern, you may have to reverse you knits and purls on the inside rows, **and**, as the front of this sweater will be minus one row of work and also minus the second half of the decrease at the left front seamline (because you couldn't get there), you **must** work a catch-up row:

◆ With a separate length of yarn, and with the outside facing, work the unworked front: Starting with the left half of the left front seamline, slip 1, SSK (the missing decrease), work across to the right seamline.

◆ Now, back to the body yarn at the left front seamline: With the inside facing, work the inside row to the end. The end is the center of the left front seamline.

◆ Turn.

Stop. Read.

As you work back and forth on the needle, the rows will start and end in the center of the decrease at the left front seamline. Work the raglan seamline decreases in proper order, starting and ending the decrease rows this way:

Outside rows: Slip 1 (as if to purl, yarn in back), SSK, work to within 3 stitches of the end, K2 tog, K1.

Inside rows: Slip 1 (as if to purl, yarn in front), work to the end.

The Neck Shaping

- ◆ Work until 20 or 21 stitches remain to be decreased on each sleeve.

Stop at the beginning of an outside row.

- ◆ Run a scrap through all the front stitches *except for 14 on each side next to the sleeves.*

Read.

The left-side neck shaping is worked separately, and last. The body yarn is attached in a position to work this small triangle of stitches. Do not break it. If you must use the same ball to work the right side shaping first, wind off a small amount and leave it attached here.

- ◆ Slip all the stitches for the left-side neck onto a holder.
- ◆ Remove the needle from the center front stitches.
- ◆ With a new ball of yarn, and starting with the 14th stitch before the right front seamline, work a decrease row to the center of the left front seamline.
- ◆ *Turn.*
- ◆ Work an inside row. You will now be working back and forth on the needle from the right neck edge to the center of the left front seamline.
- ◆ Start the *next 4 outside rows only* as:
    Slip 1, K2 tog, work to the end.
- ◆ *Then,* continue the decreases at the raglan seamlines until the seamlines come together and the sleeves are gone.

Stop at the end of an outside row.

- ◆ Slip the stitches at the left side neck from the holder onto a body-size double-point.
- ◆ Using body-size double-points and the reserved yarn, and with the outside facing, work an outside row over these stitches:
    Slip 1, SSK, work to the end.
- ◆ Turn. Work an inside row.

Stop. Read.

You will now be working back and forth over the left-side neck stitches. To duplicate the right-side neck shaping, you must decrease at the end of the outside rows (as well as continuing the raglan decrease at the beginning):

- ◆ *End* the next 4 outside rows only:
    Work to within 3 stitches of the end, SSK, K1.

Then continue the decrease at the left front seamline until this triangle of stitches matches the shaping of the right neck edge.

Stop at the beginning of an outside row—all 2 stitches of it.

The Neck Ribbing

Using a ribbing-size 24" circular needle in your right hand:

- ◆ Knit the seamline stitches from the double-point.
- ◆ Knit into the left-side neck chain selvedge.
- ◆ Knit the stitches from the scrap (slip them onto a double-pointed needle).
- ◆ Knit into the right-side neck chain selvedge.
- ◆ Knit the back neck stitches from the body needle.

Finally, you are all back together again. Count the stitches on the needle. As the open edges of the ribbing must match,

> ***For K1, P1,*** you must have an uneven number;
> ***For K2, P2,*** you must have a number divisible by 4, plus 2.

Keeping in mind the number of stitches to adjust, if necessary, in the first row of ribbing near a seamline, ***and, thinking in reverse*** for this inside row, ***and*** substituting a slip 1 for the first stitch of your ribbing pattern:

- ◆ Start the ribbing (inside row): Slip 1 as if to purl, yarn in front (this slip subs for a purl—your next stitch is a knit for K1, P1, or another purl for K2, P2).
- ◆ Work to the end of the row, ending either P1 or P2.
- ◆ ***Turn.***
- ◆ The outside row: Slip 1 as if to purl, yarn in back (this slip subs for a knit—your next stitch is a purl for K1, P1, or another knit for K2, P2).
- ◆ Work to the end of the row, ending either K1 or K2.
- ◆ Work the neck ribbing loosely for about an inch.
- ◆ Bind off in ribbing loosely.
- ◆ Crochet button loops on the front edge of the opening.
- ◆ Sew the buttons on the back edge of the opening.

THE LOW V-NECK

In this variation of the V-neck, the opening begins with a 2-button placket, and the sides of the V veer off from there. Optional decorative buttons (and buttonholes) may be added along the sloping sides of the V.

Decision Point

<<<

◆ Work the body of the Basic Sweater (p. 94) to a depth of about 7", including the ribbing.

Stop at the right seamline.

◆ Put a marker at the left seamline.

The Set-Up for Beginning the Placket

Note: The directions assume a 6-stitch Cardigan Border on each side of the V-neck. For wider borders, refer to Placket Neck Variations, p. 182.

◆ Count the number of front stitches between the markers. You must have an even number. K2 tog before the right seam marker if you need to adjust.

◆ Tie a yarn marker around the needle at the center of the front. Check to be sure there is an equal number of stitches in each half of the front section.

◆ Starting at the right seamline, work to within 3 stitches of the center front marker.

◆ *Turn.* You now have the inside of the sweater facing you.

◆ Insert the right needle between the first two stitches on the left needle and proceed to . . .

◆ Cast 6 stitches onto the left needle.

Stop. Read.

You will now be working back and forth on the needle. If you are working in a pattern, you may have to reverse your knits and purls on the inside rows, *and*, before the next inside row, you may have to work a catch-up row (p. 114) over the unworked front stitches to the marker at the right front seamline.

◆ Purl the 6 cast-on stitches and work the inside row to the end. The end is the point where the opening has been made— 3 stitches beyond the yarn marker.

◆ *Turn.*

◆ On this next outside row, work the first 6 stitches and the last 6 stitches (the cast-ons) in K1, P1 Cardigan Border (see p. 32).

(When completed, the 6 cast-on stitches will be tacked down inside the sweater. This is the button side of the placket. The 6 stitches at the beginning of the outside rows form the buttonhole side of the placket.)

◆ Work straight for 3", keeping the first and last 6 stitches in Cardigan Border on both the inside and the outside rows. At the same time, work one buttonhole about an inch above the opening and another about 2" above the first. (Refer to Buttonholes, p. 33.)

Stop at the beginning of an outside row. **Read**.

The two buttonholes you have worked in the straight placket are the only ones that truly button. If you intend to decorate the sweater with buttons to the top of the V, you might continue the buttonholes—for effect—working one about every 2". If the sweater is to be *sans* buttons, discontinue the buttonholes after this point.

From now on, work a decrease at the neck edges every 8th row in a fine yarn, every 6th row in a medium yarn. These decreases at the neck edges start the V shaping.

◆ On the next outside row, and on every neck edge decrease row thereafter: Work the first 6 stitches in Cardigan Border, K2 tog, work across to within 8 stitches of the end, SSK, work the last 6 stitches in Cardigan Border.

◆ Continue to work back and forth on the needle, keeping the first and the last 6 stitches in Cardigan Border, and work a decrease at the neck edges every 6th or 8th row.

◆ Work the body to the underarm.

Stop at the beginning of an outside row.

The Sleeves

◆ Referring to the Basic Sweater directions, pp. 102–08, work the sleeves to the underarm.

◆ **Joining—Sleeve Preparation:** See the Basic Sweater directions, pp. 108–09.

Joining—Body Preparation

The seamline is the center of the underarm stitches; one-half are to the right, one-half are to the left. Run a scrap yarn through the underarm stitches at each side of the body. Tie loosely. The underarm stitches at each side of the body remain on both the scrap *and* the needle for the moment.

The Joining Row

- ◆ Work the outside row to the right underarm stitches.

- ◆ Remove the left needle from the underarm stitches.

- ◆ Refer to p. 110 of the Basic Sweater directions (The Joining Round) and attach the sleeves to the body.

- ◆ Work to the end of the outside row.

- ◆ Work the inside row.

Stop. Read.

You must figure how many times to work the neck edge decreases. Count the number of stitches in the right front of the sweater. Do not include the 6 stitches of the Cardigan Border in this count. Count the number of stitches on the right sleeve; divide by 2. Subtract the one-half sleeve from the right front. The difference is the number of times to decrease at each neck edge.

Once the excess number of front stitches has been decreased at the neck edge, discontinue the neck edge decreases. The remaining front stitches are decreased at the raglan seamlines.

Keep a careful count of the number of times (or stitches) you decrease at the neck edge. If you decrease too many, you will run out of front stitches before the sleeve is gone. If you decrease too few, some front stitches will remain after the sleeve is gone. The sleeve stitches and the front stitches must disappear at the same time.

- ◆ Continue working back and forth on the needle, keeping the first and last 6 stitches in Cardigan Border. *At the same time,* work a decrease at the neck edges—every 6th row in a fine yarn or every 4th row in a medium yarn—as many times as necessary, *and* start the raglan seamline decreases. As you near the top, check to be sure that your math for the V-neck shaping is on target.

Stop at the beginning of an outside row when the seamlines come together and the fronts and the sleeves are gone.

- ◆ Work the first 6 stitches in Cardigan Border, then slip them onto a holder.

- ◆ Bind off all the neck stitches, loosely, to within the last 6 stitches.

- ◆ With double-points, work back and forth over the last 6 stitches of Cardigan Border until the strip is long enough to reach the center of the back of the neck.

- ◆ Slip the other 6 stitches of Cardigan Border from the holder and, with double-points, work the strip until it is long enough to reach the center of the back of the neck.

◆ Sew the border strips to the bound-off back neck edge, and sew or graft the 6 border stitches to each other at the center of the back of the neck. If you opt to graft, treat the 6 stitches as 3; in other words, graft the 6 stitches two at a time, scooping a purl with a knit. True, this double-dip grafting will not be perfect, but to graft the 6 singly would spread them to full width, whereas grafting them two at a time preserves the ribbing with its hidden purls.

CREW NECK CARDIGAN

◆ Work a gauge sample.

◆ Determine the Key Number of stitches.

The Body Ribbing

This requires a bit more math than the usual Basic Sweater pullover, as the knit-along Cardigan Border stitches must be added to the number of stitches to cast on for the ribbing. By doing so, the front of the sweater has its full complement of stitches—none are used up for the borders.

These directions assume 6-stitch-wide Cardigan Borders, but you can make them wider, if you wish. For 8-stitch borders, add a total of 16 stitches. For 10-stitch borders, add 20 stitches.

(Now, 12, 16, or 20 stitches may seem like a large number to be adding, but remember, the borders overlap when the sweater is buttoned. Also, as the purl stitches "hide" in K1, P1 ribbing, the width of the border is further reduced to the equivalent of only 3, 4, or 5 stitches.)

The directions remain the same, *except* substitute your 8 or 10 border stitches for the 6 and add an appropriate number of K1, P1s at each end of the first row.

◆ Subtract 10% from the Key Number to determine the number of ribbing stitches. Now, adjust the number of ribbing stitches accordingly for your selected ribbing pattern:

> K1, P1 requires an uneven number of stitches.
>
> K2, P2 requires a number of stitches divisible by 4, plus 2.
>
> The adjusted number of ribbing stitches equals _____ .

◆ Add 12 stitches to this number for Cardigan Borders: _____ .

This final figure is the number of stitches to cast on to a 24" circular ribbing-size needle.

Stop. Read.

The First Row

The body of the cardigan sweater is worked back and forth in the flat on the circular needle. In order that the body cast-on presents the same face as the sleeve cast-on, a preliminary inside row must be worked. Therefore, at the outset, the 6 stitches of Cardigan Border at each end of the needle are worked as row 2.

◆ Work the preliminary row according to your chosen ribbing:

For K1, P1 ribbing—P1, K1, P1, K1, P1, K1 for Cardigan Border, then P1, K1, across to the last 7 stitches, end P1, K1, P1, K1, P1, K1, P1.

For K2, P2 ribbing— P1, K1, P1, K1, P1, K1 for Cardigan Border, then P2, K2 across to the last 8 stitches, end P2, K1, P1, K1, P1, K1, P1.

Left: *This* **Crew Neck Cardigan** *has an added Knitted Cord drawstring. The Cardigan Border is worked in K1b, P1 Twisted Rib to coordinate with the body and sleeve ribbings. Raglan Seamline E enhances the yoke, its "feathers" complementing the twisted knit stitches in the ribbing.*

Right: *The Steps and Moss pattern makes an ideal "front" for a* **Sleeveless U-Neck** *sweater (p. 136).*

The fabric was woven by Nancy Cook from the same medium-weight wool Harrisville Designs yarn used for the sweaters. (Warp color sequence: aster, cinnabar, oatmeal, oatmeal. Weft sequence: cinnabar, oatmeal, oatmeal, oatmeal.)

◆ Turn your work. The outside of the sweater is now facing you. Notice that the six stitches of Cardigan Border are now balanced with a knit, or knits, beside them—the result of figuring on an uneven number of stitches for a K1, P1 ribbing, or a number of stitches divisible by 4, plus 2, for a K2, P2 ribbing. Without this extra stitch or two, the purl of the border would be next to a purl of the ribbing.

◆ Now, refer to The Cardigan Border on pp. 32–33, and start with row 1—the outside row. Throughout the ribbing, you will be working the stitches for what they are as they face you, knitting the knits, and purling the purls, but keep an eye on the slip stitches for a neat selvedge.

◆ Work in ribbing for ½".

Stop at the beginning of an outside row.

The Buttonholes

◆ On this next outside row, work a buttonhole (p. 33) in the ribbing.

> *Woman's sweater:* Work the buttonhole at the beginning of this row.
>
> *Man's sweater:* Work the buttonhole at the end of this row.

◆ Continue the ribbing, and work one more buttonhole ½" before you intend to stop the ribbing.

◆ Then, work the ribbing to within one row of the desired depth.

Stop at the beginning of an outside row.

◆ On this last outside row of ribbing, increase the number of body stitches by 10%, spacing them evenly between the borders. The number of stitches on the needle should equal the Key Number plus 12.

The Body

The body of the sweater starts on an inside row. (Continue working the Cardigan Border on the 6 stitches at each end of the needle.)

◆ Change to the body-size needle. If you are working the body of the sweater in stockinette stitch, purl the stitches between the borders for this inside row. If you are working in a pattern, you are on your own.

Stop at the beginning of the next outside row.

To position the right and left seamline markers, refer to the *Key Number* of stitches. Do not include the 12 Cardigan Border stitches; these are excess to the front—6 on each side.

◆ Divide the Key Number by 2 to find the number of stitches in the back and the front. Then divide the front by 2 to give the number of stitches in each side front.

◆ As you work this next outside row, put markers at the side seams. Remember, do not start counting the front stitches until you are past the Cardigan Border.

◆ Continue working back and forth on the needle, keeping the first and last 6 stitches in Cardigan Border, **and** continue working buttonholes. About 3" above the ribbing, **stop** at the beginning of an outside row.

Checkpoint   <<<

Slip half of the stitches onto a spare circular needle. This move opens the sweater to its full width so you can check your gauge. In a cardigan sweater, there is less chance of a gauge change, as the sweater is worked back and forth the same as the gauge sample.

◆ Measure the full width of the body. If in doubt, wrap the piece around you. Remember that the ribbing is still holding the body in somewhat.

◆ If all is well, slip the stitches back on the body needle and work to the underarm.

Stop at the beginning of an outside row. Do not break the body yarn. Start the sleeves with a new ball.

The Sleeves

◆ Referring to the Basic Sweater directions, p. 102, work the sleeves to the underarm.

◆ **Joining—Sleeve Preparation:** See the Basic Sweater directions, p. 108.

Joining—Body Preparation

The left and right seamlines mark the center of the underarm stitches on each side. One-half are to the right; one-half are to the left. Run a scrap yarn through the underarm stitches at each side of the body. Tie loosely. The underarm stitches at each side of the body remain on **both** the scrap and the needle for the moment.

The Joining Row

◆ Work the outside row to the right underarm stitches.

◆ Remove the left needle from the underarm stitches.

- ◆ Referring to the Basic Sweater directions for The Joining Round (p. 108), attach the sleeves to the body.
- ◆ Work to the end of the outside row.
- ◆ Work the inside row.

Stop. Read.

- ◆ Continue working back and forth on the needle, keeping the first and last 6 stitches in Cardigan Border, and, after the straight 1½" have been worked, start the decreases at the raglan seamlines.
- ◆ Work until 20 or 21 stitches remain to be decreased on each sleeve.

Stop at the beginning of an outside row.

The Neck Shaping and the Neck Ribbing

Refer to the Placket Neck directions, p. 178.

CREW NECK LACED CARDIGAN

Shown on p. 176

For a pleasing decorative effect, a Crew Neck Cardigan may be worked with paired buttonholes in the Cardigan Borders, then laced like a shoe.

- ◆ Follow the directions for the Crew Neck Cardigan, beginning on p. 194, but instead of making one front edge with buttonholes and the other with buttons, work a buttonhole in the Cardigan Border at *each* side front on an outside row, following the buttonhole directions on p. 196 for both Woman's and Man's.
- ◆ For the lacing, work 80" (or more) of Knitted Cord (p. 53) or other cord of your choice.

CREW NECK CARDIGAN WITH SEAGULL PATTERN

These big birds are shown on a hefty cardigan—great for cool days by the shore. The gulls parade around body and sleeves just before the joining row. Since this is a cardigan, the birds are worked in flat knitting on the body; however, on the sleeves they are worked in the round. Conceivably, they could be placed anywhere (except the yoke), possibly lower down as a border on the body and sleeves, or just one bird could be worked with Swiss Darning.

The gull is 21 stitches wide, so allow for a multiple of at least 22 stitches in order to have one stitch for separation. Its skinny 4-row legs are Swiss-Darned after the fact, covering only half a stitch (covering a whole stitch would make them too fat). Including 3 rows for the "waves" in which it is wading, this proud bird stands 20 rows/rounds high.

An oversize cardigan is a fitting roost for an oversize bird. Note the placement of these gulls, just below the joining of the body and sleeves; they are much too big to settle in the yoke. The sweater is knit of a blue/tan tweed wool from Bartlettyarns, with a natural white band as backdrop for the birds.

Also note the two buttonholes in the body ribbing—a must for the start of a neat closure, leaving no "gaposis" between the body ribbing and the body.

For flat knitting, read the graph from the bottom up, working the first row from right to left and the next from left to right. In round knitting, read every row of the graph from right to left.

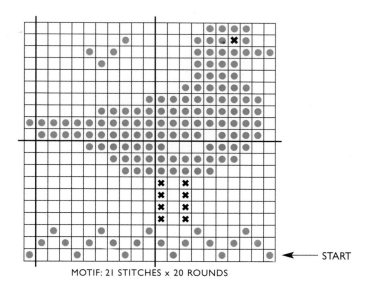

MOTIF: 21 STITCHES x 20 ROUNDS

Or, if you prefer the written word: For flat knitting, work the rows as written, *adding* one or more stitches for separation. For round knitting, work the even-numbered rows in reverse, again *adding* one or more stitches for separation.

Note: The written directions below do not include the 3 rows/ rounds of "waves" or the rows/rounds for the legs; the graph is easy to follow for those. Row 1 is the beginning of the gull's body.

The Seagull Design for Flat Knitting: A multiple of 21 stitches. Repeat * to * across row or round, adding one separator stitch (or more) between birds.

Row 1: *5L, 8D, 8L*

Row 2: *7L, 11D, 3L*

Row 3: *2L, 4D, 3L, 7D, 5L*

Row 4: *1L, 14D, 1L, 4D, 1L*

Row 5: *1L, 20D*

Row 6: *6L, 14D, 1L*

Row 7: *1L, 10D, 10L*

Row 8: *13L, 6D, 2L*

Row 9: *3L, 4D, 14L*

Row 10: *6L, 1D, 7L, 4D, 3L*

Row 11: *7D, 6L, 1D, 1L, 1D, 5L*

Row 12: *8L, 1D, 5L, 3D, 1L, 1D, 2L*

Row 13: *2L, 4D, 15L*

V-NECK CARDIGAN

Front: *The ribbings on this **V-Neck Cardigan** are K1b, P1 Twisted Rib, which is the best choice for a knit-along Cardigan Border.*

Back: *The pullover's simple Harris Tweed stitch (p. 129) pattern is ideal for a reversible sweater. Raglan Seamline A shapes the yoke so as to avoid a prominent seamline interrupting the sequence of the pattern. Both sweaters are knit from yarn handspun by the author.*

>>>   **Decision Point**

♦ Work the Cardigan Sweater (p. 194) to the start of the first raglan decrease row.

Stop. Read. Find a pencil.

One stitch is decreased at the neck edges of every other outside row, or every 4th row—however you want to think of it. You must figure how many times to work the neck edge decreases:

♦ Count the number of stitches in the right front. Do not include the 6-stitch border in this count.

♦ Also count the number of stitches on one sleeve and divide that number by 2.

♦ Subtract the one-half sleeve from the right front. The difference is the number of times to decrease at each neck edge.

Once the excess number of stitches on each side front has been decreased at the neck edge, you will discontinue working neck edge decreases. The remaining front stitches are decreased at the raglan seamline.

Keep a careful count of the number of times (stitches) you decrease at the neck edge. If you decrease too many, you will run out of front stitches before the sleeve is gone. If you decrease too few, you will have front stitches remaining after the sleeve is gone. The sleeve stitches and the front stitches must disappear at the same time.

♦ On this next outside row, work a decrease at the neck edges *and* start the raglan seamline decreases. Continue working neck decreases every other outside row thereafter for as many times as necessary.

♦ Start and end the neck edge decrease rows this way: Work the first 6 stitches in Cardigan Border, K2 tog, work to within the last 8 stitches, SSK, work the last 6 stitches in Cardigan Border.

As the raglan seamline decreases are worked every 4th row for a while, and the neck edge decreases are also worked every 4th row, combining them in this outside row starts you off in orderly fashion and gives you 3 straight rows to follow. Once the raglan seamline decreases start their every-other-row sequence, this respite of 3 straight rows will end.

♦ Continue working the raglan seamline decreases in their proper order, and the neck edge decreases every 4th row as many times as necessary until the seamlines come together and the sleeves are gone. Do not decrease into the Cardigan Border stitches.

Stop at the beginning of an outside row.

◆ Work the first 6 stitches in Cardigan Border, then slip them onto a holder.

◆ Bind off all the neck stitches, loosely, to within the last 6 stitches.

◆ With double-points, work back and forth over the last 6 stitches of Cardigan Border until the strip is long enough to reach the center of the back of the neck. Slip these 6 stitches onto a holder.

◆ Slip the first 6 stitches of Cardigan Border from the holder and, with double-points, work the strip until it also is long enough to reach the center of the back of the neck. Slip these 6 stitches onto a holder.

◆ Sew the border strips to the bound-off back neck edge, and sew or graft the 6 end stitches to each other at the center of the back of the neck. If you opt to graft, treat the 6 stitches as 3; in other words, graft the 6 two at a time, scooping a purl with a knit. True, this double-dip grafting will not be perfect, but to graft the 6 singly would spread them to full width. Grafting them two at a time preserves the ribbing with its hidden purls.

THE HAPPY SWEATER

Shown on p. 204

The Happy Sweater is truly a case of one thing leading to another. If you look closely at the Crew Neck Sweater with Two-Color Sleeve Designs (p. 149), you'll see that the small motif that borders the large sleeve design resembles little "smiles"—little smiles that can fill a sweater with color and at the same time use up lots of yarn scraps. (This cheery motif is adapted from Dover Publications' *Needlework and Alphabet Designs*.) The crescents can be oriented to smile either at the wearer—as in the photo—or at the rest of the world, by working the graph in reverse. You might even choose a half-and-half arrangement, alternating the bands of crescents so that half look at the world and half smile at you.

Filling a sweater, yoke and all, with two-color knitting means having to switch from the raglan style, but even though the drop-shoulder style means working back and forth for the yoke, you can still calculate your dimensions using the same percentage system as for raglan-style sweaters.

◆ Follow the directions for the Basic Sweater (p. 94) up to the underarm.

The Happy Sweater. *Well, it really is all in how you look at it. In this model, the wearer (most likely the knitter) can look down at the little smiles and feel very happy that all those scrap yarns in many colors are now out of the basket and into a cheerful sweater. If you would rather that the rest of the population see the crescents as smileys rather than frownies, simply work the graph upside down. Of course, a third option is to work smileys in one round and frownies in the next—just as long as everyone is happy!*

The drop-shoulder construction is one of three included in this book—a departure from the raglan. In this case, it is due to all the two-color work in the yoke. And, yes, it does mean you are working two-color knitting in the flat from the underarm to the shoulder, but that little distance should be manageable.

The sleeves are the full style, to accommodate the design, and 4 stitches are decreased at the neck edges when shaping the crew neckline.

◆ Slip the sweater front stitches onto an extra needle.

Stop. Read.

You now will be working flat rows, beginning with the back, while the front stitches are left on hold. ***Remember to work a chain selvedge stitch*** (p. 31) at the armhole edges, keeping the 3 edge stitches in the background color. By working the back of the sweater first, you will know when to start the neck shaping for the front—approximately 3 inches shy of the height of the back.

◆ Work the back until it is the desired length to top of shoulder. Put the back stitches on hold on an extra needle.

◆ Return to the sweater front stitches, slipping them onto a body-size needle (if they aren't already on one). Work back and forth until the front measures about 3 inches shorter than the back, stopping ***after an outside row***.

Stop. Read.

Try to begin the front neck shaping after completing one set of smiles. When you reach that point, divide the front into 3 sections with markers as you work the next *inside* row. ***Note:*** These are not equal divisions; instead, include 4 to 6 additional stitches (depending on diameter of yarn) in each of the two shoulder sections. These additional stitches will be decreased for the neck shaping: one stitch on each side of the neck in every other row. The right and left shoulder sections are worked separately.

◆ Starting on the next (outside) row, work across the left shoulder stitches to within 3 stitches of the marker, SSK, K1.

◆ Slip the center section of stitches, the front neck, onto a piece of scrap yarn. Slip the right shoulder stitches onto another needle or a holder.

◆ ***Turn*** and work an outside row.

◆ Work the neck edge decrease 3 or more times, depending on the number of stitches you allowed for the neck shaping.

◆ Continue working the left shoulder straight until it matches the height of the back, ending after an inside row. Break the yarn, leaving a yard-long tail for shoulder grafting.

◆ Tie in the yarn on the outside row at the neck edge of the right shoulder. Start this row as Sl1, K2 tog, then work to the end.

◆ Continue as for the left shoulder, decreasing at the neck edge 3 or more times. Then work the right shoulder straight until it matches the height of the back, ending after an inside row. Break the yarn, leaving a yard-long tail for shoulder grafting.

◆ Divide the back stitches into thirds with markers. Graft front and back shoulders together using Kitchener stitch (p. 71), working from the shoulder edges in toward the neck edges.

♦ With a 16" ribbing-size needle, knit into the left-side neck chain selvedge, knit the center stitches from the scrap, knit into the right-side neck chain selvedge, and knit the back neck stitches from the needle. Work the neck ribbing for about an inch and bind off in ribbing.

To add sleeves to this now sleeveless sweater, knit into the chain selvedge around the armholes (you **did** work the chain selvedge, didn't you?). Count the number of knit-up stitches and add (or subtract) by increasing (or decreasing) in the next round to achieve your usual number of upper-arm stitches. Work the sleeves from the top down, decreasing to the required cuff number. Be sure to follow the pattern graph *in reverse order*, so the smiles on the sleeves will be oriented the same as those on the body.

Pattern

The smiles are only 7 stitches wide, with 3 spacer stitches, for a total of 10 stitches per pattern repeat: a multiple that will fit into most any Key Number. They are 5 rows/rounds high, with 2 rows/rounds of plain knitting between, and because they are arranged in staggered bands, this makes a total of a 14-row/round repeat.

Repeat * to * across rounds/rows. *Note:* For flat knitting in the yoke, reverse the even-numbered rounds.

Round 1: *1D, 2L, 1D, 2L, 4D*
Round 2: *2L, 3D, 2L, 3D*
Round 3: *3L, 1D, 3L, 3D*
Round 4: *1D, 5L, 4D*
Round 5: *3D, 1L, 6D*
Round 6: *10D*
Round 7: *10D*
Round 8: *1L, 5D, 2L, 1D, 1L*
Round 9: *2L, 3D, 2L, 3D*
Round 10: *2L, 3D, 3L, 1D, 1L*
Round 11: *1L, 5D, 4L*
Round 12: *8D, 1L, 1D*
Round 13: *10D*
Round 14: *10D*

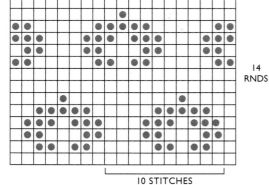

14 RNDS

10 STITCHES

● pattern
☐ background

In the photographed sweater and the written directions at right, the background is dark (D) and the pattern motifs are light (L).

JANETTA DEXTER SAMPLER SWEATER

Over the years, Janetta Dexter did us all a great favor—she collected tried and true two-color knitting designs from knitters throughout her native Nova Scotia. The resulting book, *Traditional Nova Scotian Knitting Patterns*, was first published by the Nova Scotia Museum in 1985. (Now available from Nimbus Publishing Company Ltd., 3731 Mackintosh Street, P.O. Box 9501, Station A, Halifax, Nova Scotia, Canada B3K 5N5.)

The appeal of these traditional patterns is that, for the most part, they have tiny multiples and therefore will make pleasing designs in small projects such as mittens and hats. (Many of you are already familiar with these designs from Robin Hansen's mitten books, *Fox and Geese and Fences*, and *Flying Geese and Partridge Feet*.) A further benefit of these tiny multiples is that they do not require a long carrying of the waiting yarn. You will notice that even in the patterns with large multiples of 14 or 18 stitches, the contrasting yarn is kept waiting for only a stitch—or two or three—before being worked. The result is that, even in the larger multiples, the "carrys" are very short, which makes for quick and easy

Though 15 of Janetta Dexter's splendid and sensible double-knitting patterns arranged themselves in this drop-shoulder sweater, 8 more of her patterns had to be left behind, with regret. It is plain to see why these patterns have stood the test of time—they are straightforward, handsome, and simple to work. Their distinctiveness is strikingly evident as they are worked in Bartlettyarns' 2-ply Fisherman wool— midnight against oatmeal.

two-color work and does away with the long strandings that so often catch in the fingers when putting the garment on and off.

Janetta always has described these patterns as "double-knitting patterns," as the two-color work indeed renders a double-thick fabric; a decorative method of achieving extra warmth.

Sweater Construction

Figure your gauge for your Key Number. Use the drop-shoulder method as described in the Happy Sweater directions (p. 204).

For the Kitchener-stitch grafting at the shoulders, refer to the Sampler instructions, p. 71. However, as this sweater is quite sturdy, with all the two-color knitting, you may prefer a less stretchy seam made by binding off the shoulder stitches together and thus connecting the back and the front.

METHOD

♦ Hold the needles parallel, with the purl sides of the fabric together. With a third needle, enter the first stitch on the front needle and the first stitch on the back needle, and knit them off together. Repeat with the next stitches on each needle, then pass the first stitch over the second stitch. Continue knitting off together the first two stitches on each needle and passing the first stitch over the second.

The resulting knitted seam is a ridge with a knit stitch facing you as you work and therefore a purl stitch on the back side of the ridge. In order that the shoulder seams are identical, work the bind-off in the same direction all the way across the sweater, i.e., from one shoulder edge to the neck, then from the neck to the edge of the other shoulder.

This is particularly important if you choose to accent the ridge by using the contrast color. As you can readily see in the photo, the denim color at the shoulder seam bind-off was worked from the shoulders in toward the neck on both sides; thus, one shoulder has purl ridges facing toward the front of the sweater and the other shoulder has knit stitches facing toward the front—a word to the wise, unless you are not bound to be symmetrical.

Of course, in this drop-shoulder sweater the few 2-color patterns in the yoke have to be worked back and forth: knitting a row, purling a row. However, the bulk of the sweater is worked in the round.

Planning the Patterns

It is an exciting challenge to settle on a Key Number that is divisible by many smaller numbers. Take 180 body stitches, for example: It is evenly divisible by 2, 3, 4, 5, 6, and 9, and is only off by 2 stitches for a divisor of 7 and off by 4 stitches for a divisor of 8.

For a Key Number of body stitches of 180, 64 stitches would be the number for the sleeves, and 64 is divisible by 2, 4, and 8, but only off by 1 stitch for a divisor of 3 or 5, and off by only 4 for a divisor of 6 stitches.

(Another number that is a joy to work with is 96; being divisible by 2, 3, 4, 6, and 8, and only off by 1 stitch for a divisor of 5 or by 2 stitches for a divisor of 7.)

The Sampler Sweater presented here includes Janetta's patterns in the following order:

The Body (from the ribbing up)

Zig-Zag	a multiple of 4
Houndstooth	a multiple of 4
Flying Geese	a multiple of 10

The Yoke

Old German Pattern	a multiple of 5
Goose Eye	a multiple of 18

The Left Sleeve (from the top down)

Checkerboard	a multiple of 6
Double Diamond	a multiple of 12
Sawtooth Variant	a multiple of 4
Maplewood	a multiple of 14
Pinwheels	a multiple of 6

The Right Sleeve (from the top down)

Sawtooth	a multiple of 5
Fox and Geese	a multiple of 6
Snail's Trail & Fleur-de-Lis	a multiple of 4
Candlelit Windows	a multiple of 14
Broken Stripes	a multiple of 4

As you can see, by juggling—increasing or decreasing a few stitches in the plain stockinette sections between patterns (in this case 5 rounds/rows)—the designs are amazingly eager to jump into whatever number you can make available to them. So, as they say, "go figure," have fun, and produce a wondrous sampler sweater from Janetta's significant designs.

Note: Though Janetta's directions are labeled for "rows" in her original booklet, they are here labeled and written for round knitting, with alternative flat-knitting directions given only for the two yoke patterns. If you prefer to work from the graphs, read them from the bottom to the top and from right to left for every round. However, for the yoke of this sweater (or any other project where you'll be working back and forth), you'll still read the graph from bottom to top, and you'll need to work the even-numbered rows from left to right.

Janetta Dexter's Patterns

The Body

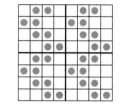

REPEAT: 4 STITCHES, 4 ROUNDS

Zig-Zag: A multiple of 4 stitches, a repeat of 4 rounds.

    Round 1: (2D, 2L).
    Round 2: (1L, 2D, 1L).
    Round 3: (2L, 2D).
    Round 4: Same as round 2.

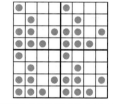

REPEAT: 4 STITCHES, 4 ROUNDS

Houndstooth: A multiple of 4 stitches, a repeat of 4 rounds.

    Round 1: (1L, 3D).
    Round 2: (1D, 1L, 2D).
    Round 3: (2L, 1D, 1L).
    Round 4: (3L, 1D).

REPEAT: 10 STITCHES, 4 ROUNDS

Flying Geese: A multiple of 10 stitches, a repeat of 4 rounds.

    Round 1: (1L, 3D, 1L, 3D, 1L, 1D).
    Round 2: (2L, 2D, 1L, 2D, 2L, 1D).
    Round 3: (3L, 1D, 1L, 1D, 3L, 1D).
    Round 4: (4L, 1D, 4L, 1D).

The Left Sleeve

Checkerboard: A multiple of 6 stitches.
>>**Rounds 1, 2, and 3:** (3D, 3L).
>>**Rounds 4, 5, and 6:** (3L, 3D).

REPEAT: 6 STITCHES, 6 ROUNDS

Double Diamond:
>A multiple of 12 stitches, a repeat of 12 rounds.
>>**Round 1:** (2L, 2D, 2L, 1D, 2L, 2D, 1L).
>>**Round 2:** (1L, 2D, 2L, 1D, 1L, 1D, 2L, 2D).
>>**Round 3:** (2D, 2L, 1D, 3L, 1D, 2L, 1D).
>>**Round 4:** (1D, 2L) 4 times.
>>**Round 5:** (2L, 1D, 2L, 3D, 2L, 1D, 1L).
>>**Round 6:** (1L, 1D, 2L, 2D, 1L, 2D, 2L, 1D).
>>**Round 7:** (1D, 2L, 2D, 3L, 2D, 2L). This is the center of the diamond.
>>**Round 8:** Same as round 6.
>>**Round 9:** Same as round 5.
>>**Round 10:** Same as round 4.
>>**Round 11:** Same as round 3.
>>**Round 12:** Same as round 2.
>Repeat rounds 1–12 as many times as desired.

REPEAT: 12 STITCHES, 12 ROUNDS

Sawtooth Variant: A multiple of 4 stitches, a repeat of 6 rounds.
>>**Round 1:** (3L, 1D).
>>**Round 2:** (2L, 2D).
>>**Round 3:** (1L, 3D).
>>**Round 4:** (1D, 3L).
>>**Round 5:** (2L, 2D).
>>**Round 6:** (3D, 1L).

REPEAT: 4 STITCHES, 6 ROUNDS

REPEAT: 14 STITCHES, 10 ROUNDS

Maplewood: A multiple of 14 stitches, a repeat of 10 rounds.

Round 1: (3L, 1D, 3L, 3D, 1L, 3D).
Round 2: (2L, 3D, 2L, 2D, 3L, 2D).
Round 3: (1L, 5D, 1L, 1D, 5L, 1D).
Round 4: Same as round 2.
Round 5: Same as round 1.
Round 6: (3D, 1L, 3D, 3L, 1D, 3L).
Round 7: (2D, 3L, 2D, 2L, 3D, 2L).
Round 8: (1D, 5L, 1D, 1L, 5D, 1L).
Round 9: Same as round 7.
Round 10: Same as round 6.

REPEAT: 6 STITCHES, 8 ROUNDS

Pinwheels: A multiple of 6 stitches, a repeat of 8 rounds.

Round 1: (3L, 3D).
Round 2: (1D, 2L, 2D, 1L).
Round 3: (2D, 1L, 1D, 2L).
Round 4: (3D, 3L).
Round 5: (3L, 3D).
Round 6: (2L, 1D, 1L, 2D).
Round 7: (1L, 2D, 2L, 1D).
Round 8: (3D, 3L).

The Right Sleeve

REPEAT: 5 STITCHES, 6 ROUNDS

Sawtooth: A multiple of 5 stitches, a repeat of 6 rounds.

Round 1: All L.
Round 2: (1D, 4L).
Round 3: (2D, 3L).
Round 4: (3D, 2L).
Round 5: (4D, 1L).
Round 6: All D.

Fox and Geese: A multiple of 6 stitches, a repeat of 6 rounds.

    Round 1: All D.

    Round 2: (2D, 3L, 1D).

    Round 3: (1D, 1L) 3 times.

    Round 4: (1D, 2L, 1D, 2L).

    Round 5: Same as round 3.

    Round 6: Same as round 2.

REPEAT: 6 STITCHES, 6 ROUNDS

Snail's Trail & Fleur-de-Lis:

A multiple of 4 stitches, a 9-round border.

    Round 1: (1L, 3D).

    Round 2: (2D, 1L, 1D).

    Round 3: All L.

    Round 4: (2L, 1D, 1L).

    Round 5: (1L, 3D).

    Round 6: Same as round 4.

    Round 7: All L.

    Round 8: Same as round 2.

    Round 9: Same as round 1.

REPEAT: 4 STITCHES
A 9-ROUND BORDER

Candlelit Windows: A multiple of 8 stitches, a repeat of 8 rounds.

    Round 1: All D.

    Round 2: (3L, 1D, 1L, 1D, 1L, 1D).

    Round 3: (3L, 2D, 1L, 2D).

    Round 4: Same as round 2.

    Round 5: All D.

    Round 6: (1L, 1D, 1L, 1D, 3L, 1D).

    Round 7: (1D, 1L, 2D, 3L, 1D).

    Round 8: Same as round 6.

REPEAT: 8 STITCHES, 8 ROUNDS

REPEAT: 4 STITCHES, 2 ROUNDS

Broken Stripes: A multiple of 4 stitches, a repeat of 2 rounds.

    Round 1: (2D, 2L).

    Round 2: (1L, 2D, 1L).

    Repeat as many times as desired.

The Yoke

Note: In the featured drop-shoulder sweater, the yoke is worked in the flat (rows), so the following written directions are presented both in the round and in the flat.

Old German Pattern:

REPEAT: 5 STITCHES, 9 ROUNDS

    A multiple of 5 stitches, 9-round/row repeat.

    Round 1: (2L, 2D, 1L).

    Round 2: (1L, 1D, 2L, 1D).

    Round 3: Same as round 2.

    Round 4: Same as round 2.

    Round 5: Same as round 1.

    Round 6: (2D, 2L, 1D).

    Round 7: Same as round 1.

    Round 8: Same as round 1.

    Round 9: Same as round 6.

    Repeat as many times as desired.

    Row 1: (2L, 2D, 1L).

    Row 2: (1D, 2L, 1D, 1L).

    Row 3: (1L, 1D, 2L, 1D).

    Row 4: Same as row 2.

    Row 5: Same as row 1.

    Row 6: (1D, 2L, 2D).

    Row 7: Same as row 1.

    Row 8: (1L, 2D, 2L).

    Row 9: (2D, 2L, 1D).

Goose Eye: A multiple of 18 stitches, a repeat of 16 rounds/rows.

    Round 1: (1D, 2L, 2D, 2L, 3D, 2L, 2D, 2L, 2D).
    Round 2: (2D, 2L, 2D, 2L, 1D, 2L, 2D, 2L, 2D, 1L).
    Round 3: (1L, 2D, 2L, 2D, 3L, 2D, 2L, 2D, 2L).
    Round 4: (2L, 2D, 2L, 2D, 1L, 2D, 2L, 2D, 2L, 1D).
    Round 5: Same as round 1.
    Round 6: Same as round 2.
    Round 7: Same as round 3.
    Round 8: Same as round 4.
    Round 9: Same as round 1.
Work rounds 8 to 2 in reverse to complete pattern.

    Row 1: (1D, 2L, 2D, 2L, 3D, 2L, 2D, 2L, 2D).
    Row 2: (1L, 2D, 2L, 2D, 2L, 1D, 2L, 2D, 2L, 2D).
    Row 3: (1L, 2D, 2L, 2D, 3L, 2D, 2L, 2D, 2L).
    Row 4: (1D, 2L, 2D, 2L, 2D, 1L, 2D, 2L, 2D, 2L).
    Row 5: Same as row 1.
    Row 6: Same as row 2.
    Row 7: Same as row 3.
    Row 8: Same as row 4.
    Row 9: Same as row 1.
Work rows 8 to 2 in reverse to complete pattern.

REPEAT: 18 STITCHES, 16 ROUNDS

THE PATCHWORK SWEATER

Shown on p. 216

Circular knitting limits the working of a single-color design or motif into the fabric because the yarn remains at the last stitch for which it was used, and when you have knit around to the design/motif again, the yarn is not there—it's at the rear end of whatever it is you are attempting to add. Mary Thomas mentions a solution in *Mary Thomas's Knitting Book* on p. 111, where she discusses tartan patterns. She suggests that tartan patterns can be worked in the round provided that the knitting is turned after each round. To quote: "[A]fter completing a round, knit to the seam stitch, knit this[,] turn, slip it, and purl back in pattern." Without Mary looking over our shoulder to explain further, this method causes a separation of the work, but it does start one thinking of a means to accomplish the feat of creating a seamless sweater while working back and forth. (Thank you, Christajo Lowes, of West Cork, Ireland, for instigating this thought process.)

The Patchwork Sweater is the result of this thinking. It uses two

*The **Patchwork Sweater**. With its Key Number of stitches divided into fourths and four colors at the ready, this drop-shoulder sweater starts off by working the body to the underarms back and forth in the round to preserve its seamlessness. By working in this seemingly contradictory manner, you'll find that the patchwork color you need is always right there waiting for you, rather than being at the tail end of that section from the previous round. The front and back sections of the yoke are worked separately in the flat. The sleeve stitches are knitted up around the armhole and worked in the round to the cuff, with blocks of the same color going all the way around. It is the combination of the three methods of knitting that produces the seamless sweater of patchwork blocks.*

stitches knit together at the right seamline, which does cause a bit of irregularity, but it is a consistent irregularity and no worse than a sewn seam. It may not appeal to perfectionists who are bothered by jogs at the seamline, but does anyone really look that closely? And what fun to be knitting back and forth in the round.

For practice, this sweater uses the "K2 tog" technique only in the body, as it is a simple drop-shoulder style with the yoke worked flat—the back, then the front. It features a boat neck (p. 172) and the full sleeve (p. 106).

Body

Work your ribbing as for the Basic Sweater (p. 99). Your Key Number of stitches should be divisible by four to work the sweater in four colors or four yarns, so adjust, if necessary, in the last round of ribbing.

Change to body-size needle and work a set-up round as follows, remembering that you are working across the back of the sweater first: With color A, knit one-quarter of your stitches, putting a marker after the first stitch; work the next quarter with color B;

work the next quarter with color C; then work the last quarter with color D, putting a marker on the needle before the last stitch in this section. (Your right seamline, between colors A and D, is flanked by the two markers; this is where you will knit two stitches together each time you turn your work. The left seamline is the boundary of colors B and C.)

Now, knit the last color D stitch together with the first color A stitch, using the D yarn. With the tip of the left needle, pick up the strand of A yarn from the K2 tog stitch and put it on the left needle. Turn your work.

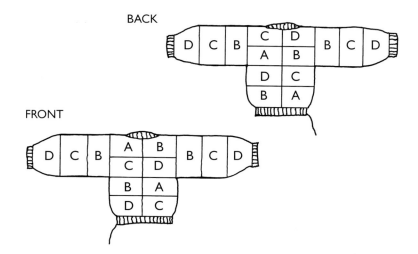

Color blocks layout for the Patchwork Sweater

From now on, you'll be alternating an "inside" round with an "outside" round. Bring the new colors under the old at all color changes except the right seamline, which takes care of itself with the following directions:

Inside Rounds: Purl 1 color D stitch, slip marker, purl remaining color D stitches; with color C, purl established C stitches; with color B, purl established B stitches; with color A, purl established A stitches to marker, slip marker. Purl the next A stitch together with next D stitch, using A yarn. With the tip of the left needle, pick up the strand of D yarn from the K2 tog stitch and put it on the left needle. Turn your work.

Outside Rounds: Knit 1 color A stitch, slip marker, knit remaining color A stitches; with color B, knit established B stitches; with color C, knit established C stitches; with color D, knit to marker, slip marker. Knit the last D stitch together with the first A stitch, using the D yarn. With the tip of the left needle, pick up the strand of A yarn from the K2 tog stitch and put it on the left needle. Turn your work.

Continue alternating inside and outside rounds for the desired depth of blocks (one-quarter the length of the sweater, in the example shown), then switch colors on the next outside round, substituting C for A, D for B, A for C, B for D, or at your pleasure.

Work to the underarm, stopping at the right seamline after an inside round. Turn your work.

Yoke

Divide the front and back: Starting at the right seamline, change colors and work around to the left seamline. Slip the sweater front stitches onto a holding needle. Work "in the flat" on the sweater back stitches, slipping the first stitch of every row as if to purl (yarn in back on the knit rows, yarn in front on the purl rows). Change colors at the halfway point to the shoulder, or whenever.

Work the back stitches to the top of the shoulder, ending with a purl row. Break the working yarn, leaving a yard-long tail for shoulder grafting. Break and secure the middle yarn. Put the back stitches on a holding needle.

Work the sweater front stitches in the same manner to the top of the shoulder, ending with a knit row. Do not break the working yarn.

Using the reserved lengths of yarn at the shoulder edges, graft one-third of the front stitches to one-third of the back stitches for each shoulder, working from the outer shoulder in toward the neck edge. (See p. 71 for grafting technique.)

The Neck Ribbing

Starting at the left neck edge, and using your choice of color, knit around all neck stitches remaining on the front and back needles, picking up an extra two or three stitches at the neck edges where the grafting ends. Work an inch of ribbing and bind off.

Sleeves

The sleeves can be worked the same as the body, i.e., knitting "back and forth in the round" with two (or more) colors so the front and back of the sleeves are different colors, or they may be simply worked in broad one-color stripes, as shown in the photograph.

With your choice of color and a circular needle, and starting at the base of the armhole, knit into the chain selvedge all around the armhole. On the next round, add (or subtract) by increasing (or decreasing) to the required number of upper-arm stitches. Work the full sleeve (p. 106), decreasing in the last round to the required number of stitches for the cuff ribbing. Change to ribbing-size double-pointed needles and work the ribbing. Bind off loosely in ribbing.

Using This Technique for Other Designs

This technique is also helpful for sweaters with a single background color and motif(s) in contrast color(s). You will isolate two right-side seamline stitches just as described here, though in this case both stitches would be the same color. Knit the seamline stitches together and lift one strand to put on the left needle, turn, and work the inside and outside rounds in the same manner as for the Patchwork pattern described above. The working end of your different-color yarn will always be right where you need it—or very nearby, depending on your design.

THE INFANT VEST

This tiny sleeveless vest keeps baby's back snug and warm while allowing those busy arms the freedom to explore the air. The straight welt version "grows," and may still fit as he/she begins to crawl around on cold floors. Both patterns are reversible—no seams. The vest is knit back and forth, beginning on a circular needle.

Yarn: 3 ounces Bartlettyarns' 2-ply Fisherman, or similar
       heavy worsted-weight yarn

Needles: one #6 24-inch circular, two #6 double-pointed

Note: The vest may be worked in either the Waved Welt or the Straight Welt pattern. (Waved Welt is from *Reader's Digest Complete Book of Needlework*, 1979.)

Waved Welt: A multiple of 8, plus 1. Repeat * to *.

Row 1: Slip 1 (yib),*K7, P1*.
Row 2: Slip 1 (yib), K1, *P5, K3* ending P5, K2.
Row 3: Slip 1 (yif), P2, *K3, P5* ending K3, P3.
Row 4: Slip 1 (yib), K3, *P1, K7* ending P1, K4.
Row 5: Slip 1 (yif), *P7, K1*.
Row 6: Slip 1 (yif), P1, *K5, P3* ending K5, P2.
Row 7: Slip 1 (yib), K2, *P3, K5* ending P3, K3.
Row 8: Slip 1 (yif), P3, *K1, P7* ending K1, P4.

*The **Infant Vest** at the top is knit in a Straight Welt pattern—the purl stitches are hiding. As the baby grows, the vest may be elongated by washing it and lightly steaming the purl stitches into view. The Waved Welt (bottom) holds itself more open, as the knits and purls wave up and down.*

Straight Welt. No multiple.

> **Row 1:** Slip 1 (yif), knit across.
> **Row 2:** Slip 1 (yif), purl across.
> **Row 3:** Slip 1 (yib), knit across.
> **Row 4:** Slip 1 (yif), purl across.
> **Row 5:** Slip 1 (yib), purl across.
> **Row 6:** Slip 1 (yib), knit across.
> **Row 7:** Slip 1 (yif), purl across.
> **Row 8:** Slip 1 (yib), knit across.

Body

- Cast 81 stitches onto circular needle. Work a preliminary row of knit before starting pattern, to keep the bottom edge from curling.

- Slip all first stitches as if to purl, with the yarn either in the front (yif) or in the back (yib), as specified, for the chain selvedge.

- Work the 8 rows of pattern 5 to 7 times, depending on desired length. *Mark the outside rows with a safety pin* as soon as possible. (The odd-numbered rows are the outside rows.)

- On the next outside row, work 20 stitches, then slip them onto a holder (right front). Work across the next 41 stitches (back), then slip the remaining 20 stitches onto a holder (left front).

For Waved Welt pattern only: After the division of the fronts from the back, this pattern will not work as written. The "waves" dip up and down in bands of 4 knits and 4 purls. At the beginning of each subsequent row, visually locate the multiple and count back in pattern to find the correct starting point.

Back

- Starting with row 2 (the inside row), continue in pattern over the 41 back stitches, decreasing 1 stitch at each armhole edge of every outside row 4 times. Work decrease rows as: Slip 1, K2 tog, work across to last 3 stitches, SSK, K1.

- Work the 8 rows of pattern 4 times. At the end of row 8, break the yarn, leaving a 2-yard length. Keep the 41 back stitches on hold on the circular needle.

Right Front (as worn)

- Slip the 20 stitches onto a double-pointed needle and, with the inside facing, tie in a new yarn at the first stitch on the right end of the needle—the armhole edge.

- ◆ Starting with row 2 (the inside row) and using the double-pointed needles, work in pattern over the 20 right front stitches, decreasing 1 stitch at the armhole edge on the next 4 outside rows. Work to within 3 stitches of the end, SSK, K1.
- ◆ At the beginning of the next outside row, bind off 4 stitches for the neck shaping.
- ◆ At the beginning of the next 4 outside rows, decrease 1 stitch at the neck edge: Slip 1, K2 tog.
- ◆ Continue pattern over the remaining 8 stitches, *4 times in all*, to match the back, ending after an inside row. Break the yarn, leaving a 1-yard length. Graft (or sew) the 8 right-front shoulder stitches to the corresponding stitches on the back.

Left Front

- ◆ Slip the 20 stitches onto a double-pointed needle and, with the outside facing, tie in a new yarn at the first stitch on the right end of the needle—the armhole edge.
- ◆ Starting with row 1 (the outside row), work the left front the same as the right front, decreasing 1 stitch at the armhole edge on the next 4 outside rows by starting: Slip 1, K2 tog. Then, at the beginning of the next inside row, bind off 4 stitches for the neck shaping. At the end of the next 4 outside rows, decrease 1 stitch at the neck edge, work to 3 stitches from the end, SSK, K1. Continue pattern over the remaining 8 stitches 4 times in all, to match right front.
- ◆ Using the back yarn, graft (or sew) the 8 left-front shoulder stitches to the corresponding 8 stitches on the back, and with the same yarn, bind off the remaining back stitches.

Tie Cords (optional)

Pick up 3 stitches at the corners of the neck edges and work the Knitted Cord (p. 53) for 6 inches. Then, about 3 inches down from the neck edge, work another set of ties, if desired.

MUSHROOM CAP

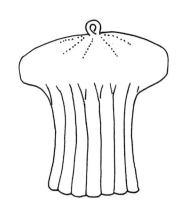

The Mushroom Cap is so named because when it stands on its ribbing, the shape is like a puffball mushroom. Simply changing from K2, P2 rib to stockinette stitch causes the cap to develop as from a stem. The stretchy K2, P2 fits snugly for warmth, yet "gives" to fit most any head.

Note: If you're not into mushrooms and a snug-fitting "stem" of K2, P2, the 4" of ribbing may, of course, be reduced to just one 1", or changed to K1, P1, or completely eliminated, to allow the cap edge to roll. (A cap with the rolled edge is shown on p. 153.)

You may use any yarn, and cap size is adjustable by changing the size of the needles. (See chart at right.) For the cap, you may gently toss gauge to the wind.

The cap is blank, waiting for your design ideas.

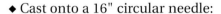

- ◆ Cast onto a 16" circular needle:

    Fine Yarn — 120 stitches
    Medium Yarn — 96 stitches
    Heavy Yarn — 80 stitches

- ◆ Work K2, P2, for 4", more or less.
- ◆ Knit around in stockinette stitch for 4", more or less.
- ◆ Try on the cap. Start to decrease when there is not too much of your head left to cover; there are 13 more rounds to the top.
- ◆ Put a marker on the needle at the seamline. Start the decrease rounds at the marker.
- ◆ Decreases:

    Round 1: K6, K2 tog around.
    Round 2 and all other even-numbered rounds: Knit.
    Round 3: K5, K2 tog around.
    Round 4: K4, K2 tog around. Change to double-points.
    Round 5: K3, K2 tog around.
    Round 6: K2, K2 tog around.
    Round 7: K1, K2 tog around.
    Round 8: K2 tog around.
- ◆ Endings:

    (A) Break yarn and run it through remaining stitches; pull them gently together and secure. Add pompom or tassel.

    (B) Continue decreasing to 3 stitches, work a Knitted Cord loop (p. 58), and hang.

Needle Sizes According to Yarn Weight & Cap Size

Yarn	Small	Medium	Large
Fine	#3	#4	#5
Medium	#5	#6	#7
Heavy	#8	#10	#10½

BARN BONNET

Here is a cozy cap and neck-warmer all rolled into one handy head covering to hang by the back door and grab on the way to the barn to bottle-feed little lambies at −40° windchill. It's also good for walking the dog at midnight.

Yarn: About 3 ounces medium (worsted) weight

Needles: #4 or #5 24-inch circular (or 2 straights), and one set of #4 or #5 double-pointed

(For an infant's version, use "baby yarn" and finer needles.)

Face Edge

The first part of the bonnet is worked flat, in rows. Therefore, either work back and forth on the circular needle or use straight needles.

The bonnet shown in the photo has K2, P2 ribbing at the face opening. Directions are also given for a picot edge, which gives an old-fashioned look.

For a ribbed edge:

◆ Cast on 78 stitches.

> **Row 1:** Slip 1, K1, P2, then *K2, P2* across, end K2.
>
> **Row 2:** Slip 1, P1, K2, then *P2, K2* across, end P2.

◆ Continue ribbing for one inch.

For a picot edge:

◆ Cast on 77 stitches. Work 4 rows of stockinette stitch, beginning with a knit row.

◆ K1, *YO, K2 tog* across. Increase one stitch in the next row. (When the bonnet is completed, fold at yarn-over row to form picot hem and stitch hem loosely to the inside.)

Body

◆ Work body of bonnet in stockinette, continuing to slip the first stitch of each row (slip as if to purl, yarn in back for knit rows; in front for purl rows) for about 6½ inches or to mid-head, ending after a purl row and decreasing 1 stitch, to 77 stitches.

◆ Change to double-pointed needles by knitting the stitches onto 3 needles (22, 33, 22), join your work, and knit 1 round.

◆ Work decrease rounds:

> **Round 1:** *K9, K2 tog* around.
>
> **Round 2 and all even-numbered rounds:** Knit around.

The close-fitting **Barn Bonnet** stays put when tied under the chin. The extended back ribbing prevents heat loss at the nape of the neck—if your neck is warm, you'll be warm. As its name implies, there is no need to be stylish at –30° out in the barn. To perk it up, add a few stripes or make one in blaze orange to be safe in hunting season. Its construction is seamless and quick.

The pullover shown here is a good example of how decorative patterns can be added to the Basic Sweater. Narrow borders of contrasting gray with a dash of jade are kept to a minimum and out of the yoke. They appear above the body and sleeve ribbings and are repeated just before the round where body and sleeves are joined. The neck is worked in the contrast yarn and hemmed with a picot edge (p. 54, under The Lacing Round).

Round 3: *K8, K2 tog* around.

Round 5: *K7, K2 tog* around.

Round 7: *K6, K2 tog* around.

Round 9: *K5, K2 tog* around.

Round 11: *K4, K2 tog* around.

Round 13: *K3, K2 tog* around.

Round 15: *K2, K2 tog* around.

◆ Thread yarn through remaining stitches, draw together, and fasten off.

Neck Ribbing

◆ With the outside facing you, and with either the circular needle or the straight needles, knit into the chain selvedge across the back (nape) neck edge, adjusting the number of knit-up stitches to be a multiple of 4, plus 2.

◆ Work flat in K2, P2 rib for 2½ to 3 inches (or as long as you want), starting with an inside row, as follows:

Inside rows: *P2, K2* across, end P2.

Outside rows: *K2, P2* across, end K2.

◆ Bind off in ribbing.

Tie Cords

◆ Pick up 3 stitches at the front corners and work the Knitted Cord (p. 53) until long enough to tie under your chinny-chin-chin. To bind off cord: K1, K2 tog, pass the first stitch over the second, secure the yarn, and tuck the tail into the cord.

BEADED RIB SCARF

Shown on p. 179

Fair warning: Once you knit this narrow, shortish scarf, you may never take it off—indoors or out. It sits well on, or under, a blazer or a coat, and in a cold house it's wonderfully warm around the neck—especially when knit in a soft handspun. The Beaded Rib pattern complements any sweater ribbing.

The pattern is a multiple of 5, plus 2, **plus** 3 extra stitches at each end of the needle for a garter stitch border. The casting-on and casting-off are accomplished on fewer stitches than the scarf proper to avoid "fanned fringe."

The scarf may be made wider or narrower by increasing or decreasing in multiples of 5, plus 2. And it can, of course, be made longer or shorter. Fringe is optional.

(The Beaded Rib pattern is from *The Knitting Dictionary*.)

Beaded Rib Pattern: A multiple of 5, plus 2, plus 6 (3 + 3).

Work on 2 double-points.

- ◆ Cast on:

Fine yarn	34 stitches
Medium yarn	24 stitches
Heavy yarn	14 stitches

- ◆ Knit one row.
- ◆ Knit the next row, increasing 9 stitches, evenly spaced, for a total of:

Fine yarn	43 stitches
Medium yarn	33 stitches
Heavy yarn	23 stitches

- ◆ Repeat rows 1 and 2 for pattern:

  Row 1: Slip 1 (as if to purl, yarn in front), K2, *K2, P3*, repeat * to *, end K2, K3.

  Row 2: Slip 1 (as if to purl, yarn in front), K2, *P2, K1, P1, K1*, repeat * to *, end P2, K3.

- ◆ Work 42" more or less. (Keep a safety pin in the row 1 side so you will know where you're at.) Stop at the end of row 1.
- ◆ Knit the next row, decreasing 9 stitches, evenly spaced, to return to your original number of stitches.
- ◆ Knit one row.
- ◆ Cast off, treating the last 2 stitches on the needle as one, to further refine and square the corner.

Needle Sizes According to Yarn Weight

Fine	#3, #4, or #5
Medium	#5, #6, or #7
Heavy	#8, #10, or #10½

Bibliography

Abbey, Barbara. *Knitting Lace*. New York: The Viking Press, 1974.

Adrosko, Rita J. *Natural Dyes and Home Dyeing*. New York: Dover Publications, 1971.

Albers, Josef. *Interactions of Color*. New Haven: Yale Univ. Press, 1975.

Bernat Book of Irish Knits (Book #145). Uxbridge, Mass.: Emile Bernat & Sons Co., 1967

Bernat Irish Knits (Book #516). Uxbridge, Mass.: Bernat Yarn & Craft Corp., 1983.

Chamberlain, John, and James H. Quilter. *Knitted Fabrics*. London: Sir Isaac Pitman and Sons Ltd., 1924.

Complete Book of Needlework. New York: Reader's Digest, 1979.

Compton, Rae. *The Complete Book of Traditional Knitting*. New York: Charles Scribner's Sons, 1983.

Debes, Hans M. *Foroysk Bindingarmynstur*. Torshavn, 1932.

Dexter, Janetta. *Double Knitting Patterns*. Halifax, N.S.: Nimbus Publishing. Orig. pub. by the Nova Scotia Museum, 1985.

Fleisher's Knitting and Crochet Manual. Philadelphia: S. B. & B. F. Fleisher, 1918.

Gombrich, E. H. *The Sense of Order*. New York: Cornell Univ. Press, 1979.

Good Shepherd Fingering Yarns and Their Use, Being a Modern Treatise on the Art of Hand Knitting and Crocheting, and Containing the Most Advanced Designs. Newton, Mass.: Shepherd Worsted Mills, 1917.

Harmony Guide to Knitting Stitches. London: Lyric Books Ltd, 1983.

Hollingsworth, Shelagh. *The Complete Book of Traditional Aran Knitting*. New York: St. Martin's Press, 1982.

Karush, William. *The Crescent Dictionary of Mathematics*. New York: The Macmillan Co., 1962.

Kidwell, Claudia B. *Cutting a Fashionable Fit*. Washington, D.C.: Smithsonian Institution, 1979.

Kiewe, Heinz Edgar. *History of Folk Cross Stitch*. Nuremburg: Sebaldus Verlag, 1967.

Kiewe, Heinz Edgar. *The Sacred History of Knitting*. Oxford, England: Art Needlework Industries Ltd., 1967.

Knitting Dictionary, The. New York: Crown Publishers, Inc., 1970.

Kovel, Ralph and Terry. *The Kovel's Collector's Guide to American Art Pottery*. New York: Crown Publishers, Inc., 1974.

Latest Novelties in Fancy Work, with Directions for Making. Isaac D. Allen Co., c. 1871.

Modern Needlecraft Knitting, 10th ed. New York: Needlework Publications, Inc., 1950.

Mon Tricot 1300 Pattern Stitches. West Caldwell, N.J.: Curtis Circulation, 1981.

Morgan, Gwyn, *Traditional Knitting Patterns of Ireland, Scotland, and England*. New York: St. Martin's Press, 1981.

Needlework and Alphabet Designs. New York: Dover Publications, Inc., 1975.

New Grove Dictionary of Music and Musicians. London: Macmillan Publishers Ltd., 1980.

Norbury, James. *Traditional Knitting Patterns*. New York: Dover Publications, Inc., 1973.

Nylen, Anna Maja. *Swedish Handcrafts*. New York: Van Nostrand Reinhold Co., 1977.

Price, Leslie. *Kids' Knits*. New York: Ballantine Books, 1986.

Prospect Yarn Manual. New York: Prospect Sales Co., Inc., 1923.

Roosevelt, Eleanor. Topical Files, 1945–1962. Box 4642, The Franklin D. Roosevelt Library, Hyde Park, New York.

17th Century Knitting Pattern. The Weaver's Guild of Boston, 1978.

Thomas, Mary. *Mary Thomas's Book of Knitting Patterns*. New York: The Macmillan Co., 1945.

———. *Mary Thomas's Knitting Book*. New York: Dover Publications, Inc., 1972.

Thompson, Gladys. *Patterns for Guernseys, Jerseys, and Arans*. New York: Dover Publications, Inc., 1971.

Walch, Margaret. *The Color Source Book*. New York: Charles Scribner's Sons, 1979.

Walker, Barbara. *Knitting from the Top*. New York: Charles Scribner's Sons, 1972.

Whitney's Treatise on Crocheting and Knitting in Yarns and Worsteds. Boston: T. D. Whitney Co., n.d.

Williams, Susanne R. *The Scotch Wool Shop Book*. Haverford, Pa., 1943.

Zimmermann, Elizabeth. *Knitting Without Tears*. New York: Charles Scribner's Sons, 1971.

———. *Knitter's Almanac*. New York: Charles Scribner's Sons, 1974.

———. *Wool Gathering*. Sept. 1979.

Index

Page numbers in boldface refer to photographs.

11/03

Jackie Fee could be referred to simply as the author of a much-loved knitting book, but that would be telling only part of the story. She is also a designer, spinner, instructor at workshops (including Rhode Island School of Design's continuing education classes), and collector of antique knitting tools and textiles. She enjoys tracing the traditions of the craft, finding new sources of inspiration, and sharing the excitement of creative knitting with others. Some 55,000 fortunate knitters who own the first edition of *The Sweater Workshop* can attest to her ability to both explain and inspire.

Jackie and her husband, Peter, live in New England—sweater country—dividing their time between Hingham, Massachusetts, and Deer Isle, Maine.

Send e-mail messages to Jackie Fee
c/o books@downeast.com